Desserts

Caroline Bretherton
Kristan Raines

DK | Penguin Random House

DK LONDON
Project Editor Martha Burley
Senior Art Editor Sara Robin
Project Art Editor Vicky Read
Editorial Assistant Alice Kewellhampton
Design Assistant Laura Buscemi
Managing Editor Dawn Henderson
Managing Art Editor Christine Keilty
Senior Jacket Creative Nicola Powling
Pre-Production Producer Dragana Puvacic
Senior Producer Stephanie McConnell
Creative Technical Support Sonia Charbonnier
Deputy Art Director Maxine Pedliham
Publisher Peggy Vance

DK US
US Editor Christy Lusiak
US Senior Editor Margaret Parrish
US Consultant Kate Ramos

DK INDIA
Senior Art Editor Ira Sharma
Editors Neha Samuel, Seetha Natesh
Art Editors Zaurin Thoidingjam, Tashi Topgyal Laya
Deputy Managing Editor Bushra Ahmed
Managing Art Editor Navidita Thapa
Pre-production Manager Sunil Sharma
DTP Designer Rajdeep Singh

First American Edition, 2015
Published in the United States by DK Publishing
345 Hudson Street, New York, New York 10014

Copyright © 2015 Dorling Kindersley Limited
A Penguin Random House Company
15 16 17 18 19   10 9 8 7 6 5 4 3 2 1
001–278606–Sept/2015

Published in Great Britain by Dorling Kindersley Limited.

A catalog record for this book is available from the Library of Congress.
ISBN 978-1-4654-3802-7

DK books are available at special discounts when purchased in bulk for sales promotions, premiums, fund-raising, or educational use. For details, contact: DK Publishing Special Markets, 345 Hudson Street, New York, New York 10014
SpecialSales@dk.com

Color reproduction by Altaimage Ltd.
Printed and bound in China

A WORLD OF IDEAS:
SEE ALL THERE IS TO KNOW
www.dk.com

Contents

Sweet success

Desserts are more indulgent, daring, and fabulous than ever. Treat yourself to dinner at a good restaurant, and you can choose a dessert that is just as exciting as your main course. Today's dessert recipes draw influences from all cuisines, play with new ingredients, and introduce flavor pairings. They are the finishing touch to a great meal, and showstoppers in their own right.

Recipes to impress

To celebrate the buzz around desserts, *Desserts* is a unique collection of over 400 recipes. With a comprehensive collection of luscious recipes and simple guidance to help you on your way, here are endless ideas and inspiration for that sweet treat at the end of a meal.

Within the three chapters—Hot, Cold, and Frozen—you can find every classic dessert recipe that a home cook needs, shown step by step. Each classic is followed by creative variations, so if you are looking for inspiration for a midweek dessert or wish to prepare an impressive finale to a celebration dinner, you can find the ideal recipe. Alongside the recipes are fun feature panels that share ideas for decoration techniques—so you

can drip, drizzle, melt, marble, pipe, crimp, skewer, shape, or dust your way to truly sensational desserts.

Making desserts is creative and fun, but it does require attention to detail and precision. Before you begin to cook, read the recipe carefully and make sure you have all the ingredients, time, and equipment you need. If your dessert needs to be baked in the oven, set the rack at the correct height before you heat it up, and keep in mind that the top of the oven can be a lot hotter than the bottom. Unless stated otherwise in the recipe, you should bake your dessert on the center rack so that it cooks evenly. Here is some more expert guidance that can help you.

Dough know-how

Homemade dough can become tough, crumbly, or difficult to handle. Don't panic—before you resort to store-bought dough, there are some simple steps that can give you fabulous results.

- **Chill dough**, well wrapped in plastic wrap, for at least 30 minutes before rolling. This allows the gluten in the flour to relax and keeps the dough from being tough when baked.
- **Do not over-flour** the work surface. Use as little flour as you can—extra flour is absorbed by the dough and makes it dry once baked.
- **Do not overwork** the dough. For all stages of dough making, use as light a hand as possible. Avoid re-rolling where possible, because the dough may toughen and be liable to shrinkage.
- **Roll your dough** into a pan or onto a baking sheet using a rolling pin. Transferring dough to a pan is tricky, so to prevent breakage, simply roll it up around your rolling pin, then unroll it gradually into the pan.

Rolled dough is delicate, so handle it with care.

For best results, beat the egg whites until they are stiff and glossy.

Mastering meringue

Delicate meringue is a very simple combination of egg whites and sugar, but it can be difficult to perfect. From preparing your bowl to separating eggs, here are some expert tips to help you.

- **Separate the eggs** one by one in a smaller bowl before combining them. Any trace of egg yolk will spoil a meringue—so this method means that even if a yolk breaks, only a single egg is lost.
- **Remove small pieces of eggshell** from the egg whites using another broken egg shell. The albumen inside the shell attracts the smaller piece, making it easy to scoop out.
- **Beat egg whites** in a scrupulously clean bowl. If in doubt, run the cut-side of a lemon around the inside of the bowl to remove any residual grease, then dry with a paper towel.

All about cakes and tortes

Baking itself is a science, but there is an art to a light and airy sponge cake or a rich and dense torte—choosing your ingredients carefully is key.

- **Make sure your eggs** are at room temperature. They beat more easily, so this means you can incorporate more air into your cake.
- **Start with butter** that is softened at room temperature, unless otherwise stated in the recipe. If you are short of time, dividing it into small cubes helps it to soften more quickly.
- **Use unsalted butter.** If the recipe calls for additional salt, use good-quality sea salt, which has a softer flavor than table salt.
- **Measure your pans.** The size is vital because the depth of the batter can affect a cake's cooking time.

Make sure that all your ingredients are at room temperature.

HOT

Cobblers, crumbles, and crisps ▪ Patisserie
Brownies and batters ▪ Cakes and tortes
Puddings ▪ Cooked fruit

INGREDIENTS

1½lb (675g) blueberries
2 tbsp cornstarch
3–4 tbsp granulated sugar
pinch of salt
grated zest of 1 lemon
2 tsp lemon juice

For the topping

1½ cups all-purpose flour
1¾ tsp baking powder
pinch of salt
4 tbsp granulated sugar
6 tbsp unsalted butter, chilled and diced
¾ cup heavy cream, plus extra for brushing
¼ tsp ground cinnamon
whipped cream, to serve (optional)

SPECIAL EQUIPMENT

1½ quart deep ovenproof dish

🕐 **55 mins**
plus cooling

🍴 **SERVES 6**

COBBLER blueberry

A cobbler is a simple alternative to a pie or crumble—perfect for when you are short on time in the kitchen. You can choose any seasonal fruit filling, top it with this sweetened biscuit crust, and bake to create a warm and comforting dessert.

1

Preheat the oven to 375°F (190°C). Combine the blueberries, cornstarch, sugar, salt, and lemon zest and juice in a bowl.

2

For the topping, sift the flour, baking powder, salt, and 3 tablespoons of the sugar into a large bowl. Rub in the butter until the mixture resembles coarse bread crumbs. Add the cream and bring the mixture together to form a dough.

3

Transfer the blueberry mixture to the ovenproof dish, spreading it out evenly. Divide the dough into six equal portions and place it on top of the blueberries. Combine the cinnamon and remaining sugar in a small bowl.

Make sure you leave enough space for the dough to spread.

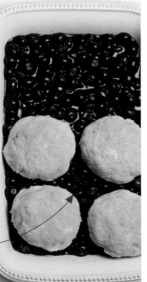

Brush the dough with a little heavy cream, then sprinkle with the cinnamon mixture. Bake for 25–30 minutes, until golden and bubbling. Insert a skewer into the topping—it should come out clean. Remove and let cool for 5 minutes. Serve warm with whipped cream, if desired. You can store the cobbler in the fridge for up to 2 days.

4

⏱ **1 hr** plus cooling   🍴 **SERVES 6**

COBBLER cranberry and pear

The combination of tart cranberries and sweet pears gives this recipe a tempting contrast of color, flavor, and texture.

INGREDIENTS
½ cup light brown sugar
½ tsp ground cardamom
¼ tsp ground cinnamon
2 tbsp cornstarch
salt
4oz (115g) cranberries
2lb (900g) pears, peeled, cored, and thinly sliced
juice of ½ orange
whipped cream, to serve

For the topping
1½ cups all-purpose flour
1¾ tsp baking powder
4 tbsp granulated sugar
6 tbsp unsalted butter, chilled and diced
¾ cup heavy cream, plus extra for brushing
¼ tsp ground cinnamon

SPECIAL EQUIPMENT
1½ quart ovenproof dish

1 Preheat the oven to 375°F (190C°). Combine the brown sugar, cardamom, cinnamon, cornstarch, and a pinch of salt in a large bowl. Add the cranberries, pears, and orange juice. Mix well, spread the mixture in the ovenproof dish, and set aside.

2 For the topping, sift the flour, baking powder, 3 tablespoons of granulated sugar, and a pinch of salt into a large bowl. Rub in the butter until the mixture resembles bread crumbs. Add the cream and bring the mixture together to form a soft, sticky dough.

3 Place 6 heaping tablespoons of the dough over the fruit, leaving space for it to spread. Brush with a little cream. Mix the cinnamon and remaining sugar in a bowl and sprinkle over the dough.

4 Bake for 35–40 minutes, until the cobbler is golden and bubbling and an inserted skewer comes out clean. Cover with foil if the topping browns too quickly. Cool for 5 minutes, then serve warm with whipped cream. You can store the cobbler in the fridge for up to 2 days.

⏱ **55 mins** plus cooling   🍴 **SERVES 6**

COBBLER peach

Fragrant summer peaches require nothing more than this soft and yielding topping to soak up their juices.

INGREDIENTS
¼ cup granulated sugar
8 ripe peaches, peeled, pitted, and quartered
1 tsp cornstarch
juice of ½ lemon

For the topping
1½ cups all-purpose flour
1¾ tsp baking powder
⅓ cup granulated sugar
pinch of salt
½–¾ tsp ground cinnamon, to taste

5 tbsp unsalted butter, chilled and diced
1 egg
½ cup buttermilk
1 tbsp light brown sugar
custard or cream, to serve (optional)

SPECIAL EQUIPMENT
1½ quart ovenproof dish

1 Preheat the oven to 375°F (190°C). Heat the sugar and ¼ cup of water in a large, heavy-bottomed saucepan with a lid. Add the peaches once the sugar has dissolved. Cover and cook for 2–3 minutes over medium heat, stirring occasionally, until the peaches are well coated in the mixture. Reduce the heat to low.

2 Mix the cornstarch and lemon juice in a bowl to a paste. Add to the pan and cook the mixture, uncovered, until thickened to a syrup-like consistency. Transfer to the ovenproof dish and spread out the peach filling into an even layer.

3 For the topping, sift the flour, baking powder, granulated sugar, salt, and cinnamon into a bowl. Rub in the butter until the mixture resembles bread crumbs. Whisk the egg and buttermilk in a separate bowl and combine with the dry ingredients to form a dough. Use to cover the fruit (see Cranberry and pear cobbler, step 3).

4 Sprinkle with the brown sugar. Bake for 25–30 minutes, until done (see Cranberry and pear cobbler, step 4). Cool for 5 minutes, then serve with custard or cream, if desired. You can store the cobbler in the fridge for up to 2 days.

🕐 **1 hr 20 mins**
plus cooling

🍴 **SERVES 6**

COBBLER apple and blackberry

Enhance the flavor of your cobbler with a mix of tart and sweet apples. This blend ensures that some apple pieces stay firm enough to have a nice bite to them.

INGREDIENTS

2lb (900g) mixed tart and sweet apples, peeled, cored, and thinly sliced

½ cup dark brown sugar

2 tbsp cornstarch

1 tsp ground cinnamon

¼ tsp ground cloves

juice of ½ lemon

12oz (350g) blackberries

whipped cream, to serve

For the topping

1½ cups all-purpose flour

1¾ tsp baking powder

pinch of salt

4 tbsp granulated sugar

6 tbsp unsalted butter, chilled and diced

¾ cup heavy cream, plus extra for brushing

¼ tsp ground cinnamon

SPECIAL EQUIPMENT

1½ quart ovenproof dish

1 Preheat the oven to 375°F (190C°). Combine the apples, brown sugar, cornstarch, cinnamon, cloves, and lemon juice in a large bowl. Transfer the mixture to the ovenproof dish and bake for 20 minutes, until the apples are slightly tender. Remove and fold in the blackberries.

2 For the topping, sift the flour, baking powder, salt, and 3 tablespoons of granulated sugar into a bowl. Rub in the butter until the mixture resembles bread crumbs. Add the cream and bring the mixture together to form a dough. Use to cover the fruit (see Cranberry and pear cobbler, step 3).

3 Combine the cinnamon with the remaining sugar in a bowl. Brush the dough with cream and sprinkle with the cinnamon and sugar mixture.

4 Bake for 35–40 minutes, or until done (see Cranberry and pear cobbler, step 4). Cool the cobbler for 5 minutes, then serve it warm with whipped cream. You can store the cobbler in the fridge for up to 2 days.

1 hr 10 mins plus resting   **MAKES 6-8**

CRUMBLE apple and cinnamon

This is a beloved dessert, and deservedly so. A good crumble topping should be loosely patted down over the filling and made with irregular-sized lumps of butter that melt and create a fudge-like texture while baking.

INGREDIENTS

1¾ cup all-purpose flour
⅔ cup granulated sugar
1 tsp cinnamon
11 tbsp unsalted butter, softened and diced

For the filling
8-10 apples, peeled, cored, and diced into ¾in (2cm) pieces
2 heaping tbsp light brown sugar

1 heaping tbsp all-purpose flour
½ tsp ground cinnamon
2 tbsp butter, softened and diced
heavy cream, to serve (optional)

SPECIAL EQUIPMENT
9in (23cm) ovenproof dish, about 3in (7.5cm) deep

1 Preheat the oven to 350° (180°C). Combine the flour, sugar, and cinnamon in a large bowl. Rub in the butter until the mixture resembles coarse bread crumbs, making sure you leave a few small lumps of butter.

2 For the filling, place the apple pieces in the ovenproof dish. Scatter with the sugar, flour, and cinnamon. Toss well to combine. Gently pack the filling into the dish.

3 Dot the filling with butter, then spoon the flour topping over and spread it out gently. Lightly shake the dish to help settle the topping into an even layer.

4 Bake for 45 minutes, until the top is golden brown and the filling is soft when pierced with a sharp knife. Remove and let rest for 5 minutes. Serve warm with cream, if desired. You can store this, covered, for up to 3 days in the fridge.

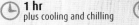

1 hr
plus cooling and chilling   **MAKES 4**

CRISPS summer berry

These are ideal when you need to plan ahead. Prepare the components in advance for a no-fuss finish to a meal.

INGREDIENTS
1 cup rolled oats

1 tsp cinnamon

3 tbsp light brown sugar

4 tbsp unsalted butter, melted

¾ cup half-and-half

2 egg yolks

½ tsp vanilla extract

4 tbsp granulated sugar

1lb 2oz (500g) mixed berries, chopped into small pieces

½ cup heavy cream

SPECIAL EQUIPMENT
4 x 12fl oz (350ml) wide-mouthed jam jars

PLAN AHEAD
You can prepare and store the oat mixture in an airtight container up to 2 days ahead. You can prepare and store the custard in an airtight container in the fridge up to 2 days ahead.

1 Preheat the oven to 350°F (180°C). Combine the oats, cinnamon, brown sugar, and butter in a bowl. Spread the mixture on a heavy baking sheet. Bake on the top rack of the oven for 12–15 minutes, until golden. Let cool.

2 Heat the half-and-half in a heavy-bottomed saucepan over low heat, until steaming. Whisk the egg yolks, vanilla extract, and 3 tablespoons granulated sugar in a heatproof bowl. Pour in the hot cream and whisk until the sugar melts.

3 Pour the mixture back into the pan. Cook over low heat for 8–10 minutes, stirring continuously, until it is thick enough to coat the back of a spoon. Transfer the custard to a bowl and let cool. Cover the surface with plastic wrap and chill until needed.

4 Combine the berries and remaining granulated sugar in a bowl and let macerate for 20 minutes. In a separate bowl, whisk the heavy cream to form stiff peaks. Then whisk in the chilled custard until well combined.

5 Place one-eighth of the berries in each jam jar in an even layer. Top with one-eighth each of the custard and the oat mixture. Repeat to add one more layer each of the fruit, custard, and oat mixture. Chill for at least 30 minutes before serving on the same day.

---

50 mins
plus resting   **SERVES 4-6**

SMULPAJ rhubarb

A Swedish favorite, smulpaj features a layer of fruit topped with an oaty crumble.

INGREDIENTS
⅓ cup all-purpose flour

⅓ cup light brown sugar

5 tbsp unsalted butter, softened

¾ cup oats

½ tsp ground cinnamon

For the filling

10oz (300g) rhubarb, trimmed and chopped into ¾in (2cm) chunks

¼ cup granulated sugar

1 tsp cornstarch

For the custard

1⅔ cups whole milk

¼ cup heavy cream

3 large egg yolks, at room temperature

1½ tbsp granulated sugar

1 tbsp cornstarch

½ tsp vanilla extract

SPECIAL EQUIPMENT
8in (20cm) round ovenproof dish

1 Preheat the oven to 375°F (190°C). Combine the flour and brown sugar in a bowl. Rub in the butter until the mixture resembles coarse bread crumbs. Add the oats and cinnamon, mix well, and set aside.

2 For the filling, combine the rhubarb, granulated sugar, and cornstarch in the ovenproof dish. Gently pack the filling down, spread the flour topping over the top, and shake the dish lightly to help it settle evenly. Place it on a baking sheet.

3 Bake for 30 minutes, until the top is golden and the filling is soft when pierced with a knife. Remove and let rest for 5–10 minutes. Meanwhile, for the custard, heat the milk and cream in a heavy-bottomed saucepan for 5–6 minutes, until steaming.

4 In a heatproof bowl, whisk the egg yolks, granulated sugar, cornstarch, and vanilla extract until well combined. Gradually add the milk mixture, whisking until the sugar has melted. Pour the custard back into the pan.

5 Cook the custard over gentle heat for another 5–8 minutes, stirring constantly, until it is thick enough to coat the back of a spoon. Remove from the heat and serve warm with the smulpaj. You can store the smulpaj, covered, in the fridge for 1–2 days.

⏱ **1 hr 20 mins**
plus cooling and resting   🍴 **SERVES 6–8**

CRUMBLE fall fruit

The walnuts in this filling give the crumble fantastic crunch and texture, and cranberries add a tangy brightness to the flavor.

INGREDIENTS

2 cups all-purpose flour

¾ cup light brown sugar

½ tsp ground cinnamon

12 tbsp unsalted butter, softened and diced

1 cup rolled oats

vanilla custard, to serve

For the filling

⅓ cup walnuts

½ tsp cinnamon

2 heaping tbsp light brown sugar

4–5 apples, peeled, cored, and cut into cubes

2–3 pears, peeled, cored, and cut into cubes

3½oz (100g) cranberries

1 heaping tbsp all-purpose flour

SPECIAL EQUIPMENT

9in (23cm) ovenproof dish, about 3in (7.5cm) deep

1 Preheat the oven to 350°F (180°C). Combine the flour, brown sugar, and cinnamon in a large bowl. Rub in 11 tablespoons of the butter until the mixture resembles coarse bread crumbs. Add the oats, mix well, and set aside.

2 For the filling, spread the walnuts on a baking sheet and bake for 5 minutes. Gently rub them with a paper towel to remove the skin. Let cool before chopping them into small pieces. Transfer to the ovenproof dish along with the cinnamon, sugar, and fruit.

3 Mix the filling and pack it down gently. Dot with the remaining butter, then spread the flour topping over the top (see Rhubarb smulpaj, step 2).

4 Bake for 45–50 minutes, until the top is golden and the filling is soft when pierced with a knife. Remove the crumble from the heat and let rest. Serve it warm with the custard. You can store the crumble, covered, in the fridge for 1–2 days.

Simple alternatives

A simple Apple and cinnamon crumble (see pp14–15) is a time-honored classic, but you can substitute a variety of fruits and spices to create fabulous alternatives.

Pear and nutmeg Omit the cinnamon from the recipe (see Apple and cinnamon crumble, pp14–15). Use 8 peeled, cored, and diced, just-ripe pears instead of the apples. Add ½ tsp grated nutmeg to the filling and 1 tsp to the topping and continue.

Plum Replace the apples (see Apple and cinnamon crumble, pp14–15) with 16–18 halved and pitted firm plums and continue with the recipe.

Damson These are a little-known fruit, smaller and tarter than plums. Use 18–20 halved and pitted damsons instead of the chopped apples (see Apple and cinnamon crumble, pp14–15).

Peach Omit the cinnamon from the recipe (see Apple and cinnamon crumble, pp14–15). Use 10 halved, pitted, and quartered peaches instead of the apples. Serve the crumble at room temperature with vanilla ice cream.

Gooseberry and elderflower For this summertime recipe, toss 1¾lb (800g) hulled, ripe gooseberries in a little elderflower cordial and ¼ cup granulated sugar, and omit the cinnamon (see Apple and cinnamon crumble, pp14–15).

Banana and mango Omit the cinnamon from the recipe (see Apple and cinnamon crumble, pp14–15). Use 2–3 large bananas, cut into ¾in (2cm) thick slices with 2 mangos, diced into ¾in (2cm) pieces instead of the apples. For best results, use fruit that is just ripe.

Rhubarb and strawberry Use 14oz (400g) rhubarb, cut into 1in (2.5cm) pieces, and 14oz (400g) hulled strawberries, and omit the cinnamon (see Apple and cinnamon crumble, pp14–15).

Cherry and almond Omit the cinnamon from the recipe (see Apple and cinnamon crumble, pp14–15). Use 1lb 8oz (700g) pitted cherries and 1 cup coarsely chopped raw almonds instead of the apples.

🕐 **1 hr 25 mins**
plus resting

🍴 **SERVES 6–8**

🌡 Also great
COLD

STRUDEL apple and almond

Strudel dough is tricky to get right, but this recipe guarantees success. The bread crumbs in the filling help to soak up juices from the apple that could make the pastry soggy—leaving you with perfectly crisp and flaky pastry.

INGREDIENTS
1½ cups all-purpose flour, plus extra for dusting

¼ tsp salt

1 tsp granulated sugar, plus extra for dusting

7 tbsp unsalted butter, diced, plus extra for greasing

1 large egg, beaten

½ tsp cider vinegar

1 tbsp confectioners' sugar, for dusting

For the filling
2lb (900g) tart apples, such as Granny Smith, peeled, cored, and thinly sliced

grated zest of ½ lemon

¼ cup bread crumbs

½ cup granulated sugar

3 tbsp dark brown sugar

1 tsp ground cinnamon

¼ tsp grated nutmeg

½ cup sliced almonds

¼ tsp vanilla extract

1

Combine the flour, salt, and granulated sugar in a large bowl. Rub in 2 tablespoons of the butter until the mixture resembles coarse bread crumbs. Whisk the egg, vinegar, and ¼ cup water in a separate bowl. Add the liquid mixture to the dry ingredients and mix well to form a loose dough.

2

Add 1–2 teaspoons of flour if the dough seems too wet. Throw the dough against a lightly floured work surface repeatedly for about 10-15 minutes until it is shiny, smooth, and elastic. Place it in a lightly greased bowl, cover, and let rest for 30 minutes.

3

Preheat the oven to 375°F (190°C). Line a baking sheet with parchment paper and set aside. For the filling, combine all the ingredients in a large bowl and set aside. Cover a work surface with a large, clean, kitchen towel and flour it lightly. Place the dough on top.

Start at the center and work outward to stretch out the dough.

4

Roll out the dough to a large rectangle of even thickness, then gently stretch it out, until it is very thin and translucent. The stretched dough should be about 16 x 24in (40 x 61cm) in size.

5

Melt the remaining butter in a saucepan over low heat and brush generously over the dough. Place the filling at one end of the dough, leaving a wide edge. Lift the edges of the kitchen towel and slowly roll up the strudel, working gently but firmly, making sure the filling does not fall out.

6

Place the strudel on the baking sheet. Curve it into a crescent and brush with butter. Sprinkle with the granulated sugar and trim the edges. Bake for 35–40 minutes, until golden. Sprinkle with confectioners' sugar and serve warm. Best served on the same day.

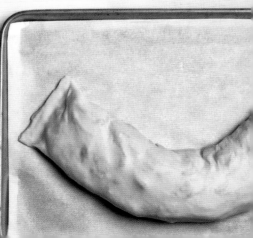

🕐 **1 hr 20 mins** plus resting and cooling   🍴 **SERVES 6–8**   🌡 Also great **COLD**

STRUDEL ricotta and raisin

In the style of Eastern European sweetened-cheese strudels, this recipe uses ricotta for a sweet, creamy, and delicious filling.

INGREDIENTS

1½ cups all-purpose flour, plus extra for dusting

¼ tsp salt

1 tsp granulated sugar

7 tbsp unsalted butter, softened, plus extra for greasing

1 large egg, beaten

½ tsp cider vinegar

1–2 tbsp confectioners' sugar, to serve

For the filling

½ cup raisins

3 tbsp rum or Port

12oz (350g) ricotta cheese

¼ cup granulated sugar, plus extra for dusting

1 tsp vanilla extract

⅛ tsp salt

grated zest of 1 lemon

1 large egg

1½ tbsp bread crumbs

1. Preheat the oven to 375°F (190°C). Combine the flour, salt, and granulated sugar in a bowl. Rub in 2 tablespoons butter until the mixture resembles bread crumbs. In a separate bowl, whisk the egg, vinegar, and ¼ cup water. Add it to the dry mixture and bring together to form a smooth dough.

2. Add 1–2 teaspoons of flour if the dough seems too wet, then throw it against a floured surface repeatedly for 10–15 minutes, until shiny, smooth, and elastic. Place it in a lightly greased bowl, cover, and let rest for 30 minutes.

3. For the filling, combine the raisins and rum in a bowl and let soak. In a separate bowl, combine the ricotta, granulated sugar, vanilla extract, salt, lemon zest, and egg. Cover a work surface with a large kitchen towel and flour it lightly. Place the dough on top and roll it out to a large rectangle.

4. Gently stretch the dough, working outward from the center to form a 16 x 24in (40 x 61cm) translucent rectangle. Use a slotted spoon to combine the raisins with the ricotta mixture. Melt the remaining butter and use to brush over the dough.

5. Scatter 1 tablespoon of the bread crumbs at one end of the dough, leaving a wide edge. Top with the filling, and then the remaining bread crumbs. Lift the edges of the cloth to roll the strudel, gently but firmly, making sure the filling does not fall out. Place it on a baking sheet lined with parchment paper.

6. Shape the strudel into a crescent and brush with the remaining butter. Sprinkle with granulated sugar and trim the excess dough. Bake for 30–35 minutes, until golden. Cool for 5–10 minutes. Dust with confectioners' sugar and serve warm. You can keep the strudel in an airtight container in the fridge for up to 1 day.

🕐 **1 hr 20 mins** plus resting   🍴 **SERVES 6–8**   🌡 Also great **COLD**

STRUDEL plum

For a twist on classic fruit strudel, finely dice plums and mix them with walnut and fragrant cardamom.

INGREDIENTS

1½ cups all-purpose flour

¼ tsp salt

1 tsp granulated sugar

7 tbsp unsalted butter, softened

1 large egg, beaten

½ tsp cider vinegar

1–2 tbsp confectioners' sugar, to serve

½ cup bread crumbs

½ cup light brown sugar

3 tbsp granulated sugar

1 tsp ground cinnamon

¼ tsp cardamom

½ cup chopped walnuts

¼ tsp vanilla extract

For the filling

1½lb (675g) plums, pitted and thinly sliced

1. Preheat the oven to 375°F (190°C). Prepare the dough, transfer it to a greased bowl, and let rest for 30 minutes (see Ricotta and raisin strudel, steps 1–2).

2. For the filling, combine all the ingredients in a large bowl and set aside. Cover a work surface with a large kitchen towel and flour it lightly. Place the dough on top and roll it out to a large rectangle.

3. Gently stretch out the dough to form a 16 x 24in (40 x 61cm) translucent rectangle (see Ricotta and raisin strudel, step 4). Melt the remaining butter and brush generously over the dough.

4. Place the filling at one end of the dough, leaving a wide edge. Roll the strudel and transfer to a lined baking sheet (see Ricotta and raisin strudel, step 5). Sprinkle with granulated sugar and trim the excess dough at the ends.

5. Bake for 30–35 minutes, until golden. Remove the strudel from the heat and let rest for 5–10 minutes. Dust with confectioners' sugar and serve warm. You can keep it in an airtight container in the fridge for up to 1 day.

2 hrs 5 mins—2 hrs 25 mins plus cooling   **MAKES 36**   Also great **COLD**

BAKLAVA

This crisp Middle Eastern pastry is layered with chopped nuts and spices, then drenched in orange-flower honey syrup. Serve it for an exotic flourish to any meal.

INGREDIENTS

2½ cups walnut pieces, coarsely chopped

2 tsp ground cinnamon

large pinch of ground cloves

¼ cup granulated sugar

2½ cups unsalted and skinned pistachios, coarsely chopped

1 x 18oz (500g) pack of phyllo dough

18 tbsp unsalted butter

For the syrup

¾ cup granulated sugar

1 cup honey

juice of 1 lemon

3 tbsp orange flower water

SPECIAL EQUIPMENT

12 x 16in (30 x 40cm) deep baking pan

1 Preheat the oven to 350°F (180°C). For the filling, place the walnuts, cinnamon, cloves, and sugar in a large bowl. Add the pistachios, reserving 3–4 tablespoons, and stir to mix. Set aside.

2 On a damp kitchen towel, unroll the pastry sheets and cover with a second dampened towel. Melt the butter in a saucepan over low heat. Brush the baking pan with a little butter and line it with a sheet of phyllo dough. Fold over the ends to fit the pan.

3 Brush the phyllo dough with butter and gently press it into the corners and sides of the pan. Repeat to form layers with one-third of the dough, brushing each layer with butter. Scatter with half the filling.

4 Repeat with another third of the phyllo sheets. Sprinkle with the remaining filling and layer with the remaining phyllo dough. Trim off any excess and pour over any remaining butter.

5 Gently score 1½in (4cm) wide and ½in (1cm) deep diamond shapes into the phyllo dough. Bake on the bottom rack of the oven for 1¼–1½ hours, until golden on top and an inserted skewer comes out clean.

6 For the syrup, heat the sugar and 1 cup water in a saucepan, stirring occasionally, until dissolved. Add the honey, stir to mix, and bring to a boil. Cook for 25 minutes, without stirring, until drops of the cooled mixture can be shaped into soft balls.

7 Remove and cool the syrup to lukewarm, stir in the lemon juice and orange flower water, and pour over the phyllo dough. Use a sharp knife to cut along the marked lines, almost to the bottom, and let cool.

8 Cut through the marked lines and carefully place the pastries on a large serving plate. Sprinkle with the reserved pistachios and serve warm. You can store the baklava in an airtight container for up to 5 days.

1 hr
plus chilling

MAKES 8

GALETTES apple and almond

This classic French dessert features layers of light, flaky pastry decorated with a sweet topping and baked in the oven. Quicker to prepare than a tart or pie, galettes are equally stunning—the open form beautifully showcases the apple filling.

INGREDIENTS
flour, for dusting
1lb 5oz (600g) store-
   bought all-butter puff
   pastry

For the filling
7½oz (215g) marzipan
8 small, tart apples,
   peeled, cored,
   and thinly sliced

juice of ½ lemon
¼ cup granulated sugar
confectioners' sugar, for
   dusting
heavy cream, to serve
   (optional)

PLAN AHEAD
You can chill the pastry and
marzipan rounds for up to
2 hours before baking.

1

On a floured surface, roll out half the pastry to a 14in (35cm) square, about ⅛in (3mm) thick. Use a 6in (15cm) plate to cut out four rounds. Place them on a baking sheet lightly sprinkled with water.

2

Make four more rounds with the remaining dough and place them on another baking sheet. Prick them with a fork, avoiding the edges, and chill all the pastry for 15 minutes. Cut the marzipan into eight equal portions and roll them into balls.

Leave a border of at least ½in (1cm) around the edge.

3

Set one of the marzipan balls between two sheets of parchment paper and roll it out to a 5in (12cm) round. Place it on top of a pastry round and repeat with the remaining marzipan. Chill for 15 minutes.

4

Preheat the oven to 425ºF (220ºC). Toss the apple slices with the lemon juice in a bowl. Arrange them in an overlapping spiral over the marzipan, leaving a thin border around the edge.

5

Bake for 15–20 minutes, until the pastry edges have risen around the marzipan and are lightly golden. Sprinkle the apples evenly with granulated sugar and return the galettes to the oven.

6

Bake for another 5–10 minutes, until the apples have caramelized around the edges and are tender when tested with a knife. Transfer the galettes to warmed serving plates and dust with confectioners' sugar. Serve immediately, with heavy cream if desired.

🕐 **50 mins**   🍴 **MAKES 4**

GALETTES pineapple and rum

Grilling the pineapple first helps to caramelize it, and produces this attractive charred design. A sweet, heady, rum-laced sauce adds a tropical twist.

INGREDIENTS

½ ripe pineapple, skin removed and cored

3 tbsp unsalted butter, melted, for brushing

flour, for dusting

10in (25cm) square sheet of store-bought, all-butter puff pastry

2 tbsp light brown sugar

For the sauce

4 tbsp unsalted butter

¼ cup golden rum

¼ cup packed brown sugar

⅔ cup heavy cream

vanilla ice cream, to serve

PLAN AHEAD

You can wrap the pastry squares in plastic wrap and chill for up to 2 days ahead.

1 Heat a grill pan to very hot. Cut the pineapple in half. Slice each piece into eight thin slices, each 3in (7.5cm) in length. Pat the slices dry with paper towels and brush them lightly with the butter on both sides. Grill the slices for 2 minutes on each side until golden.

2 Preheat the oven to 400°F (200°C). On a floured surface, cut the pastry into four equal-sized squares. Prick each square with a fork, leaving a ¾in (2cm) border around the edge. Sprinkle with the brown sugar and transfer them to a baking sheet sprinkled with a little water.

3 Layer each pastry with four overlapping pineapple slices, leaving the border. Brush the galettes with butter and place them on the top rack of the oven. Bake for 17–20 minutes, until the pastry is golden and puffed up and the pineapple is soft.

4 For the sauce, gently heat the butter, rum, and sugar in a saucepan, stirring occasionally, until the sugar has melted. Bring to a boil, then reduce the heat to a simmer. Add the cream and cook for 10 minutes, until the sauce is thick and syrup-like. Drizzle the sauce over the galettes and serve warm with vanilla ice cream.

🕐 **55 mins** plus cooling   🍴 **SERVES 6–8**

GALETTES des rois

This layered galette from France was traditionally prepared to celebrate the feast of Epiphany.

INGREDIENTS

flour, for dusting

1lb 2oz (500g) store-bought, all-butter puff pastry

1 egg, beaten, to glaze

For the frangipane

7 tbsp unsalted butter, softened

½ cup granulated sugar

1 egg

¾ cup ground almonds

1 tsp almond extract

1 tbsp brandy

PLAN AHEAD

You can prepare and chill the frangipane for up to 3 days ahead.

1 Preheat the oven to 400°F (200°C). For the frangipane, place the butter and sugar in a large bowl and beat until light and fluffy. Add the egg and mix well until combined. Then add the ground almonds, almond extract, and brandy and beat the mixture to form a thick paste.

2 On a lightly floured surface, roll out the pastry to a 20 x 10in (50 x 25cm) rectangle, at least ⅛–¼in (3–5mm) thick. Fold it in half and use a 10in (25cm) plate to cut out two rounds.

3 Place one of the rounds on a nonstick baking sheet. Spread the frangipane on the pastry, leaving a ½in (1cm) border along the edges. Brush the border with a little of the beaten egg.

4 Place the remaining pastry round on top and pinch together the edges to seal. Use a sharp knife to score spiraling slivers on the top of the pastry, making sure they do not meet in the center.

5 Brush the top with beaten egg. Bake on the top rack of the oven for 30 minutes, until golden brown and puffed up. Let the galette cool on the baking sheet for about 5 minutes. Serve warm. You can store the galette in an airtight container in the fridge for up to 3 days.

🕐 **1 hr**
plus chilling and cooling

🍴 **SERVES 6–8**

GALETTE plum and thyme

Fold over the pastry edges to make this free-form tart—this process helps to contain the juices of the sweet, sticky plums. You can also replace the plum with another orchard fruit.

INGREDIENTS

1⅓ cups all-purpose flour, plus extra for dusting

2 tbsp granulated sugar

9 tbsp unsalted butter, chilled and diced

pinch of salt

1 tbsp milk

3 sprigs of thyme

half-and-half, to serve

For the filling

1 tbsp ground almonds

3 tbsp granulated sugar

3 large ripe plums, pitted and thinly sliced

1 Sift the flour and sugar into a large bowl and mix well. Rub in the butter until the mixture resembles fine bread crumbs. Add the salt and 3 tablespoons of ice-cold water to the bowl.

2 Use your fingertips to bring the mixture together to form a dough, adding more cold water if needed. Transfer the dough to a lightly floured surface and knead it gently and briefly until smooth. Wrap it in plastic wrap and chill for at least 1 hour.

3 Preheat the oven to 400°F (200°C). On a lightly floured surface, roll out the pastry to a 12in (30cm) round. Transfer it to a large baking sheet sprinkled with a little water.

4 For the filling, combine the almonds and 1 tablespoon of the sugar in a bowl. Sprinkle it over the pastry, leaving a 2in (5cm) border.

5 Arrange the plum slices over the filling in a spiral pattern. Fold the pastry edges over them, pressing down lightly to enclose the filling. Brush the pastry edges with the milk, sprinkle the plums with the remaining sugar, and place the thyme in the center.

6 Bake in the oven for 35–40 minutes, until the plums are soft and the pastry is golden. Remove from the heat and let cool for 10 minutes. Then remove the thyme and serve warm with half-and-half.

 1 hr 40 mins
plus chilling

SERVES 8

Also great
COLD

DOUBLE-CRUST PIE
cherry

This pie is an all-American classic. Ripe cherries give off
a lot of luscious juice once cooked, so add cornstarch
to transform the liquid into a thick, sticky sauce that
keeps the filling together when you slice it.

INGREDIENTS

2½ cups all-purpose flour,
   plus extra for dusting

1 tsp salt

2 tbsp granulated sugar

16 tbsp unsalted butter,
   chilled and diced

2 tsp apple cider vinegar

For the filling

¼ cup granulated sugar,
   plus extra for sprinkling

¼ cup cornstarch

1 tbsp lemon juice

zest of ½ lemon

pinch of salt

½ tsp vanilla extract

2lb (900g) sweet cherries,
   pitted

1 tbsp unsalted butter,
   chilled and diced

1 large egg, lightly beaten,
   to glaze

SPECIAL EQUIPMENT

9in (23cm) round pie dish,
   about 2in (5cm) deep

PLAN AHEAD

You can store the prepared
dough, wrapped, in the
fridge for up to 2 days ahead.

Gently stir the liquid and flour mixtures until clumps form.

Knead the dough only until it is just smooth.

Make sure that one portion of the dough is roughly double the size of the other.

1 For the dough, place the flour, salt, and sugar in a large bowl and mix well. Rub in the butter and mix well until the mixture resembles coarse bread crumbs. Combine the vinegar with ⅔ cup chilled water in a separate bowl.

2 Gradually add ¼ cup of the liquid mixture to the dry ingredients, using two forks to fluff and stir, until well combined. The mixture should resemble coarse crumbs. If the dough seems dry, add a little more of the liquid mixture and combine.

KNOW-HOW Handle the dough very gently and be careful not to knead it too much. Overworking the pastry can cause the dough to become tough.

3 Transfer the mixture to a lightly floured work surface, and bring it together to form a loose dough. Knead gently for 4–5 minutes, until soft.

4 Divide the dough into one-third and two-thirds of the total quantity so you have two portions. Wrap them both in plastic wrap and chill for at least 30 minutes, or preferably overnight.

5 On a floured surface, roll out the larger portion of the dough to a 12–13in (30–33cm) circle, about ⅛in (3mm) thick. Use it to line the pie dish, leaving a ¾in (2cm) overhang. Chill the pie crust until needed.

6 Preheat the oven to 400°F (200°C). For the filling, place the sugar, cornstarch, lemon juice, zest, salt, and vanilla extract in a large bowl and stir well to combine. Add the cherries, toss well to coat, and let macerate for 10–15 minutes.

Crimp the edges of the dough to your liking (see p35).

KNOW-HOW It is important to cut slits in the pie before baking, as it allows steam to escape and prevents the filling from leaking.

7 Transfer the filling to the pie crust and dot with the butter. Roll out the smaller portion of the dough to a circle slightly larger than the pie dish. Place it on top of the filling and seal the edges. Chill in the freezer for 15–20 minutes.

8 Brush with the beaten egg and sprinkle with the sugar. Cut four slits on top of the pie. Bake for 35–45 minutes, then reduce the temperature to 350°F (180°C). Bake for another 15–20 minutes, until golden. Remove and serve warm. You can store the pie in the fridge for 1–2 days.

🕐 **1 hr 20 mins**
plus chilling 🍴 **SERVES 6–8** 🌡 Also great
COLD

DOUBLE-CRUST PIE
pear and walnut

Nuts are a delicious addition to pie crust. Here, the mellow flavors of pear contrast with the nutty dough.

INGREDIENTS
⅓ cup walnut pieces

⅔ cup granulated sugar, plus extra for sprinkling

1⅓ cups all-purpose flour, sifted, plus extra for dusting

1 egg

11 tbsp unsalted butter, softened, plus extra for greasing

½ tsp salt

1 tsp ground cinnamon

For the filling

1lb 15oz (875g) pears, trimmed, cored, and quartered

½ tsp freshly ground black pepper

juice of 1 lemon

SPECIAL EQUIPMENT
9in (23cm) loose-bottomed tart pan

PLAN AHEAD
You can prepare and store the dough, covered in the fridge, up to 2 days ahead.

1 In a food processor, pulse the walnuts and half the sugar to a fine powder. Combine with the flour in a bowl. Make a well in the center. Add the egg, butter, salt, cinnamon, and the remaining sugar. Combine well.

2 Gradually work the flour into the egg mixture until it resembles coarse bread crumbs. Bring the mixture together to form a dough and knead gently on a floured surface for 1–2 minutes until smooth. Shape into a ball, wrap in plastic wrap, and chill for 30 minutes until firm.

3 Preheat the oven to 375°F (190°C). Grease the pan. On a floured surface, roll out two-thirds of the dough to an 11in (28cm) circle. Use it to line the pan, pressing it up the sides. Trim and chill for 1 hour. Add the trimmings to the reserved dough, rewrap, and chill.

4 For the filling, remove any hard fibers from the pears and place them in a bowl. Toss to coat with the pepper and lemon juice. Shake off any excess juice and arrange them in a spiral pattern in the pie crust.

5 Roll out the reserved dough to a 10in (25cm) circle and drape over the pears. Trim the edges, brush with water, and seal. Sprinkle with sugar and chill for 15 minutes. Place on a baking sheet and bake for 35–40 minutes, until brown on top. Remove and serve hot.

🕐 **1 hr 5 mins**
plus chilling and cooling 🍴 **MAKES 6** 🌡 Also great
COLD

HAND PIES peach

These individual pies, filled with gently spiced peaches, are perfect for picnics.

INGREDIENTS
1 cup all-purpose flour, plus extra for dusting

½ tsp salt

1 tbsp granulated sugar, plus extra for sprinkling

8 tbsp unsalted butter, chilled and diced

1 tsp apple cider vinegar

For the filling

12oz (350g) peaches, peeled and cut into 1in (2.5cm) pieces

1 vanilla bean, seeds removed

⅓ cup dark brown sugar

1 tsp cinnamon

¼ tsp salt

1 tbsp all-purpose flour

1 large egg, lightly beaten

PLAN AHEAD
You can prepare and store dough, covered in the fridge, up to 2 days ahead.

1 Combine the flour, salt, and granulated sugar in a bowl. Rub in the butter until the mixture resembles coarse bread crumbs. Combine the vinegar with ½ cup chilled water in a separate bowl. Gradually add ¼ cup of the liquid mixture to the dry ingredients, using two forks to fluff, until it resembles loose crumbs.

2 Add a little more liquid, if needed. On a floured surface, bring the mixture together to form a dough and gently knead it 3–6 times. Shape into a ball and wrap in plastic wrap. Chill for 30 minutes, preferably overnight.

3 For the filling, combine the peaches and vanilla bean seeds in a bowl. Mix the brown sugar, cinnamon, salt, and flour in a separate bowl and toss with the peaches.

4 On a floured surface, roll out the dough to a 9½ x 15in (24 x 37cm) rectangle, about 1in (2.5cm) thick. Cut out 6 x 5in (12cm) squares. Transfer to a baking sheet and lightly dampen the edges of the dough.

5 Use a slotted spoon to place equal quantities of the filling on one side of each square. Fold the dough over to enclose the filling and seal the edges. Crimp the edges and chill the pies for about 20 minutes. Preheat the oven to 375°F (190°C).

6 Brush the pies with the beaten egg. Cut two small slits on top of each pie. Sprinkle the pies with granulated sugar and bake them for 30–35 minutes, until golden brown. Remove from the heat and let cool slightly. Serve warm.

DOUBLE-CRUST PIE
Alternative fillings

A homemade Cherry double-crust pie (see pp26–29) is a comforting treat, but there are so many alternative fillings to try using the same dough as a crust.

◄ Blueberry and peach
Instead of the cherries, combine 1lb 5oz (600g) peeled, pitted, and thickly sliced ripe peaches with 10oz (300g) blueberries. Add them to the other filling ingredients (see pp26–29, step 6).

▲ Apricot and pistachio
Use 2lb 8oz (1.1 kg) halved, pitted, and quartered just-ripe apricots in place of the cherries. Combine them with ⅓ cup coarsely chopped shelled raw pistachios and add to the other filling ingredients (see pp26–29, step 6).

◄ Apple and cinnamon
Use 3lb (1.35kg) peeled and diced tart apples instead of the cherries. Add ⅓ cup dark brown sugar, ½ tsp cinnamon, ¼ tsp cloves, and ¼ tsp grated nutmeg to the rest of the filling ingredients (see pp26–29, step 6).

◄ Blackberry and apple
Replace the cherries with 1lb (450g) each of blackberries and peeled, cored, and diced apples. Add them to the rest of the filling ingredients (see pp26–29, step 6).

Rhubarb and strawberry ▶
For the perfect summer filling, chop 1lb (450g) rhubarb into ¾in (2cm) chunks and combine with the same quantity of hulled strawberries. Add them to the rest of the filling ingredients (see pp26–29, step 6).

▲ Yellow plum
In place of cherries, add the same amount of halved and pitted yellow plums to the rest of the filling ingredients (see pp26–29, step 6). Plums can give off a lot of liquid if they are very ripe, so use only just-ripe smaller plums.

🕐 **1 hr 35 mins**
plus chilling and cooling

🍴 **SERVES 8**

🌡️ Also great
COLD

SINGLE-CRUST PIE
blueberry and apple

A simple streusel topping is quick to make, and creates a beautifully textured topping for this soft blueberry filling. You need to blind bake the pie crust before filling to give the pie a crisp and golden crust.

INGREDIENTS
1½ cups all-purpose flour, plus extra for dusting

7 tbsp unsalted butter, chilled and diced

1 egg, beaten

For the topping
½ cup all-purpose flour

2 tbsp light brown sugar

½ tsp cinnamon

5 tbsp unsalted butter

¼ cup rolled oats

⅓ cup chopped pecans

salted caramel ice cream, to serve (optional)

For the filling
9oz (250g) blueberries

9oz (250g) apples, peeled, cored, and diced into about ½in (1cm) cubes

2 tbsp cornstarch

3 tbsp granulated sugar

SPECIAL EQUIPMENT
9in (23cm) deep-sided, loose-bottomed tart pan

PLAN AHEAD
You can line the pan with dough and chill for up to 2 days ahead.

1

Place the flour in a bowl and rub in the butter until the mixture resembles fine bread crumbs. Add the egg and bring together to form a smooth dough. Wrap in plastic wrap and chill for 30 minutes. Preheat the oven to 350°F (180°C).

2

On a floured surface, roll out the dough to a circle, ¼in (5mm) thick, and use to line the tart pan. Trim the overhang, prick the crust, line it with parchment paper, and fill with baking beans. Bake for 20 minutes. Remove the beans and parchment and bake for another 5 minutes. Remove and let cool.

3

Leave a few small lumps of butter in the flour mixture.

Increase the oven temperature to 375°F (190°C). For the topping, combine the flour, sugar, cinnamon, and butter into a coarse mixture. Stir in the oats and pecans.

4

For the filling, place all the ingredients in a bowl. Toss well to coat the fruit in the cornstarch and sugar.

KNOW-HOW The apple cubes should be small enough to cook through while baking but not lose their texture.

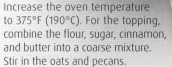

5

Spread the filling in the pie crust evenly and pack it down slightly. Then heap the topping in the center and spread it out loosely and evenly.

6

Bake for 40–45 minutes. Cover loosely with foil if it browns too quickly. Cool for 30 minutes. Remove from the pan and serve warm with salted caramel ice cream, if desired. You can store the pie in the fridge for up to 2 days.

🕐 **1 hr** plus chilling   🍴 **SERVES 6**   🌡 Also great **COLD**

SINGLE-CRUST PIE mincemeat

Many people find Christmas cake dense and heavy. Try this flaky pie instead—it features all the familiar festive flavors.

INGREDIENTS

²/₃ cup dried cranberries

1½ cups each golden raisins and raisins

3 tbsp candied peel

5½oz (150g) apples, peeled, cored, and grated

2 tbsp brandy

¼ cup walnuts, chopped

grated zest and juice of 1 orange

½ tsp ground cinnamon

¼ tsp grated nutmeg

⅛ tsp ground cloves

2 tbsp sliced almonds

confectioners' sugar, to dust

1 cup all-purpose flour, plus extra to dust

2 tbsp granulated sugar

6 tbsp unsalted butter, chilled and diced

1 egg, beaten

For the frangipane

7 tbsp unsalted butter, softened

½ cup granulated sugar

2 large eggs

1 cup ground almonds

⅓ cup all-purpose flour

SPECIAL EQUIPMENT

9in (23cm) loose-bottomed tart pan

baking beans

1 For the filling, chop the cranberries, golden raisins, raisins, and candied peel finely. Mix them with the apples, brandy, walnuts, orange zest and juice, and spices in a large bowl. Cover with plastic wrap and chill overnight.

2 For the dough, combine the flour and granulated sugar in a bowl. Rub in the butter until the mixture resembles bread crumbs. Add the egg and bring the mixture together to form a smooth dough. Wrap it in plastic wrap and chill for 30 minutes. Preheat the oven to 350°F (180°C).

3 On a floured surface, roll out the dough to a circle, ¼in (5mm) thick, and use to line the pan. Prick the dough, line with parchment paper, and fill with baking beans. Bake for 20 minutes. Remove the beans and paper and bake for 5 more minutes, until lightly colored. Remove and set aside.

4 For the frangipane, whisk the butter and granulated sugar in a bowl until light and fluffy. Add the eggs, one at a time, and whisk well after each addition until combined. Fold in the almonds and flour and combine well.

5 Spread the filling evenly in the pie dough. Top with an even layer of the frangipane and sprinkle the sliced almonds over the top. Bake for 40 minutes, until light brown all over. Cool in the pan for 10 minutes before removing it from the pan. Dust with confectioners' sugar and serve warm. You can store the pie in an airtight container for up to 3 days.

🕐 **35 mins** plus chilling and cooling   🍴 **MAKES 4**   🌡 Also great **COLD**

PIES plum and blackberry

These freeform pies are open in the center, and so make the most of an attractive fall fruit filling.

INGREDIENTS

1½ cups all-purpose flour, plus extra for dusting

¼ cup granulated sugar

7 tbsp unsalted butter, chilled and diced

2 large plums, pitted and coarsely chopped into ¾in (2cm) cubes

7oz (200g) blackberries

1 tbsp ground almonds

1 tbsp light brown sugar, plus extra for dusting

½ tsp lemon zest

1 egg, beaten to glaze

custard, to serve

1 Sift the flour and granulated sugar into a bowl. Rub in the butter until the mixture resembles coarse bread crumbs. Add 3–4 tablespoons of chilled water and bring the mixture together to form a smooth dough. Wrap in plastic wrap and chill for 30 minutes.

2 Preheat the oven to 400°F (200°C). Combine the plums, blackberries, almonds, brown sugar, and lemon zest in a large bowl. Divide the dough into four equal portions and shape them into balls. On a lightly floured surface, roll out each ball to an 8in (20cm) round.

3 Place one-quarter of the filling in the center of each round. Pull up the dough edges and crimp them together, leaving an opening in the center to show the filling. Brush the pies with the beaten egg and sprinkle with brown sugar.

4 Place the pies on a large nonstick baking sheet and bake for 20 minutes, until they are crisp underneath and golden brown on top. Remove from the heat and let cool for 10 minutes. Serve warm with custard. Best served on the same day.

Crusts and crimping

Add style to a pie dough. Line a traditional pie dish with dough and trim the excess. Just before you blind bake, embellish the crust.

Crimped Pinch the dough with the thumb and forefinger of one hand, from the outside in, to create a lip. At the same time, use your other forefinger to push the dough between the thumb and forefinger from the inside out. Repeat the process around the dish.

Braided Use a sharp knife to cut three ½ x 9in (1 x 23cm) dough strips. Braid them on a flat surface and use egg wash to stick one braid down on top of your crust. Repeat this process with two more braids of the same size, until the braid reaches around the whole circumference.

Leaf Cut out about 40 leaves using a small leaf-shaped cookie cutter, and use the tip of a small, sharp knife to score a vein design on each one. Use egg wash to attach them to the dough, overlapping as you go. Brush the top with egg wash.

Twisted ribbon Cut two 1 x 15in (2.5 x 38cm) dough strips. Twist one loosely between your hands and use egg wash to fix it around the crust, pressing it down lightly to secure it. Twist and adhere the second strip to complete the circumference of the pie.

🕐 **40 mins** plus cooling   🍴 **MAKES 6**   🌡 Also great **COLD**

PIES peach and raspberry

Thanks to store-bought phyllo dough, these delicacies are so easy to make. They are the perfect ending to a summer meal.

INGREDIENTS

3 sheets store-bought phyllo dough

flour, for dusting

2 tbsp unsalted butter, melted, plus extra if needed

⅓ cup ground almonds

Greek yogurt, to serve

1 tbsp pistachios, finely chopped

For the filling

2 ripe peaches, peeled, pitted, and thinly sliced

4½oz (125g) raspberries

1 heaping tbsp light brown sugar

SPECIAL EQUIPMENT

6-hole muffin pan, about 2½in (6cm) deep

1 Preheat the oven to 375°F (190°C). On a well-floured work surface, roll out one sheet of the phyllo dough and brush with a little butter. Cover with a second layer of dough, brush with butter, and cover with the final sheet. Cut it into 6 equal pieces.

2 Grease the muffin pan and line with the dough pieces. Gently push the dough into the sides, until it ruffles up in places. Brush the edges of the dough with butter and cover the pan with a damp paper towel. For the filling, combine all the ingredients in a large bowl.

3 Divide the almonds evenly between the crusts and top with equal quantities of the filling, allowing it to pile up in the center. Bake for 15–20 minutes, until the pies are crisp and golden and the filling is soft.

4 Remove from the heat and let the pies cool in the pan for 5 minutes. Then transfer to a wire rack to cool slightly before serving them warm with Greek yogurt and topped with pistachios. Best served on the same day.

 **1 hr 10 mins** plus chilling   **SERVES 4-6**   Also great **COLD**

TARTE TATIN apple

According to legend, this tart is named after two French sisters who created the recipe by accident in the 19th century. To create an even layer of caramelized fruit on top of the pastry, fill all the gaps between the apple slices with smaller apple pieces.

INGREDIENTS

1 cup all-purpose flour, sifted, plus extra for dusting

2 tbsp granulated sugar, sifted

7 tbsp unsalted butter, chilled and diced

vanilla ice cream, to serve

For the topping

⅔ cup granulated sugar

2 tbsp unsalted butter

4–5 apples, such as Gala or Fuji, peeled, cored, and cut into eighths

SPECIAL EQUIPMENT

9in (23cm) ovenproof frying pan

Place the flour and sugar in a large bowl. Rub in the butter until the mixture resembles coarse bread crumbs. Add 3 tablespoons of ice-cold water and bring together to form a smooth dough. Wrap in plastic wrap and chill for 30 minutes.

1

For the topping, spread the sugar in the frying pan and heat gently until melting at the edges. Cook, stirring occasionally, until golden. Do not over-stir or the sugar will harden. Remove from the heat.

2

Stir in the butter until combined. Spread the caramel evenly in the pan, then let cool and harden. Preheat the oven to 400°F (200°C).

3

4

Place the apple slices evenly over the cooled caramel in a tight layer. Plug any gaps with small pieces of apple.

5

On a floured surface, roll out the dough. Use a 9½in (24cm) plate to cut out a circle and drape over the apples. Tuck in the edges, creating a small lip around the fruit.

Bake on the top rack of the oven for 30–35 minutes until golden. Cool for 5 minutes before carefully turning the tart onto a large plate. Pour the excess caramel over the apples. Serve immediately with vanilla ice cream.

6

⏱ **30 mins**
plus cooling and chilling   🍴 **SERVES 4–6**   🌡 Also great **COLD**

TARTE TATIN
fig with goat cheese mascarpone

Sweet, ripe figs create a wonderfully sticky topping for this tart. Serve it with mild tangy goat cheese and creamy mascarpone for a delicious Middle Eastern take on the French classic. It looks showstopping and is so easy to make.

INGREDIENTS

4 tbsp unsalted butter

¼ cup granulated sugar

8 ripe figs, trimmed and halved lengthwise

flour, for dusting

10in (25cm) square store-bought puff pastry

For the mascarpone

5½oz (150g) mascarpone, at room temperature

3½oz (100g) soft goat cheese, at room temperature

6 tbsp half-and-half

6 tsp confectioners' sugar

SPECIAL EQUIPMENT

9in (23cm) cast-iron frying pan

PLAN AHEAD

You can prepare and chill the mascarpone up to 3 days ahead.

1 Preheat the oven to 425°F (220°C). Place the butter and sugar in the frying pan over medium heat. Cook, stirring constantly, until the sugar dissolves and the mixture is well combined. Remove and let cool.

2 Place the figs, cut-side down, over the caramel. On a floured surface, roll out the pastry and use a 9½in (24cm) plate to cut out a circle. Drape the pastry over the figs, tucking in the edges to create a small lip around the fruit.

3 Bake the tart on the top rack of the oven for 20 minutes, until golden brown. Let cool for 5 minutes before transferring it to a serving plate. Pour over any excess caramel.

4 Meanwhile, for the mascarpone, place all the ingredients in a large bowl. Beat the mixture until smooth and well combined. Chill until needed. Serve the tart warm, on the same day, along with the mascarpone.

🕐 **35 mins** plus cooling　　🍴 **SERVES 4–6**　　🌡 Also great **COLD**

TARTE TATIN
banana, maple, and rum

This tart is unashamedly sweet, with deep, rich notes of maple syrup alongside the soft sweetness of banana. Serve with good-quality vanilla ice cream.

INGREDIENTS

2 tbsp maple syrup

¼ cup dark brown sugar

2 tbsp unsalted butter

2 tbsp rum

4 slightly underripe bananas, cut into ¾in (2cm) slices

flour, for dusting

10in (25cm) square store-bought puff pastry

SPECIAL EQUIPMENT

9in (23cm) cast-iron frying pan

1 Preheat the oven to 425°F (220°C). Place the maple syrup, sugar, butter, and rum in the frying pan over medium heat. Cook, stirring constantly, until the sugar dissolves and the mixture is well combined.

2 Bring to a boil, then reduce the heat to a simmer. Cook for 2–3 minutes, until the caramel has reduced. Remove and let cool. Place the banana slices over the cooled caramel in tight concentric circles.

3 On a floured surface, roll out the pastry and use a 9½in (24cm) plate to cut out a circle. Drape the pastry over the bananas, tucking in the edges to create a small lip around the fruit.

4 Bake the tart on the top rack of the oven for about 20 minutes, until golden brown. Let cool for 5 minutes before transferring it to a large serving plate. Pour over any excess caramel and serve immediately.

Simple alternatives

There are many fruits that lend themselves to caramelizing. All you require is a good sweet pastry tart recipe (see pp36–37) and an ovenproof frying pan.

Apple and blackberry Fill the gaps between the apple slices with blackberries (see p37, step 4). You will need one less apple, and 3½oz (100g) blackberries.

Pear Use slightly underripe pears in a tarte tatin. Peel, core, and quarter the same quantity of pears as apples (see pp36–37).

Pineapple The flavor of caramel works well with sweet and rich pineapple. Trim, core, and chop 1 medium-sized pineapple into ¾in (2cm) cubes and use in place of the apple (see pp36–37).

Apricot Halve and pit 8 large apricots. Use them instead of the apples in the recipe (see pp36–37). As with all soft fruit, make sure the apricots are not overripe or they may disintegrate before the tart is fully cooked.

Plum Halve and pit 8 plums, and place them skin-side down over the caramel layer instead of the apples (see pp36–37). Choose dark and firm plums.

Peach Halve, pit, and thickly slice 4–6 perfectly ripe peaches. Use in place of the apples for a summery alternative (see pp36–37).

INGREDIENTS

5 tbsp unsalted butter, softened and diced, plus extra for greasing

1 cup all-purpose flour, sifted, plus extra for dusting

3 egg yolks

¼ cup granulated sugar

pinch of salt

½ tsp vanilla extract

3–4 ripe pears, peeled, cored, and cut into wedges

juice of 1 lemon

heavy cream, to serve

For the frangipane

5 tbsp unsalted butter, softened

½ cup granulated sugar

1 egg, plus 1 egg yolk, lightly beaten

1 tbsp Kirsch

1¼ cups ground almonds

2 tbsp all-purpose flour, sifted

For the glaze

⅔ cup apricot jam

2–3 tbsp Kirsch or water

SPECIAL EQUIPMENT

9in (23cm) loose-bottomed, fluted tart pan

PLAN AHEAD

You can store the tart crust in an airtight container in the fridge for up to 3 days ahead, or freeze it for up to 12 weeks.

🕐 **1 hr 30 mins**
plus chilling and cooling

🍴 **SERVES 8**

TART Normandy pear

Rich, crisp butter pastry makes this elegant French tart irresistible. The pairing of pears and frangipane is a classic of the Normandy region, but you can use apples instead for another traditional choice.

Preheat the oven to 400°F (200°C) and grease the tart pan. Place the flour in a large bowl and make a well in the center. Place the butter, egg yolks, sugar, salt, and vanilla extract in the well and mix to combine.

1

2

Use your fingertips to work the ingredients together to form a sticky dough, adding water if needed. Lightly knead the dough on a floured surface for 1–2 minutes, wrap in plastic wrap, and chill for 30 minutes.

Knead the dough gently and work it only until the texture is just smooth.

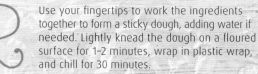

3

On a floured surface, roll out the dough to an 11in (28cm) circle. Use it to line the pan and trim any overhang. Prick the crust with a fork and chill the tart crust for 15 minutes, or until firm.

For the frangipane, beat the butter and sugar in a large bowl for 2–3 minutes until fluffy. Add the egg and yolk, a little at a time, beating well after each addition. Stir in the Kirsch, ground almonds, and flour.

4

Toss the pears with the lemon juice in a small bowl. Spread the frangipane in the tart crust evenly and top with the pears in a spiral pattern. Place the tart on a baking sheet and bake for 12–15 minutes. Then reduce the heat to 350°F (180°C) and bake for another 25–30 minutes, until the filling is set and golden.

5

6

Let cool slightly, then remove the tart from the pan. For the glaze, push the jam through a strainer into a heatproof bowl. Add the Kirsch, melt over a saucepan of hot water, and brush over the tart. Serve warm with heavy cream. You can store the tart in an airtight container for up to 2 days.

🕐 **1 hr 15 mins**
 plus chilling and cooling   🍴 **SERVES 8**

TART French apple

This stunning tart combines a layer of pureed cooked apple, topped with an overlapping spiral of finely cut fresh apple. Glazing makes a homemade tart look as appetizing as one in a French patisserie—use apricot jam for this recipe.

INGREDIENTS
flour, for dusting

13oz (375g) store-bought pie crust

2 tbsp apricot jam, strained

For the filling

4 tbsp unsalted butter

1lb 10oz (750g) apples, cored and coarsely chopped

½ cup granulated sugar

finely grated zest and juice of ½ lemon

2 tbsp Calvados or brandy

2 sweet apples, cored and thinly sliced

SPECIAL EQUIPMENT
9in (23cm) loose-bottomed tart pan

PLAN AHEAD
You can store the blind-baked pie crust in an airtight container in the fridge for up to 3 days ahead, or freeze it for up to 12 weeks.

1 On a lightly floured surface, roll out the crust to an 11in (28cm) large and ⅛in (3mm) thick circle. Use the circle to line the pan, leaving an overhang of ¾in (2cm). Prick the bottom and chill for 30 minutes. Preheat the oven to 400°F (200°C).

2 Prick the crust and line it with parchment paper. Fill with baking beans, and place on a baking sheet. Blind bake the tart crust for 20 minutes, then remove the beans and paper and bake for another 5 minutes, until it is a light golden color. Remove and set aside.

3 For the filling, melt the butter in a lidded saucepan over low heat and add the apples. Then cover and cook for 15 minutes, stirring, until soft. Push the cooked apple through a strainer to make a smooth puree.

4 Return the puree to the pan. Reserve 1 tablespoon of the sugar and stir the rest into the pan. Add the lemon zest and Calvados, and reduce the heat to a simmer. Cook the puree, stirring frequently, until thickened.

5 Spread the puree evenly in the tart crust and top with the dessert apples in a spiral pattern. Brush with the lemon juice and sprinkle with the reserved sugar. Bake for 30–35 minutes, until the apples are a pale gold in color.

6 Trim the crust and let cool slightly in the pan before removing the tart. Warm the jam and brush over the top. Serve warm. You can store the tart in an airtight container in the fridge for up to 2 days.

⏱ **1 hr 10 mins**
plus chilling and cooling   🍴 **SERVES 8**

TART custard

Delicious and simple to make, this tart is made with gently set homemade custard that is delicately flavored with nutmeg.

INGREDIENTS

1 cup all-purpose flour, plus extra for dusting

7 tbsp unsalted butter, chilled and diced

¼ cup granulated sugar

2 egg yolks

½ tsp vanilla extract

For the filling

2 eggs

2 tbsp granulated sugar

½ tsp vanilla extract

¼ tsp grated nutmeg

1 cup milk

⅔ cup heavy cream

SPECIAL EQUIPMENT

9in (23cm) loose-bottomed tart pan

PLAN AHEAD

You can store the blind-baked tart crust in an airtight container in the fridge for up to 3 days ahead, or freeze it for up to 12 weeks.

1 Place the flour in a large bowl and rub in the butter until the mixture resembles bread crumbs. Stir in the sugar. In a separate bowl, beat together the egg yolks and vanilla extract until combined. Add the egg mixture to the dry ingredients and bring together to form a soft dough. Wrap in plastic wrap and chill for 1 hour.

2 Preheat the oven to 350°F (180°C). Roll out the dough and use it to line the tart pan (see French apple tart, step 1). Prick the bottom, chill, and then blind bake the tart crust until light golden in color (see French apple tart, step 2). Trim the overhanging dough. Reduce the oven temperature to 340°F (170°C).

3 For the filling, beat the eggs, sugar, vanilla extract, and nutmeg in a bowl until combined. Place the milk and cream in a saucepan, bring to a boil, and pour the hot mixture over the egg mixture, mixing to combine.

4 Place the tart crust on a baking sheet and put in the oven. Carefully pour in the filling and spread it out evenly. Bake for 20–25 minutes, until just set but with a slight wobble. Let cool in the pan for 15 minutes, before removing the tart. Serve warm. You can store the tart in an airtight container in the fridge for up to 1 day.

⏱ **1 hr 50 mins**
plus chilling and cooling   🍴 **SERVES 8**

TART treacle

The fillings for most classic treacle tarts include little more than bread crumbs and syrup. This version is given a French twist with the addition of cream and eggs, for a just-set texture.

INGREDIENTS

1 cup all-purpose flour, plus extra for dusting

7 tbsp unsalted butter, chilled and diced

½ tsp vanilla extract

1 egg yolk

¼ cup granulated sugar

For the filling

¾ cup corn syrup

¾ cup heavy cream

2 eggs

finely grated zest of 1 orange

1 cup brioche or croissant crumbs

whipped cream, to serve

SPECIAL EQUIPMENT

9in (23cm) loose-bottomed tart pan

PLAN AHEAD

You can store the blind-baked tart crust in an airtight container in the fridge for up to 3 days ahead, or freeze it for up to 12 weeks.

1 Place the flour in a large bowl and rub in the butter until the mixture resembles bread crumbs. Beat the vanilla extract and egg yolk in a separate bowl. Add the egg mixture and sugar to the flour mixture and bring them together to form a soft dough, adding water if it seems dry. Wrap in plastic wrap and chill for 30 minutes.

2 Preheat the oven to 350°F (180°C). Roll out the dough and use it to line the tart pan (see French apple tart, step 1). Prick the bottom, chill it, and then blind bake the tart crust until light golden in color (see French apple tart, step 2). Reduce the heat to 340°F (170°C).

3 For the filling, mix the corn syrup, cream, eggs, and orange zest in a large bowl until combined. Gently fold in the brioche crumbs and combine well. Place the tart crust on a baking sheet and then on an oven rack. Carefully pour the filling into the tart crust, ensuring that it spreads out evenly.

4 Carefully slide the rack into the oven and bake for 30 minutes, until the filling is just set. Trim the overhanging dough while still warm. Let cool in the pan for 15 minutes, before removing the tart. Serve warm with whipped cream. You can store the tart in an airtight container for up to 2 days.

🕐 **1 hr 35 mins**
plus cooling   🍴 **SERVES 8**   🌡 Also great
COLD

PIE pumpkin

Dark, rich, and sweet, this quintessentially American pie has all the fragrance and flavors of fall wrapped in a crisp pie crust. It is the perfect dessert to bring to the Thanksgiving table.

INGREDIENTS

8 tbsp butter, chilled
  and diced, plus
  extra for greasing
1¼ cups all-purpose flour,
  plus extra for dusting
1 tbsp granulated sugar
½ tsp salt
1 tsp apple cider vinegar
whipped cream, to serve

For the filling
1 x 14oz (400g) can
  pumpkin puree
½ cup whole milk
¾ cup dark brown sugar
1⅛ tsp ground cinnamon

½ tsp grated nutmeg
⅛ tsp ground allspice
½ tsp salt
2 large eggs

SPECIAL EQUIPMENT
9in (23cm) pie dish, about
  2in (5cm) deep
baking beans

PLAN AHEAD
You can store the blind-baked pie crust in an airtight container up to 3 days ahead.

The mixture should resemble loose crumbs.

 Grease the pie dish. Combine the flour, granulated sugar, and salt in a bowl. Rub in the butter with your fingertips until the mixture resembles coarse bread crumbs. In a separate bowl, combine the cider vinegar with ½ cup chilled water.

Gradually add ½ cup of the liquid mixture to the dry ingredients, using two forks to fluff and stir them together until clumps form. Add a little more of the liquid mixture if it seems too dry.

Knead the dough only until it is just smooth.

KNOW-HOW Chilling the dough allows the gluten to relax, making the dough easier to roll out. It also helps prevent the dough from shrinking.

On a lightly floured surface, gently knead the mixture 3–6 times, until it comes together to form a dough. Wrap the dough in plastic wrap and chill it for 30 minutes, or preferably overnight.

 On a floured surface, roll out the dough to a 12in (30cm) circle, ⅛in (2mm) thick. Use to line the pie dish, leaving an overhang of ½in (1cm). Crimp the edges of the dough (see p35) and chill for 30 minutes. Preheat the oven to 375°F (190°C).

KNOW-HOW Blind bake the pie crust to prevent the filling from creating a soggy bottom.

Prick the bottom of the pie crust, then line it with parchment paper and fill with baking beans. Place on a baking sheet and bake for about 25 minutes, until lightly brown at the edges.

Remove the beans and paper. Bake for another 6-10 minutes, until the crust is golden. Remove from the oven, trim, and let cool. Reduce the oven temperature to 350°F (180°C).

For the filling, whisk the pumpkin puree, milk, and brown sugar in a bowl until smooth. Beat in the spices, salt, and eggs until smooth and well combined.

Pour the filling into the pie crust and place on a baking sheet. Cover the edges with foil and bake for 35-40 minutes. Remove the foil and bake for another 10 minutes, until set. Let cool slightly and serve warm with whipped cream. You can store the pie in an airtight container for up to 2 days.

🕐 **1 hr 40 mins**
plus chilling and cooling

🍴 **SERVES 8**

🌡 Also great
COLD

PIE brûléed spiced pumpkin

This recipe packs a punch thanks to the cardamom and cloves. A brûlée topping is
a caramelizing technique that gives a professional finish—try it with any just-set tart.

INGREDIENTS

8 tbsp unsalted butter,
chilled and diced, plus
extra for greasing

1¼ cups all-purpose flour,
plus extra for dusting

2½ tbsp granulated sugar

½ tsp salt

1 tsp apple cider vinegar

whipped cream, to serve

For the filling

1 x 14oz (400g) can
pumpkin puree

1 x 14oz (400g) can
condensed milk

1¼ tsp ground cinnamon

½ tsp grated nutmeg

¼ tsp ground cardamom

⅛ tsp ground cloves

½ tsp pure vanilla extract

¼ tsp salt

2 large eggs

SPECIAL EQUIPMENT

9in (23cm) pie dish, about
2in (5cm) deep

baking beans

small kitchen blowtorch

PLAN AHEAD

You can store the blind-
baked pie crust in an
airtight container up
to 3 days ahead.

1 Grease the pie dish and set aside. Combine the flour,
1 tablespoon of sugar, and salt in a bowl. Rub in the
butter until the mixture resembles coarse bread crumbs.
Mix the vinegar with ½ cup chilled water in a bowl.

2 Gradually add ½ cup of the liquid mixture to the dry
ingredients. Use two forks to fluff and stir the mixture
until it forms clumps. On a floured surface, gently knead it
3-6 times to form a dough. Wrap in plastic wrap and chill
for 30 minutes, preferably overnight.

3 On a floured surface, roll out the dough to a 12–13in
(30–33cm) circle, ⅛in (3mm) thick. Use it to line the pie
dish, leaving a ½in (1cm) overhang. Crimp the edges and
chill for 30 minutes. Preheat the oven to 375°F (190°C).

4 Prick the bottom of the dough, line with parchment
paper, and fill with baking beans. Bake for 25 minutes.
Then remove the beans and paper and bake for another
6–10 minutes, until lightly golden. Remove from the heat,
trim, and let cool.

5 Reduce the temperature to 350°F (180°C). For the
filling, whisk the pumpkin puree and milk in a bowl
until combined. Then beat in the remaining ingredients
until smooth.

6 Pour the filling into the pie crust and cover the
edges with foil. Bake for 35 minutes until set,
then remove the foil and bake for another 10 minutes.
Remove from the heat and let cool completely.

7 Sprinkle the remaining sugar over the pie and
gently spread it out with the back of a spoon.
Use the blowtorch to melt the sugar, sweeping it
over gently to form a caramel. Serve at room
temperature with whipped cream. You can store
the pie in an airtight container for up to 2 days.

PIE sweet potato

🕐 **1 hr 30 mins**
plus chilling and cooling

🍴 **SERVES 8**

🌡 Also great
COLD

Another Southern holiday favorite, sweet potato pie has a light and velvet-like texture.

INGREDIENTS

1½ tbsp unsalted butter, melted, plus extra for greasing

1 recipe pie dough (see Brûléed spiced pumpkin pie, steps 1–2)

1¼lb (550g) sweet potatoes, boiled and mashed

¼ tsp salt

¾ cup condensed milk

½ cup evaporated milk

2 tbsp dark brown sugar

1¼ tsp ground cinnamon

½ tsp grated nutmeg

½ tsp vanilla extract

2 large eggs

whipped cream, to serve

SPECIAL EQUIPMENT

9in (23cm) pie dish, about 2in (5cm) deep

baking beans

PLAN AHEAD

You can store the blind-baked pie crust in an airtight container up to 3 days ahead.

1 Preheat the oven to 350°F (180°C). Grease the pie dish. Roll out the dough, use it to line the dish, and blind bake it (see Brûléed spiced pumpkin pie, steps 3–4). Beat the potatoes, butter, salt, and both types of milk in a large bowl until smooth and well combined.

2 Add the brown sugar, cinnamon, nutmeg, vanilla extract, and eggs to the bowl. Beat until smooth, and pour the filling into the pie crust evenly. Cover the edges with foil.

3 Transfer the pie to the oven and bake for about 35 minutes, until the filling is set. Then remove the foil and bake for another 10 minutes. Remove from the heat.

4 Let cool slightly in the dish, then transfer to a wire rack to cool completely. Serve at room temperature with whipped cream. You can store the sweet potato pie in an airtight container for up to 2 days.

PIE pumpkin and pecan

🕐 **1 hr 30 mins**
plus chilling and cooling

🍴 **SERVES 8**

🌡 Also great
COLD

This recipe requires a metal tart pan instead of a pie dish. The pan helps heat to conduct evenly, resulting in a super-crisp crust.

INGREDIENTS

1 cup all-purpose flour, plus extra for dusting

7 tbsp unsalted butter, chilled and diced

¼ cup granulated sugar

1 egg yolk

½ tsp vanilla extract

For the filling

3 eggs

½ cup light brown sugar

1 tsp pumpkin pie spice

¾ cup heavy cream

1 tsp ground cinnamon

2 tbsp maple syrup

1 x 14oz (400g) can pumpkin puree

½ cup pecans, coarsely chopped

SPECIAL EQUIPMENT

9in (23cm) loose-bottomed tart pan

baking beans

PLAN AHEAD

You can store the blind-baked pie crust in an airtight container up to 3 days ahead.

1 Place the flour in a bowl and rub in the butter until the mixture resembles bread crumbs. Stir in the sugar. In a separate bowl, whisk the egg yolk and vanilla extract and add to the flour mixture. Bring them together to form a dough, adding a little water if it seems dry. Wrap in plastic wrap and chill for 30 minutes.

2 Preheat the oven to 350°F (180°C). On a lightly floured surface, roll out the dough to an ⅛in (3mm) thick circle. Use it to line the pan, leaving a ¾in (2cm) overhang. Prick the bottom of the dough, line it with parchment paper, and fill with baking beans.

3 Place the pie crust on a baking sheet and bake for 20 minutes. Then remove the beans and paper and bake for another 5 minutes if the center seems uncooked. Remove from the heat, trim, and let cool.

4 For the filling, whisk the eggs, brown sugar, pumpkin pie spice, cream, cinnamon, and maple syrup in a bowl until combined, then beat in the pumpkin until well-blended. Sprinkle the pecans in the pie crust. Place the tart crust on a baking sheet.

5 Carefully pour the filling into the pie crust, spread it out evenly, and bake for 45–50 minutes until set. Let the pie cool in the pan for 15 minutes before transferring to a wire rack. Serve warm. You can store the pie in an airtight container in the fridge for up to 2 days.

40 mins plus resting   **MAKES 12**   Also great **COLD**

DOUGHNUTS jam

These airy and addictive delights are so much better than any store-bought variety you have ever tried. They are also surprisingly easy to make—the trick is to achieve the right temperature for the oil, and to maintain it throughout cooking.

INGREDIENTS

⅔ cup whole milk

5 tbsp unsalted butter

½ tsp vanilla extract

2 tsp dried yeast

⅓ cup granulated sugar, plus extra for coating

2¼ cups all-purpose flour, plus extra for dusting

½ tsp salt

2 eggs, beaten

3½ cups sunflower oil, plus extra for greasing

¾ cup good-quality raspberry, strawberry, or cherry jam, pureed until smooth

SPECIAL EQUIPMENT

oil thermometer

piping bag with thin nozzle

PLAN AHEAD

You can store the unfilled doughnuts in an airtight container up to 1 day ahead.

1

Heat the milk, butter, and vanilla extract in a saucepan over medium heat until combined. Cool to lukewarm and whisk in the yeast and 1 tablespoon of sugar. Cover and leave for 10 minutes. Sift the flour, salt, and the remaining sugar into a large bowl. Whisk the eggs into the cooled milk mixture until combined.

2

Make a well in the center of the dry ingredients. Pour in the milk mixture and bring together to form a dough. On a floured surface, knead the dough for 10 minutes until soft. Transfer to a greased bowl, cover with plastic wrap, and leave in a warm place for 2 hours to rise.

3

On a floured surface, punch down the dough until smooth. Divide it into 12 portions and shape into balls. Place them on nonstick baking sheets, spaced apart, and cover with plastic wrap and a kitchen towel. Rest the dough balls in a warm place for 1–2 hours, until they double in size.

4

Heat the oil in a large, deep saucepan to 340–350°F (170–180°C). Carefully slide the doughnuts, rounded-side down, into the oil. Fry them for 1 minute on each side, until golden brown all over. Remove with a slotted spoon. Fry in batches to avoid overcrowding the pan.

5

Drain the doughnuts on plates lined with paper towels. Roll them in some sugar while they are still hot.

6

Place the jam in a piping bag. Pierce each doughnut on the side and gently squirt in a tablespoon of the jam, until it almost spills out. Dust with a little more sugar and serve warm. You can store them in an airtight container for up to 1 day.

🕐 **25 mins** 🍴 **MAKES 25–30**

FRITTERS apple and cinnamon

It is easy and quick to transform apples and some pantry ingredients into these light and delicious fritters.

INGREDIENTS
½ cup whole milk

1 egg

2 tbsp unsalted butter, melted and cooled

½ tsp vanilla extract

1 cup all-purpose flour

½ tsp salt

1 tsp baking powder

1 tsp ground cinnamon

¼ cup granulated sugar

2 apples, peeled, cored, and finely diced

3½ cups sunflower or other flavorless oil

confectioners' sugar, for dusting

SPECIAL EQUIPMENT
oil thermometer

1 Whisk the milk, egg, butter, and vanilla extract in a large bowl until well combined. Sift the flour, salt, baking powder, cinnamon, and granulated sugar into a separate bowl and mix well. Bring the wet and dry ingredients together to form a thick batter. Fold in the apples.

2 Heat the oil in a large, heavy-bottomed saucepan to 350°F (180°C). Drop a small amount of the batter into the oil to test if it is hot enough—the batter should sizzle and turn golden brown in color.

3 Carefully drop a few heaping teaspoons of the batter into the hot oil and cook them for 2–3 minutes on each side, until golden brown all over. Do not use large amounts of the batter or overcrowd the pan.

4 Remove the fritters with a slotted spoon. Leave them to drain on a plate lined with paper towels, or keep them warm in a preheated oven. Continue cooking until you have used all of the batter. Dust the warm fritters with a little confectioners' sugar and serve immediately.

🕐 **25 mins** 🍴 **MAKES 25–30**

FRITTERS lemon and ricotta

These airy little puffs, straight from the pan, are so addictive—serve them at a dinner party and you will find it hard to cook them quickly enough for your guests.

INGREDIENTS
7oz (200g) ricotta cheese

2 eggs, beaten

½ tsp vanilla extract

2 tbsp unsalted butter, melted and cooled

¾ cup all-purpose flour

2 tsp baking powder

¼ cup granulated sugar

1 tsp lemon zest

1 tbsp lemon juice

3½ cups sunflower or other flavorless oil

confectioners' sugar, to dust

SPECIAL EQUIPMENT
oil thermometer

1 Whisk the ricotta, eggs, vanilla extract, and butter in a small bowl until well combined. Sift the flour, baking powder, and granulated sugar into a separate bowl. Add the lemon zest, then bring the dry and wet mixture together to form a thick batter. Add the lemon juice and mix well to combine.

2 Heat the oil in a large, heavy-bottomed saucepan to 350°F (180°C). Test to see if the oil is hot (see Apple and cinnamon fritters, step 2). Cook heaping teaspoons of the batter in the oil until golden brown all over (see Apple and cinnamon fritters, step 3).

3 Remove the fritters with a slotted spoon and drain them on a plate lined with paper towels, or keep them warm in a preheated oven. Continue cooking until you have used all of the batter. Dust the warm fritters with a little confectioners' sugar and serve immediately.

BEIGNETS
pumpkin spice

This is a delicious treat that is popular in New Orleans. Beignets were first brought to Louisiana by French settlers in the 1700s.

INGREDIENTS

1 heaping tsp (7g) active dried yeast

½ cup granulated sugar, plus a pinch extra

1 cup heavy cream

4 tbsp butter

2 eggs

4¼ cups all-purpose flour, plus extra for dusting

3½ cups peanut or sunflower oil

For the spice mix

1 tbsp ground cinnamon

½ tbsp ground ginger

½ tbsp grated nutmeg

½ tbsp ground cloves

⅔ cup confectioners' sugar

SPECIAL EQUIPMENT

oil thermometer

1 Place ½ cup warm water in a bowl. Add the yeast and a pinch of granulated sugar and stir to dissolve. Let stand for 5–7 minutes, until it begins to bubble. For the spice mix, combine all the ingredients in a small bowl and set aside.

2 Heat the cream and butter in a large saucepan over low heat until the butter melts. Transfer to a large bowl and add the yeast mixture, sugar, eggs, and half the flour. Stir well to combine, then gradually add the remaining flour and stir well to form a smooth dough.

3 Knead the dough for 5–7 minutes until it is smooth, adding more flour if it is sticky and difficult to handle. Place the dough in a bowl, cover with plastic wrap, and chill for 4–6 hours, until it doubles in size.

4 On a floured surface, roll out the dough to a large circle, about ½in (1cm) thick. Cut it into 40 squares, each about 1½in (4cm) in diameter. Heat the oil in a large, heavy-bottomed saucepan to 375°F (190°C).

5 Cook the squares in batches for 1–2 minutes on each side, until golden brown and puffed. Remove with a slotted spoon and place on a wire rack to cool slightly. Sprinkle the spice mix over the warm beignets and serve immediately.

CHURROS with spicy chocolate sauce

Sprinkled with cinnamon–sugar and served with a rich and spicy chocolate dipping sauce, these Spanish treats make the perfect accompaniment to after-dinner coffee.

INGREDIENTS

2 tbsp unsalted butter

1⅔ cups all-purpose flour

1 tsp baking powder

¼ cup granulated sugar

3½ cups peanut or sunflower oil

1 tsp ground cinnamon

For the sauce

1¾oz (50g) good-quality dark chocolate, broken into pieces

⅔ cup heavy cream

1 tbsp granulated sugar

1 tbsp unsalted butter

pinch of salt

¼ tsp chile powder, to taste

SPECIAL EQUIPMENT

piping bag fitted with a ¾in (2cm) star nozzle

oil thermometer

1 Place the butter and ¾ cup boiling water in a pitcher and stir well. Sift the flour, baking powder, and half the sugar into a bowl. Make a well in the center and gradually add the liquid mixture, beating continuously to form a thick batter. Let cool for 5 minutes.

2 Heat the oil in a large, heavy-bottomed saucepan to 375°F (190°C). Spoon the batter into the piping bag and pipe 2¾in (7cm) lengths into the pan, in batches, using a pair of scissors to snip off the ends. Cook them for 1–2 minutes on each side, until golden brown all over.

3 Remove them with a slotted spoon and drain on a plate lined with paper towels. Combine the cinnamon and remaining sugar in a plate and use to lightly coat the churros while still hot. Let cool for 5–10 minutes.

4 For the sauce, melt the chocolate, cream, sugar, and butter in a heatproof bowl over a pan of simmering water, making sure it does not touch the water. Stir for 3–4 minutes, until the sauce thickens.

5 Remove from the heat, add the salt, and mix well. Add the chile powder gradually, until it reaches the desired level of heat. Serve the sauce with the warm churros immediately.

🕐 **1 hr 10 mins** plus cooling 🍴 **MAKES 9** 🌡 Also great **COLD**

BROWNIES triple chocolate chip

The best kind of brownie is crisp on the surface and gently yielding on the inside. If you prefer them really soft and gooey, bake them for 5 minutes less than suggested here. If you like them firm, add 5 minutes more to the cooking time.

INGREDIENTS

8 tbsp unsalted butter, plus extra for greasing

6oz (175g) good-quality dark chocolate, finely chopped

2oz (60g) unsweetened chocolate, finely chopped

2 tsp vanilla extract

1 cup granulated sugar

¼ cup dark brown sugar

2 large eggs

1 cup all-purpose flour

3 tbsp natural cocoa powder

¾ tsp salt

¼ tsp baking powder

⅓ cup good-quality milk chocolate chips

⅓ cup white chocolate chips

vanilla ice cream, to serve (optional)

SPECIAL EQUIPMENT

8in (20cm) square cake pan

1

Preheat the oven to 350°F (180°C). Lightly grease and line the pan with parchment paper, leaving some overhang. Melt the butter and both types of chocolate in a heatproof bowl over a saucepan of simmering water, making sure it does not touch the water. Stir until smooth, then let cool.

2

Gradually add the vanilla extract and both types of sugar to the mixture and whisk well to combine. Then add the eggs, one at a time, whisking well after each addition until smooth. Place the flour, cocoa powder, salt, and baking powder in a separate bowl and mix well.

3

Use a spatula to fold the dry ingredients into the chocolate mixture and combine until smooth. Then mix in both types of chocolate chips until evenly incorporated. Pour the brownie mixture into the prepared pan and spread it out evenly.

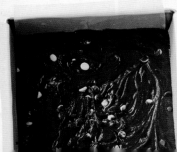

4

Bake for 40–45 minutes, until an inserted toothpick comes out clean. Let cool slightly before removing the brownie from the pan. Then cut it into nine equal-sized pieces, cleaning the knife with a damp paper towel between cuts. Serve warm with vanilla ice cream, if desired. You can store them in an airtight container for up to 5 days.

BROWNIES cheesecake

🕐 **1 hr 10 mins** plus cooling 　🍴 **MAKES 9** 　🌡 Also great **COLD**

This rich and moist variety is rippled with sweetened cream cheese to provide a pleasing contrast in flavor and texture.

1 Preheat the oven to 350°F (180°C). Grease and line an **8in (20cm) square pan** with parchment paper, leaving some overhang. Melt **6 tbsp unsalted butter**, **2½oz (75g) finely chopped dark chocolate**, and **1½oz (45g) finely chopped unsweetened chocolate** in a heatproof bowl over a saucepan of simmering water, making sure it does not touch the water. Stir until smooth.

2 Let the chocolate mixture cool, then gradually mix in **¾ cup granulated sugar** and **2 tbsp dark brown sugar** to combine. Add **2 eggs**, one at a time, beating well after each addition until smooth. Whisk in **1½ tsp vanilla extract**. Combine **½ cup all-purpose flour**, **½ tsp salt**, and **½ tsp baking powder** in a separate bowl and fold into the mixture.

3 Beat **8oz (225g) full-fat cream cheese** in a separate bowl, until smooth. Add **1 tsp pure vanilla extract**, **⅛ tsp salt**, **1 large egg yolk**, and **⅓ cup confectioners' sugar**. Mix to combine. Pour the chocolate mixture into the pan. Spoon over the cheese mixture and swirl the point of a knife through it.

4 Bake for 40–45 minutes, until a toothpick inserted into the center comes out with very few crumbs. Let cool slightly in the pan, then transfer to a large plate. Cut into nine even-sized pieces and serve warm. You can store them in an airtight container in the fridge for up to 4 days.

BROWNIES chocolate and raspberry

🕐 **1 hr 5 mins** plus cooling 　🍴 **MAKES 24** 　🌡 Also great **COLD**

There are few better flavor combinations than raspberries and dark chocolate. Served warm with whipped cream, these brownies are truly decadent.

1 Preheat the oven 350°F (180°C). Lightly grease and line a deep **9 x 13in (23 x 32cm) baking pan** with parchment paper, leaving some overhang. Melt **8 tbsp unsalted butter** and **8oz (225g) finely chopped dark chocolate** in a heatproof bowl (see Cheesecake brownies, step 1).

2 Let the chocolate mixture cool, then add **1 cup dark brown sugar**, **½ cup granulated sugar**, and **2 tsp vanilla extract**, mixing well to combine. Add **4 large eggs**, one at a time, mixing well after each addition until smooth.

3 Combine **1¼ cups all-purpose flour**, **1 tsp salt**, and **1 tsp baking powder** in small bowl and fold into the brownie mixture until incorporated. Fold in **8oz (225g) raspberries** and **¾ cup milk chocolate chips**. Mix well and pour into the pan in an even layer.

4 Bake for 30–35 minutes, until a toothpick inserted into the center comes out clean. Let cool slightly in the pan, then transfer to a large plate. Cut into 24 equal-sized squares and serve warm. You can store them in an airtight container in the fridge for up to 3 days.

Chocolate and raspberry

Cheesecake

Salted peanut

Pecan blondies

🕐 **1 hr**
plus cooling

🍴 **MAKES 9**

🌡 Also great
COLD

BROWNIES
salted peanut

A pinch of good-quality sea salt can enhance the flavor of many chocolate desserts. Here the salted peanuts give the brownies a deliciously piquant edge.

1. Preheat the oven to 350°F (180°C). Grease and line an **8in (20cm) square cake pan** with parchment paper, leaving some overhang. Melt **6 tbsp unsalted butter, 4½oz (125g) finely chopped semisweet chocolate**, and **2oz (60g) finely chopped unsweetened chocolate** in a heatproof bowl (see Cheesecake brownies, step 1).

2. Let the chocolate mixture cool, then gradually add **1 cup granulated sugar, ½ cup dark brown sugar**, and **2 tsp vanilla extract**. Mix well to incorporate. Add **2 eggs**, one at a time, mixing well after each addition until smooth.

3. Combine **¾ cup all-purpose flour, ½ tsp salt**, and **¼ tsp baking powder** in a medium bowl and fold into the chocolate mixture. Then add **½ cup chopped salted peanuts**, mix well, and pour the mixture into the pan in an even layer.

4. Bake for 40–45 minutes, until a toothpick inserted into the center comes out clean. Let cool slightly in the pan, then transfer to a plate. Cut into nine equal-sized squares and serve warm. You can store them in an airtight container for up to 5 days.

🕐 **45 mins**
plus cooling

🍴 **MAKES 24**

🌡 Also great
COLD

BLONDIES pecan

Made with white chocolate, these brownies are creamy and rich. The chopped pecans add instant crunch. You can also try hazelnuts or pistachios.

1. Preheat the oven to 350°F (180°C). Grease and line a deep **9 x 13in (23 x 32cm) baking pan** with parchment paper, leaving some overhang. Melt **10 tbsp unsalted butter** in a small saucepan over low heat.

2. Remove from the heat and add **1½ cups light brown sugar** and **1½ tsp vanilla extract**. Mix until combined. Add **3 large eggs**, one at a time, and mix well after each addition until the mixture is smooth.

3. Combine **1½ cups all-purpose flour, 1 tsp salt**, and **1¼ tsp baking powder** in a separate bowl and fold into the mixture until combined. Then fold in **1 cup chopped pecans** and **1 cup white chocolate chips**, mixing until evenly combined. Pour the mixture into the pan in an even layer.

4. Bake for 30 minutes, until a toothpick inserted into the center comes out clean. Let cool slightly in the pan, then transfer to a large plate. Cut it into 24 even-sized pieces, wiping the knife on a clean paper towel after each cut. Serve warm. You can store them in an airtight container for up to 4 days.

🕐 **45 mins**
plus resting and cooling

🍴 **SERVES 6**

CLAFOUTIS cherry

First popular in 19th-century France, clafoutis combines the simplest ingredients to stunning effect. For best results, use a cast-iron frying pan, which helps to conduct the heat and cook evenly. Serve warm, directly from oven to table.

INGREDIENTS
2 tbsp unsalted butter, melted and cooled, plus extra for greasing
½ cup all-purpose flour
¼ cup granulated sugar
2 eggs
½ cup whole milk
½ cup heavy cream
1 tsp vanilla extract
1 x 12oz (300g) can pitted cherries, drained
confectioners' sugar, for dusting

SPECIAL EQUIPMENT
10in (25cm) cast-iron frying pan or ovenproof dish

1 Preheat the oven to 400°F (200°C). Grease the frying pan and set aside. Combine the flour and granulated sugar in a large bowl. Add the eggs, one at a time, beating well after each addition until combined. Then mix in the butter until it is well incorporated.

2 Add the milk and cream alternately, a little at a time, and whisk well to form a smooth batter. Add the vanilla extract and mix well to combine. Let rest at room temperature for 30 minutes.

Whisk the mixture well after each addition.

3 *Ensure that the batter and cherries are evenly distributed.*

Spread out the cherries in the pan in an even layer and carefully pour the batter over them.

4 Bake on the top rack of the oven for 30 minutes, until the top is golden brown and the center is firm. Remove and cool for 5 minutes. Dust with confectioners' sugar and serve warm, or at room temperature. Best served on the same day.

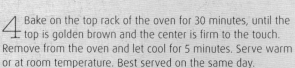

CLAFOUTIS apricot and almond

You only need pantry ingredients to make this variety, so it is ideal for a last-minute dessert.

INGREDIENTS

2 tbsp butter, melted and cooled, plus extra for greasing
½ cup ground almonds
3 tbsp all-purpose flour
¼ cup granulated sugar
2 eggs
½ cup whole milk
½ cup heavy cream
1 tsp vanilla extract
1 x 14oz (400g) can apricots, drained and halved
¼ cup sliced almonds
confectioners' sugar, for dusting

SPECIAL EQUIPMENT
10in (25cm) cast-iron frying pan

1 Preheat the oven to 400°F (200°C). Grease the frying pan and set aside. Combine the ground almonds, flour, and granulated sugar in a large bowl. Add the eggs, one at a time, mixing well after each addition. Then mix in the butter until incorporated.

2 Mix in the milk and cream gradually (see Blackberry and pear clafoutis, step 2). Then add the vanilla extract and mix well. Let rest at room temperature for about 30 minutes.

3 Spread out the apricots evenly in the pan, cut-side down. Pour the batter in carefully, making sure the apricots are not displaced and the batter is evenly distributed. Scatter with the sliced almonds.

4 Bake for 30 minutes (see Blackberry and pear clafoutis, step 4). Remove from the oven and let cool for 5 minutes. Dust with confectioners' sugar and serve warm or at room temperature. Best served on the same day.

 **45 mins**
plus resting and cooling   🍴 **SERVES 6**

CLAFOUTIS blackberry and pear

This is a fall take on classic clafoutis. Use the ripest blackberries for added juice, but avoid choosing pears that are very ripe, since you will need the slices to keep their shape.

INGREDIENTS

½ cup all-purpose flour
¼ cup granulated sugar
2 eggs
3 tbsp unsalted butter, melted and cooled
½ cup whole milk
½ cup heavy cream
1 tsp vanilla extract
2 pears, peeled, cored, and cut lengthwise into 8 slices each
5½oz (150g) blackberries

SPECIAL EQUIPMENT
10in (25cm) cast-iron frying pan

1 Preheat the oven to 400°F (200°C). Combine the flour and sugar in a large bowl. Add the eggs, one at a time, mixing well after each addition until combined. Mix in 2 tablespoons of the butter.

2 Add the milk and cream, a little at a time, and mix well to form a smooth batter. Then add the vanilla extract and mix well. Let rest at room temperature for 30 minutes.

3 Heat the remaining butter in the frying pan over medium heat. Add the pears and blackberries, toss well to coat, and remove from the heat. Shake the pan lightly to spread out the mixture evenly. Pour the batter over the fruit mixture, making sure it is evenly distributed.

4 Bake on the top rack of the oven for 30 minutes, until the top is golden brown and the center is firm to the touch. Remove from the oven and let cool for 5 minutes. Serve warm or at room temperature. Best served on the same day.

🕐 **35 mins**
plus resting and cooling

🍴 **MAKES 12**

MINI CLAFOUTIS
raspberry

Mini clafoutis require less baking time than larger ones—perfect for delicate raspberries, since they can disintegrate if baked too long.

INGREDIENTS

2 tbsp butter, melted and cooled, plus extra for greasing

½ cup all-purpose flour

¼ cup granulated sugar

2 eggs, separated

½ cup whole milk

½ cup heavy cream, plus extra for serving

1 tsp vanilla extract

48 raspberries, about 6oz (175g) in total confectioners' sugar, for dusting

SPECIAL EQUIPMENT

12-hole deep muffin pan

1 Preheat the oven to 400°F (200°C). Grease the muffin pan and set aside. Place the flour and granulated sugar in a bowl and mix well. Add the egg yolks and butter, mixing constantly until well combined.

2 Add the milk and cream, a little at a time, and mix until smooth and well incorporated. Stir in the vanilla extract. Place the egg whites in a separate bowl and whisk to form soft peaks. Fold them into the batter and mix until just combined.

3 Place a tablespoon of batter in each hole of the muffin pan. Top with 4 raspberries each and pour in the remaining batter, making sure it is evenly distributed. Bake the mini clafoutis on the top rack of the oven for about 20 minutes, until golden brown on top and firm to the touch.

4 Remove from the oven and leave them to rest for 10 minutes. Run a knife around the edge of each clafoutis to loosen and remove them from the pan. Place them on a wire rack to cool to room temperature. Dust with confectioners' sugar and serve with heavy cream. Best served on the same day.

20 mins plus resting   **MAKES 8**

CRÊPES lemon and sugar

These rich and crisp crêpes are a great choice for a family gathering. It is so easy to serve them with a variety of toppings—as alternatives to lemon and sugar, you could bring honey, corn syrup, chocolate spread, and berries to the table.

INGREDIENTS

¾ cup all-purpose flour, sifted

2 tbsp granulated sugar, plus extra for dusting

½ tsp fine salt

2 eggs

1 cup whole milk

2 tbsp unsalted butter, melted and cooled, plus extra for cooking

1 lemon, cut into quarters, to serve

SPECIAL EQUIPMENT

10in (25cm) nonstick frying pan

PLAN AHEAD

You can store the batter in the fridge, covered, for up to 1 day ahead. Bring it to room temperature and mix well before cooking.

1 Combine the flour, sugar, and salt in a large bowl. Add the eggs, one at a time, mixing well after each addition to form a smooth, thick paste.

2 Gradually pour in the milk and mix well to incorporate. Add the butter and mix well to combine. Pour the batter into a pitcher. Let rest for 30 minutes. Preheat the oven to 300°F (150°C).

3 Place the frying pan over medium-high heat and melt a small pat of butter. When the butter begins to sizzle, use paper towels to wipe off any excess. Pour in enough batter to form a thin layer, tipping the pan quickly to spread it. Cook for 2 minutes, until the edges are browning and the underside is golden.

4 Flip and cook for another 1–2 minutes. Remove from the heat, wrap the crêpe tightly in a clean paper towel, and place in the oven. Continue cooking with all of the batter. Dust the crêpes with sugar and serve warm with a squeeze of lemon.

🕐 **25 mins** 🍴 **SERVES 6–8**

CRÊPE CAKE Swedish-style

This stunning cake is a Swedish favorite. If time is short, you can use good-quality, store-bought crêpes and fill them with seasonal berries and whipped cream.

INGREDIENTS

¾ cup heavy cream
1 cup crème fraîche
3 tbsp granulated sugar
¼ tsp vanilla extract
9oz (250g) raspberries
6 crêpes (see p62, steps 1–4)
confectioners' sugar, to serve

1 Place the cream in a large bowl and whisk to form stiff peaks. Add the crème fraîche, granulated sugar, and vanilla extract, and beat well to combine. Set aside ¼ cup of the mixture.

2 Reserve a handful of the raspberries and place the rest in a bowl. Crush them with the back of a fork. Gently fold the crushed raspberries into the cream mixture to create a ripple effect.

3 Place one crêpe on a platter, spread over one-fifth of the cream, and top with a second crêpe. Repeat with the remaining crêpes, spreading equal quantities of the raspberry cream mixture between each layer.

4 Spread the reserved cream mixture on top of the crêpe cake. Scatter with the reserved raspberries, dust with confectioners' sugar, and serve immediately.

🕐 **25 mins** plus resting 🍴 **MAKES 8**

CRÊPES suzette

Give simple crêpes a flourish with a rich, buttery sauce made from fresh orange juice and orange liqueur.

INGREDIENTS

1 large orange, peeled with a vegetable peeler, then cut into julienne strips
4 tbsp unsalted butter
¼ cup granulated sugar
juice and grated zest of 2 oranges
2 tbsp Grand Marnier, or other orange liqueur
8 crêpes (see p62, steps 1–4)

1 Place the julienned orange strips in a saucepan half-full of boiling water. Let simmer for 2 minutes. Drain, then set aside to cool.

2 Heat the butter and sugar in a small, heavy-bottomed saucepan over low heat, stirring until the sugar has dissolved. Add the orange juice and zest and bring to a boil, stirring frequently.

3 Reduce the heat to a simmer and cook the sauce for 5 minutes until thick and syrup-like. Then add the Grand Marnier and cook for another 1–2 minutes, until it has reduced.

4 Remove the sauce from the heat and keep it warm. Fold the warm crêpes into quarters and pour the sauce over the crêpes. Decorate each crêpe with the cooled orange strips and serve immediately.

CRÊPES chocolate

Children and adults alike love these crêpes. Stack them with chocolate frosting for a delightful birthday cake.

INGREDIENTS

2 tbsp unsalted butter, plus extra for frying

1oz (30g) good-quality dark chocolate

¾ cup all-purpose flour, sifted

¼ cup cocoa powder

2 tbsp granulated sugar

½ tsp fine salt

2 eggs

1 cup whole milk

PLAN AHEAD

You can store the batter in the fridge, covered, for up to 1 day ahead. Bring it up to room temperature and mix well before cooking.

1 Melt the butter and chocolate in a heatproof bowl over a saucepan of simmering water. Set aside to cool completely. Mix together the flour, cocoa powder, sugar, and salt in a large bowl. Add the eggs, one at a time, mixing to form a paste.

2 Gradually add the milk and mix until incorporated. Add the cooled chocolate mixture to the bowl, a little at a time, mixing constantly to combine. Pour the batter into a pitcher and let rest for at least 30 minutes.

3 Preheat the oven to 300°F (150°C). Melt a little butter in a large nonstick frying pan over medium heat. When the butter sizzles, use paper towels to wipe off excess. Pour in a thin layer of batter, tipping the pan to help it spread.

4 Cook the crêpe for 2 minutes, until the underside looks golden. Flip and cook for another 1–2 minutes. Remove and wrap in a clean paper towel. Keep it warm in the oven while you cook with the remaining batter. Serve warm.

BLINTZ with cherry sauce

These delicate stuffed crêpes hail from Eastern Europe. The soft, creamy filling and sharp, fruity sauce provide a beautiful contrast in flavor.

INGREDIENTS

¾ cup full-fat cottage cheese

3½oz (100g) full-fat cream cheese

2 tbsp confectioners' sugar, plus extra for dusting

grated zest of ½ lemon

½ tsp vanilla extract

8 crêpes (see p62, steps 1–4)

pat of unsalted butter, for cooking

For the sauce

1 x 14oz (450g) can pitted dark cherries, quartered

¼ cup granulated sugar

2 tbsp lemon juice

1 tsp vanilla extract

1 Pulse the cottage cheese in a food processor until smooth and transfer to a large bowl. Add the cream cheese, confectioners' sugar, lemon zest, and vanilla extract. Beat the mixture until smooth. Place a tablespoon of the filling in the center of each crêpe. Fold the sides over the filling to make a package.

2 Preheat the oven to 300°F (150°C). Melt a pat of butter in a 10in (25cm) nonstick frying pan over medium heat. Cook the blintz for 2 minutes on each side, until golden brown. Remove with a slotted spoon, place on a lined plate, and keep warm in the oven.

3 For the sauce, place all the ingredients in a small saucepan with a lid and bring to a boil. Then reduce the heat to a simmer, cover, and cook for 2–3 minutes.

4 Increase the heat to medium. Cook, uncovered, for 3–5 minutes, until the sauce is thick and syrup-like and the cherries are cooked but retain their shape. To serve, dust the blintz with confectioners' sugar and pour over the cherry sauce.

1 hr 5 mins
plus cooling

SERVES 8

Also great
COLD

UPSIDE-DOWN CAKE
caramelized pear

The soft texture of lightly caramelized pears makes them a perfect match for delicate sponge cake. The cake tastes meltingly good fresh from the oven, but it is also great the next day, as the fruit continues to impart the cake with flavor and juice.

INGREDIENTS
4 tbsp unsalted butter, plus extra for greasing

½ cup packed light brown sugar

2 pears, peeled, cored, and chopped into 16 slices

half-and-half, to serve (optional)

For the sponge cake
½ cup granulated sugar

8 tbsp unsalted butter, softened

2 eggs

1 tsp vanilla extract

1¼ cups all-purpose flour

1 tsp baking powder

½ cup whole milk

SPECIAL EQUIPMENT
8in (20cm) round cake pan

1 Preheat the oven to 350°F (180°C). Grease the cake pan and set aside. Melt the butter in a small, heavy-bottomed saucepan over low heat. Increase the heat and add the sugar. Bring to a boil, stirring frequently, until the sugar has dissolved and the mixture has thickened.

2 Transfer the caramel to the cake pan and use a wooden spoon to spread it out into an even layer. Let cool slightly. Place the pear slices over the cooled caramel in a well-spaced spiral pattern. Set aside.

Beat the cake mixture until smooth.

The finished cake will be golden and well-risen.

3 For the sponge cake, beat the sugar and butter in a bowl until fluffy. Add the eggs one at a time, beat well, and stir in the vanilla extract. Sift the flour and baking powder into a separate bowl. Add the dry mixture and milk to the egg mixture, alternately, and beat to combine.

4 Spoon the mixture into the pan and place on a baking sheet. Bake in the oven for 40–45 minutes. Cool for 5 minutes before turning it out. Serve warm with cream, if desired. You can store the cake in an airtight container in the fridge for up to 3 days.

1 hr plus cooling | MAKES 4 | Also great COLD

UPSIDE-DOWN CAKES pineapple

Give this classic dessert a contemporary makeover by serving it with a light cream sauce that is laced with fresh basil.

INGREDIENTS
9 tbsp unsalted butter, plus extra for greasing
½ cup light brown sugar
1 x 4oz (125g) can pineapple chunks, in natural juice, chopped into small pieces
½ cup granulated sugar
2 eggs
½ tsp vanilla extract
1 cup self-rising flour, sifted
½ cup heavy cream
1 tsp finely chopped basil
1 tsp lime juice

SPECIAL EQUIPMENT
4 x 9fl oz (250g) ramekins

1 Preheat the oven to 350ºF (180ºC). Grease the ramekins. Melt 4 tbsp of the butter in a heavy-bottomed saucepan over medium heat. Add the brown sugar and cook for 2–3 minutes, stirring constantly, until dissolved. Divide evenly between the ramekins.

2 Drain the pineapple chunks, reserving the juice, and divide them between the ramekins. In a bowl, beat the granulated sugar and remaining butter until light and fluffy. Then beat in the eggs and vanilla extract until combined. Gently fold in the flour, until just combined.

3 Divide the mixture between the ramekins. Transfer to a baking sheet and bake for 25–30 minutes, until well-risen and golden. Remove and let cool slightly.

4 Meanwhile, bring the reserved pineapple juice to a boil in a small, heavy-bottomed saucepan. Cook for 5 minutes, until the juice has reduced by half. Invert the ramekins onto serving plates. Leave for 2–3 minutes before removing, to allow the juices to drip down.

5 Add half the cream to the pan. Cook for 5–7 minutes, until reduced by half. Remove from the heat and whisk in the basil, lime juice, and remaining cream until thick. Serve immediately along with the cakes.

1 hr 25 mins plus cooling | SERVES 8 | Also great COLD

UPSIDE-DOWN CAKE apple and blackberry

With a glorious orchard flavor, this cake is also delicious served with custard.

INGREDIENTS
⅔ cup maple syrup, plus extra to serve
11 tbsp unsalted butter, diced, plus extra for greasing
⅓ cup dark brown sugar
2 eggs
1½ cups all-purpose flour
2 tsp baking powder
½ tsp ground cinnamon
¼ tsp ground ginger
¼ tsp grated nutmeg
¼ cup light brown sugar
1 apple, peeled, cored, and quartered
3½oz (100g) frozen blackberries, halved if large
whipped cream, to serve

SPECIAL EQUIPMENT
8in (20cm) deep cake pan

1 Preheat the oven to 325°F (160°C). Melt the maple syrup, butter, and dark brown sugar in a saucepan over medium heat, stirring, until the sugar has dissolved. Transfer to a bowl and let cool.

2 Add the eggs to the cooled maple syrup, one at a time, beating well after each addition until combined. Sift the flour, baking powder, and spices into a bowl and make a well in the center. Pour the wet mixture into the well and fold into the dry ingredients until just combined.

3 Grease the pan and sprinkle the light brown sugar over the bottom evenly. Slice the apple quarters lengthwise, into 3 or 4 pieces. Place them in a well-spaced spiral over the brown sugar. Fill the spaces with the blackberries and pour the batter evenly over the top.

4 Bake for 50 minutes to 1 hour, until well-risen and golden brown. Cover loosely with foil if it browns too quickly. Cool in the pan for 5 minutes before transferring to a plate. Serve warm or at room temperature with whipped cream. You can store the cake in an airtight container for up to 2 days.

50 mins plus cooling   **MAKES 6**   Also great **COLD**

UPSIDE-DOWN CAKES blueberry with crème anglaise

These mini dessert cakes, served with a light and pourable custard, are easy to make and look very impressive.

INGREDIENTS

8 tbsp unsalted butter, softened, plus extra for greasing
¼ cup light brown sugar
3½oz (100g) frozen blueberries
½ cup granulated sugar
2 eggs
1 tsp vanilla extract
¾ cup self-rising flour

For the crème anglaise

1 vanilla bean, split in half, lengthwise
¾ cup whole milk
2 egg yolks
2 tbsp granulated sugar

SPECIAL EQUIPMENT

6-hole deep muffin pan

1 Preheat the oven to 350°F (180°C). Grease the muffin pan. Sprinkle the brown sugar into each hole and top with equal quantities of the blueberries. Beat the butter and granulated sugar in a bowl until light and fluffy.

2 Add the eggs to the butter mixture, one at a time, beating well after each addition until combined. Add the vanilla extract, sift in the flour, and fold in gently. Divide the batter evenly between the holes in the pan.

3 Bake for 20 minutes, until well-risen and golden brown. Let cool slightly. For the crème anglaise, cook the vanilla bean and milk in a saucepan over low heat for 5 minutes, until hot, but not boiling.

4 Remove the vanilla bean, scrape out the seeds, and add to the milk. In a heatproof bowl, whisk the egg yolks and granulated sugar until combined. Pour in the hot milk and whisk until the sugar has dissolved. Pour the mixture back into the pan.

5 Cook the mixture over low heat for 2–3 minutes, stirring constantly, until thick enough to coat the back of a spoon. Invert the muffin pan over a large serving plate and leave for 2–3 minutes before taking off the pan. Serve immediately with the crème anglaise.

Simple alternatives

It is very easy to adapt the Caramelized pear upside-down cake on pages 66–67 following the recipes below. You should caramelize just-ripe fruit, which will keep its shape.

Apple and cinnamon Add a pinch of ground cinnamon to the caramel and 1 tsp of it to the cake mixture. Replace the pears (see p67, step 2) with 2 peeled, cored, and sliced apples.

Plum and almond In place of the pears (see p67, step 2), scatter slivers of raw almonds over the caramel and top with 6–8 pitted and quartered plums.

Peach Instead of the pears (see p67, step 2), use 3 ripe, peeled, pitted, and quartered peaches. Top them with 1 tsp finely chopped lemon verbena or thyme.

Cranberry and raspberry Use 5½oz (150g) raspberries and 1¾oz (50g) cranberries in place of the pears (see p67, step 2).

Banana Use 2 bananas, cut into ¾in (2cm) thick slices, in place of the pears for a gorgeously sticky dessert (see p67, step 2).

Chocolate and date For a rich version of this cake, add 2 heaping tbsp cocoa powder to the cake mixture and use ¾ cup coarsely chopped dates instead of the pears (see p67, step 2).

Rhubarb, ginger, and orange Sprinkle the caramel with 1 tbsp finely diced crystallized ginger and top with 5½oz (150g) rhubarb, sliced into 1in (2.5cm) thick pieces. Add 1 tsp grated fresh ginger and the grated zest of 1 orange to the cake mixture (see p67, step 3).

Black currant Instead of the pears (see p67, step 2), place 7oz (200g) black currants, in a thick layer, over the caramel.

Apricot and lavender Use 4 halved, pitted, and quartered apricots in place of the pears (see p67, step 2). Add ¼ tsp finely chopped culinary lavender to the cake mixture.

35 mins
plus cooling

MAKES 4

SOUFFLÉ vanilla

Many people assume that a soufflé is difficult to master, yet a few simple tips can help you to achieve a beautifully light and airy dessert. Make sure the ramekin is buttered and dusted, the mixture lightly folded, and that you serve it immediately.

INGREDIENTS

2 tbsp unsalted butter, plus extra for greasing
¼ cup granulated sugar, plus extra for dusting
2 tbsp all-purpose flour
¾ cup whole milk
¾ tsp vanilla extract
pinch of salt
3 large eggs, separated
pinch of cream of tartar
confectioners' sugar, to dust

SPECIAL EQUIPMENT

4 x 5fl oz (150ml) ramekins

PLAN AHEAD

You can prepare and store the batter, covered in the fridge, up to 1 day ahead.

1

Preheat the oven to 400°F (200°C). Grease the ramekins, dust lightly with granulated sugar, and set aside. Melt the butter in a saucepan over low heat. Add the flour and cook for 1 minute. Remove from the heat and whisk in the milk until smooth.

2

Bring the mixture to a boil over low heat, stirring constantly. Reduce the heat and simmer for 1–2 minutes. Remove from the heat. Add the vanilla extract, salt, and 2 tablespoons of granulated sugar. Stir until the sugar has dissolved.

3

Cool the milk mixture slightly, then beat in the egg yolks, one at a time, until well combined and smooth. Set aside.

4

In a large bowl, beat the egg whites and cream of tartar with a handheld mixer to form medium peaks, then beat in the remaining sugar to form stiff peaks.

5

Gradually fold the egg white mixture into the milk mixture until combined. Divide the batter evenly between the ramekins, filling them to the rim. Smooth over the batter and run a finger around the edge of each ramekin.

KNOW-HOW Running a finger around the edges of the batter creates an indentation, helping the soufflés rise upward in a straight direction.

6

Place the ramekins on a baking sheet. Bake on the bottom rack of the oven for 10–12 minutes, until well-risen, golden, and an inserted toothpick comes out clean. Dust with confectioners' sugar and serve immediately.

🕐 **35–40 mins** plus cooling   🍴 **MAKES 6**

SOUFFLÉ chocolate

Served straight from the oven, this deliciously rich soufflé is fantastic with a scoop of good-quality vanilla ice cream.

1 Preheat the oven to 400°F (200°C). Grease **6 x 5fl oz (150ml) ramekins** with **softened, unsalted butter** and dust with **granulated sugar**. Dissolve **1 tsp instant espresso powder** into **3 tbsp heavy cream** in a heatproof bowl over a saucepan of simmering water until smooth.

2 Add ⅔ **cup finely chopped good-quality dark chocolate** to the pan, stirring until melted. Remove and let cool. Whisk **3 large egg whites** with a **pinch of cream of tartar** in a bowl until thick. Gradually add ¼ **cup granulated sugar**, whisking continuously until soft peaks form.

3 Beat **2 large egg yolks** into the cooled chocolate mixture until smooth. Stir in ¼ **tsp vanilla extract** and a **pinch of salt**. Fold in a little of the egg white mixture, then gently fold in the remaining until combined.

4 Divide the mixture between the ramekins. Smooth them over, run a finger around the edges, and place them on a baking sheet. Bake on the bottom rack of the oven for 12–15 minutes, until they are well-risen and an inserted toothpick comes out clean. Dust with **confectioners' sugar** and serve immediately.

PLAN AHEAD
You can prepare and store the batter, covered in the fridge, up to 1 day ahead.

Pistachio

🕐 **30 mins** plus cooling   🍴 **MAKES 6**

SOUFFLÉ pistachio

This is a fragrant dessert that combines pistachio, orange, and cardamom. Try serving it with crème fraîche, mixed with a little orange flower water.

1 Preheat the oven to 400°F (200°C) and prepare **6 x 5fl oz (150ml) ramekins** (see Chocolate soufflé, step 1). Pulse ⅓ **cup unsalted and skinned pistachios** with **2 tsp granulated sugar** in a food processor, adding **1 tbsp water** if needed, to form a smooth, thick paste. Set aside.

2 Melt **3 tbsp unsalted butter** in a saucepan over low heat. Add **2 tbsp all-purpose flour** and cook for 1 minute, then remove from the heat and whisk in ¾ **cup whole milk at room temperature**, until smooth.

3 Bring the mixture to a boil over low heat. Reduce the heat to a simmer and cook for 1–2 minutes. Then remove from the heat and add ¼ **tsp ground cardamom**, **1 tbsp orange juice**, **2 tbsp granulated sugar**, and a **pinch of salt**. Stir until the sugar has dissolved, then let cool slightly.

4 Beat 3 tbsp of the pistachio paste and **2 large egg yolks** in a bowl and combine with the milk mixture until smooth. In a separate bowl, whisk **3 large egg whites** and a **pinch of cream of tartar** to form medium peaks. Whisk in **2 tbsp granulated sugar** to form soft peaks and gradually fold it to the milk mixture until just combined.

5 Divide the mixture between the ramekins and place them on a baking sheet (see Chocolate soufflé, step 4). Bake on the bottom rack of the oven for 10–14 minutes, until they are well-risen and an inserted toothpick comes out clean. Dust with **confectioners' sugar** and serve immediately.

PLAN AHEAD
You can prepare and store the batter, covered in the fridge, up to 1 day ahead.

Chocolate

30–35 mins plus cooling   **MAKES 6**

SOUFFLÉ raspberry

This white chocolate and raspberry soufflé is a summery take on the French classic. You can serve it with a cold raspberry coulis (see p215).

1 Preheat the oven to 400°F (200°C) and prepare **6 x 5fl oz (150ml) ramekins** (see Chocolate soufflé, step 1). Melt **3oz (85g) finely chopped white chocolate**, **2 tbsp heavy cream**, and a **pinch of salt** in a heatproof bowl over a saucepan of simmering water. Remove and let cool.

2 Pulse **7oz (200g) raspberries** in a food processor until smooth and strain into a bowl. In a separate bowl, whisk **4 large egg whites** and a **pinch of cream of tartar** until thick. Gradually whisk in **¼ cup granulated sugar** to form soft peaks.

3 Whisk **3 large egg yolks** into the chocolate mixture, one at a time, until combined. Then whisk in **2 tbsp all-purpose flour**, **¼ tsp vanilla extract**, and the raspberry puree, until smooth. Fold in a little of the egg white mixture, then gently fold in the remaining mixture until combined.

4 Divide the mixture between the ramekins and place them on a baking sheet (see Chocolate soufflé, step 4). Bake for 10–12 minutes, until they are well-risen, lightly golden, and an inserted toothpick comes out clean. Dust with **confectioners' sugar** and serve immediately.

PLAN AHEAD
You can prepare and store the batter, covered in the fridge, up to 1 day ahead.

Lemon

30–35 mins plus cooling   **MAKES 6**

SOUFFLÉ lemon

A delicious palate-cleanser with a sharp–sweet flavor, this lemon soufflé works very well alongside a spoonful of cold heavy cream.

1 Preheat the oven to 400°F (200°C) and prepare **6 x 5fl oz (150ml) ramekins** (see Chocolate soufflé, step 1). Melt **2 tbsp unsalted butter** in saucepan over low heat. Add **2 tbsp all-purpose flour** and cook for 1 minute. Remove and whisk in **¾ cup whole milk, at room temperature**, until smooth.

2 Bring the mixture to a boil over low heat, then reduce to a simmer and cook for 1–2 minutes, stirring constantly. Remove from the heat. Whisk in **¼ tsp vanilla extract**, **2 tbsp granulated sugar**, and a **pinch of salt** until the sugar dissolves. Whisk in **zest and juice of 1 lemon** and let cool.

3 In a bowl, whisk **4 large egg whites** and a **pinch of cream of tartar** until thick. Gradually whisk in **2 tbsp granulated sugar** to form medium peaks. Whisk **3 large egg yolks** into the cooled milk mixture, one at a time, until smooth. Fold in a little of the egg white mixture, then gently fold in the remaining until combined.

4 Divide the mixture between the ramekins and place them on a baking sheet (see Chocolate soufflé, step 4). Bake for 10–12 minutes, until they are well-risen, lightly golden, and an inserted toothpick comes out clean. Dust with **confectioners' sugar** and serve immediately.

PLAN AHEAD
You can prepare and store the batter, covered in the fridge, up to 1 day ahead.

Raspberry

🕐 **35 mins**
plus resting and cooling

🍴 **MAKES 4**

LAVA CAKE chocolate

Baking a lava cake can seem daunting, since it is difficult to know just how molten the inside will be until you serve. However, think of it as a slightly undercooked chocolate cake—a careful eye on the clock guarantees a perfectly oozing center.

INGREDIENTS

11 tbsp unsalted butter, plus extra for greasing

5½oz (150g) good-quality dark chocolate, at least 60 percent cocoa solids

3 large eggs

⅓ cup granulated sugar

1 heaping tbsp all-purpose flour

cocoa powder, for dusting

heavy cream, to serve (optional)

SPECIAL EQUIPMENT

4 x 7fl oz (200ml) ramekins

PLAN AHEAD

You can wrap the batter in plastic wrap and chill it up to 3 days ahead, or freeze it for up to 1 month. Bring to room temperature before baking.

Preheat the oven to 400°F (200°C). Grease the ramekins and chill them in the fridge until needed. Melt the chocolate and butter in a heatproof bowl over a small saucepan of gently simmering water, making sure it does not touch the water. Let cool.

In a separate bowl, beat the eggs and sugar for 4–5 minutes until the mixture has tripled in volume and is pale and fluffy. Fold in the cooled chocolate mixture and mix well, then sift over the flour and fold it in gently.

Lightly dust the ramekins with cocoa powder, shaking off any excess. Divide the batter evenly between the ramekins, making sure that they are not filled to the top. Bake in the oven for 12 minutes, until set, but still soft to the touch in the middle.

Let rest for 1 minute. Run a sharp knife around the edges of the cakes and top with serving plates. Turn them over and gently remove the ramekins. Dust with cocoa powder and serve immediately with heavy cream, if desired.

🕐 **2 hrs 5 mins**
plus chilling and cooling   🍴 **MAKES 4**

LAVA CAKE dulce de leche

Place small amounts of homemade dulce de leche inside your chocolate lava cakes—it transforms them into a showstopping dessert.

1 Preheat the oven to 425°F (220°C). For the dulce de leche, pour **1 x 14oz (400g) sweetened can condensed milk** into a **5¾in (14cm) pie dish**. Cover tightly with two sheets of foil and place the dish in a small roasting pan. Fill the pan with enough hot water to come halfway up the sides of the pie dish, making sure the water does not splash onto the foil.

2 Bake in the middle of the oven for 1–1½ hours, stirring every 15 minutes, until small holes appear on the surface of the foil and the milk is a golden, caramel color. Check the water level regularly and add more if it has evaporated. Transfer the dulce de leche to a shallow dish. Cool completely before chilling. Reduce the oven temperature to 400ºF (200ºC).

3 Grease **4 x 7fl oz (200ml) ramekins** with **unsalted butter** and place in the fridge to chill. Melt **5½oz (150g) good-quality dark chocolate** and **11 tbsp unsalted butter** in a heatproof bowl over a small saucepan of simmering water. Make sure the bottom of the bowl does not touch the water. Stir well and let cool.

4 Beat **3 large eggs** and ⅓ cup granulated sugar in a large bowl until fluffy and tripled in volume. Stir in the cooled chocolate mixture until combined. Sift **1 heaping tbsp all-purpose flour** into the mixture and gently fold it in.

5 Lightly dust the ramekins with **cocoa powder**, shaking off any excess. Half-fill the ramekins with the chocolate mixture and spread to form an even base. Shape 4 heaping teaspoons of the dulce de leche into balls and place one in each ramekin. Divide the remaining chocolate mixture between the ramekins, covering the dulce de leche completely.

6 Bake the lava cakes in the oven for 12 minutes, until the sides are set and the center is soft to the touch. Let cool for 1 minute. To remove the cakes, run a knife around the edge of the ramekin, place a serving plate on top, and turn over. Serve the cakes immediately with **heavy cream**, if desired.

PLAN AHEAD

You can wrap the chocolate mixture in plastic wrap at the end of step 5 and chill up to 2 days ahead, or freeze them up to 1 month ahead. Bring to room temperature before baking.

Dulce de leche

LAVA CAKE
peanut butter

Peanut butter melts at high temperatures, creating a salty contrast to the interior—rather like a sophisticated peanut butter cup.

1 Grease **4 x 7fl oz (200ml) ramekins** with **unsalted butter** and place in the fridge to chill. Melt **5½oz (150g) good-quality dark chocolate** and **11 tbsp unsalted butter** in a heatproof bowl over a small saucepan of simmering water (see Dulce de leche fondant, step 3). Stir and let cool.

2 Preheat the oven to 400ºF (200ºC). Beat **3 large eggs** and **⅓ cup granulated sugar** in a large bowl until fluffy and tripled in volume. Stir in the chocolate mixture until well combined. Sift **1 heaping tbsp all-purpose flour** into the mixture and gently fold it in.

3 Lightly dust the ramekins with **cocoa powder**, shaking off any excess. Half-fill the ramekins with the chocolate mixture, spreading it out to form an even base. Shape **4 heaping tsp creamy peanut butter** into balls and place one in each ramekin. Divide the remaining chocolate mixture between the ramekins, covering the peanut butter completely.

4 Bake the lava cakes in the oven for 12 minutes, until the sides are set and the center is soft to the touch. Let cool for 1 minute before turning them out (see Dulce de leche lava cakes, step 6). Dust with cocoa powder, if desired, and serve immediately.

PLAN AHEAD
You can wrap the chocolate mixture in plastic wrap at the end of step 3 and chill up to 2 days ahead, or freeze them up to 1 month ahead. Bring to room temperature before baking.

Peanut butter

 **50–55 mins**
plus resting and cooling

SERVES 4–6

BREAD AND BUTTER
PUDDING brioche

Originally conceived as an everyday dessert that took advantage of pantry ingredients, rich and creamy versions of bread and butter pudding are now favorites at dinner parties, restaurants, and bakeries.

INGREDIENTS
unsalted butter, for
    greasing
9oz (250g) brioche, cut
    into 1in (2.5cm) cubes
2 eggs
¼ cup granulated sugar
¾ cup whole milk
¾ cup heavy cream

confectioners' sugar, for
    dusting
chocolate ice cream,
    to serve (optional)

SPECIAL EQUIPMENT
8 x 10in (20 x 25cm)
ovenproof dish

1

Preheat the oven to 350°F (180°C). Grease the ovenproof dish. Spread out the brioche pieces in the dish, pressing down gently to form an even layer.

2

Place the eggs and granulated sugar in a bowl and whisk to combine. Add the milk and cream, a little at a time, beating constantly to combine.

Pour the mixture over the brioche, pushing down to help the liquid to absorb. Rest for 5 minutes. Place the dish in a large roasting pan. Pour hot water into the pan.

3

The hot water should come halfway up the sides of the dish.

4

Bake for 40–45 minutes, until golden brown. Lift the dish out of the pan and let cool slightly. Dust with confectioners' sugar. Serve with chocolate ice cream, if desired. You can cover and store the pudding in the fridge for up to 2 days.

35 mins plus cooling   **MAKES 4**

BREAD AND BUTTER PUDDING
bourbon and pecan

Bourbon lends a warming flavor to these grown-up puddings. The caramelized pecans add a sweet crunch to the texture.

INGREDIENTS
1 tbsp unsalted butter, plus extra for greasing
1 tbsp granulated sugar
⅓ cup pecans
5½oz (150g) brioche, diced into ½in (1cm) cubes
¼ cup raisins
3 eggs
1 cup half-and-half
2 tbsp bourbon
½ tsp vanilla extract
2 heaping tbsp light brown sugar
heavy cream, to serve (optional)

SPECIAL EQUIPMENT
4 x 7fl oz (200ml) ramekins

PLAN AHEAD
You can store the candied pecans in an airtight container up to 1 week ahead.

1 Preheat the oven to 350°F (180°C) and grease the ramekins. Heat the butter, granulated sugar, and pecans in a nonstick frying pan over medium heat. Cook for 5 minutes, stirring frequently, until the caramel is golden and smooth and the pecans are well coated. Place them on a lightly greased plate and let cool.

2 Mix the brioche and raisins in a large bowl. Whisk together the eggs, cream, bourbon, vanilla extract, and brown sugar in a separate bowl and pour over the brioche mixture. Stir well to ensure that the bread is soaked in the cream mixture.

3 Divide the mixture equally between the ramekins, heaping it up in the center. Pour in any remaining liquid, making sure the ramekins are not overflowing. Bake on the top rack of the oven for 20 minutes, until they are well risen and golden brown.

4 Remove from the heat and let them cool for about 5 minutes. Chop the candied pecans and sprinkle over the puddings. Serve them warm with heavy cream, if desired. You can store the puddings, covered in the fridge, for up to 2 days.

55 mins plus resting and cooling   **SERVES 4–6**

BREAD AND BUTTER PUDDING pain au chocolat

The perfect way to use up day-old pain au chocolat. Adding white chocolate makes this dessert even more luxurious.

INGREDIENTS
unsalted butter, for greasing
7½oz (215g) chocolate croissants, torn into large chunks
¼ cup white chocolate chips
2 eggs
¼ cup granulated sugar
¾ cup whole milk
¾ cup heavy cream
1 tsp vanilla extract
vanilla ice cream or cream, to serve

SPECIAL EQUIPMENT
7 x 9in (18 x 23cm) ovenproof dish

1 Preheat the oven to 350°F (180°C) and lightly grease the ovenproof dish. Place the croissant chunks and chocolate chips in the dish. Toss well to combine and spread the mixture out in an even layer, pressing it down gently to make a packed base.

2 Whisk the eggs and sugar in a large bowl until light. Add the milk, cream, and vanilla extract. Beat to combine and pour over the base, pushing down lightly to help the liquid to absorb. Let rest for 5 minutes.

3 Place the dish in a large roasting pan. Pour hot water into the pan to come halfway up the sides of the dish. Bake for 40–45 minutes, until golden brown. Remove carefully and let cool for 5 minutes. Serve warm with vanilla ice cream or cream. You can store the pudding, covered in the fridge, for up to 2 days.

50 mins
plus resting and cooling

SERVES 4–6

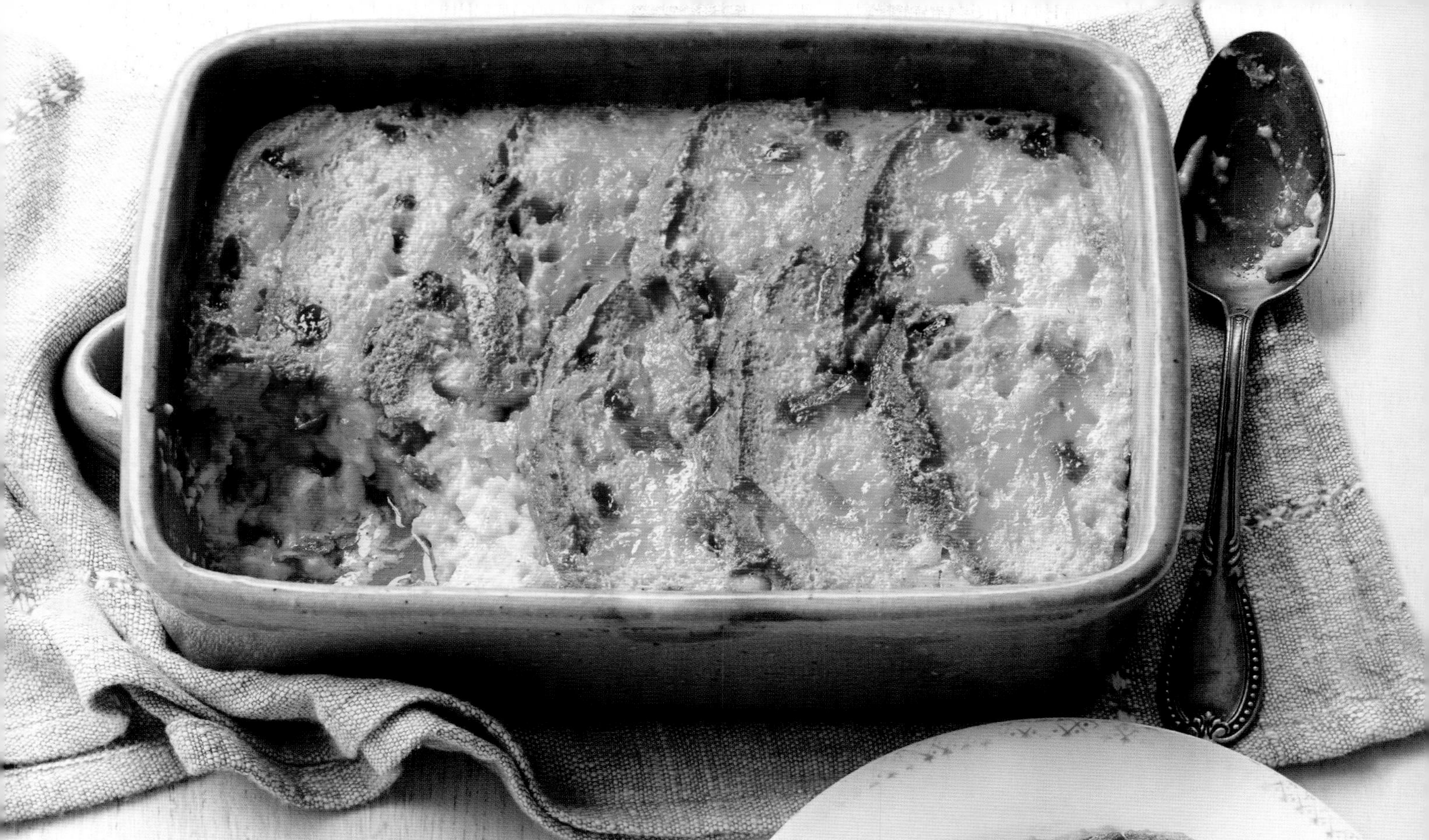

BREAD AND BUTTER PUDDING

panettone and marmalade

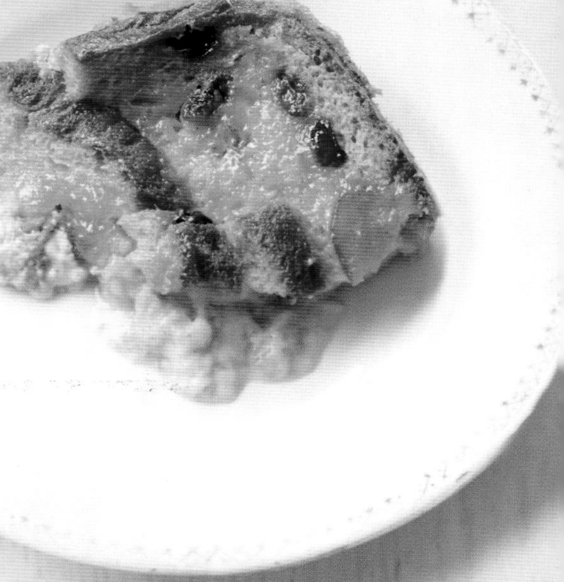

Bursting with citrus flavors, this dessert is great for serving a crowd. The pudding is cooked at a low temperature, so it is not necessary to use the classic bainmarie method in the oven.

INGREDIENTS

- unsalted butter, for greasing
- ½ cup marmalade
- 9oz (250g) panettone, thickly sliced
- ¾ cup whole milk
- 3 eggs, lightly beaten
- 3 tbsp heavy cream
- ¼ cup light brown sugar
- ½ tsp pumpkin pie spice
- finely grated zest and juice of 1 orange

SPECIAL EQUIPMENT

7 x 9in (18 x 23cm) ovenproof dish

1 Preheat the oven to 325°F (160°F) and grease the ovenproof dish. Spread the marmalade evenly over the panettone slices. Arrange the slices in the dish in a neat layer, making sure they overlap slightly.

2 Pour the milk into a large bowl. Add the remaining ingredients. Whisk to combine and pour over the panettone, pushing down lightly to help the liquid to absorb. Let rest for 15 minutes.

3 Place the dish on a baking sheet and bake for 30 minutes, until golden brown. Remove and let cool for 5 minutes. Serve warm, or at room temperature. You can store the pudding, covered in the fridge, for up to 2 days.

 30 mins
plus soaking

SERVES 6–8

Also great
COLD

TAPIOCA PUDDING vanilla

Some associate tapioca pudding with bland flavor and unappealing texture. This grown-up version is the perfect comfort food and anything but bland—it is rich and creamy with a good textural contrast from the tapioca pearls.

INGREDIENTS

3 cups whole milk

⅓ cup small pearl tapioca

2 large egg yolks

¼ tsp salt

¼ cup dark brown sugar

¼ cup granulated sugar

1 vanilla bean

30 blackberries, to serve

half-and-half, to serve

1 Pour ¾ cup milk into a heavy-bottomed saucepan. Add the tapioca pearls and stir to mix. Let the mixture soak for about 45 minutes.

2 Stir in the remaining milk. Add the egg yolks, salt, and both types of sugar and whisk well to combine. Split the vanilla bean with a sharp knife, add to the pan, and stir well to mix.

3

Bring the mixture to a boil over medium heat, stirring constantly. Reduce the heat to a simmer and cook for 15 minutes, stirring occasionally, until the tapioca pearls are soft and the pudding has thickened slightly.

4

Remove from the heat and discard the vanilla bean. Serve warm with blackberries and a swirl of cream; serve it chilled for a thicker texture. You can keep it in an airtight container in the fridge for 2–3 days.

Orange

Chocolate
and banana

🕐 **30 mins**
plus soaking   🍴 **SERVES 6–8**   🌡 Also great
COLD

TAPIOCA PUDDING
chocolate and banana

Add grated good-quality dark chocolate to still warm tapioca to create this marvelously rich dessert that is topped with banana slices.

1 Place **¾ cup whole milk** in a heavy-bottomed saucepan. Add **⅓ cup small pearl tapioca**, stir well, and let soak for about 45 minutes.

2 Add **3¼ cups whole milk** and **¼ cup heavy cream** and mix well. Whisk in **2 large egg yolks**, **¼ cup granulated sugar**, and **¼ tsp salt** until combined. Bring to a boil over medium heat, stirring constantly, then reduce the heat to a simmer and cook, stirring occasionally, for 15 minutes, or until the tapioca pearls are soft.

3 Remove from the heat. Stir in **5oz (140g) finely chopped dark chocolate** until melted, then stir in **½ tsp vanilla extract** and top with **2–3 thinly sliced bananas**. Serve warm, or chill for 2 hours before serving if a thicker texture is preferred. You can store the puddings in an airtight container in the fridge for 2–3 days.

🕐 **30 mins**
plus soaking   🍴 **SERVES 6–8**   🌡 Also great
COLD

TAPIOCA PUDDING
orange

Use both orange zest and juice to give a fresh flavor to this pudding. Blood oranges, when in season, can also add a wonderfully deep color.

1 Place **¾ cup whole milk** in a heavy-bottomed saucepan. Add **⅓ cup small pearl tapioca**, stir well, and let soak for about 45 minutes.

2 Stir in **2 cups whole milk** and **½ cup heavy cream**. Add **2 large egg yolks**, **¼ tsp salt**, **⅓ cup granulated sugar**, **grated zest of 1 orange**, and **juice of ½ orange** and mix well. Bring to a boil over medium heat, stirring constantly, then reduce the heat to a simmer and cook, stirring occasionally, for 15 minutes, or until the tapioca pearls are soft.

3 Remove from the heat. Stir in **½ tsp vanilla extract** and decorate with **¼ cup coarsely chopped pistachios**. Serve warm, or chill for 2 hours before serving if a thicker texture is preferred. You can store them in an airtight container in the fridge for 2–3 days.

Lime and mango

Coconut

🕐 **30 mins**
plus soaking   🍴 **SERVES 6-8**   🌡 Also great **COLD**

TAPIOCA PUDDING
coconut

Tapioca is made from cassava plants that are grown in Asia alongside coconut trees. This explains why this creamy pairing is so popular in Asian cuisine.

1 Place **¾ cup coconut milk** in a heavy-bottomed saucepan. Add **⅓ cup small pearl tapioca**, stir well, and let soak for about 45 minutes.

2 Add **2¼ cups coconut milk**, **1 large egg yolk**, **¼ tsp salt**, and **½ cup granulated sugar**. Whisk well to combine. Bring the mixture to a boil over medium heat, stirring constantly, then reduce the heat to a simmer and cook, stirring occasionally, for 15 minutes, or until the tapioca pearls are soft.

3 Remove from the heat. Stir in **¼ tsp vanilla extract** and sprinkle with **½ cup toasted, unsweetened, dried coconut flakes.** Serve warm, or chill for 2 hours before serving if a thicker texture is preferred. You can store them in an airtight container in the fridge for 2-3 days.

🕐 **30-35 mins**
plus chilling   🍴 **SERVES 6-8**   🌡 Also great **COLD**

TAPIOCA PUDDING
lime and mango

For a very quick tropical-flavored pudding, add cooked tapioca pearls to a puree of ripe mango, lime, and a little condensed milk.

1 Place **4 cups water** in a large saucepan, bring to a boil, and add **½ cup small pearl tapioca**. Cook for 20-25 minutes, stirring constantly, until the tapioca pearls are soft and translucent. Remove from the heat, drain, and rinse under running cold water to halt the cooking process.

2 Drain well again, place the tapioca in a small bowl, and set aside. Place **2 peeled, pitted, and coarsely chopped mangoes** in a food processor and pulse to a smooth puree. Transfer to a bowl and add **½ cup condensed milk**, **⅛ tsp salt**, and **juice of ½ lime**. Mix well until smooth.

3 Add the tapioca pearls to the mango pudding and mix until combined. Decorate with the **zest of ½ lime** and **½ pineapple, thinly sliced**. Serve warm, or chill for 2 hours before serving if a thicker texture is preferred. You can store them in an airtight container in the fridge for 2-3 days.

🕐 **1 hr 50 mins**   🍴 **SERVES 6–8**   🌡 Also great
COLD

RICE PUDDING baked

This is a sophisticated dessert of soft, fragrant, and billowy rice cooked in creamy milk. Some people associate rice pudding with baby food, but when it is cooked to perfection and infused with spices, that couldn't be further from the truth.

INGREDIENTS
2½ tbsp unsalted butter
½ cup short-grain rice
⅓ cup dark brown sugar
¼ cup granulated sugar
¾ tsp ground cinnamon
¼ tsp grated nutmeg, plus extra for sprinkling
¼ tsp salt
4 cups whole milk
½ cup heavy cream
1 tsp pure vanilla extract
1 bay leaf

SPECIAL EQUIPMENT
3-quart ovenproof dish

1 Preheat the oven to 300°F (150°C). Melt the butter in a saucepan over medium heat. Add the rice and stir well to coat.

2 Add both types of sugar, the cinnamon, nutmeg, salt, and 1–2 tablespoons of the milk. Cook, stirring frequently, until the sugar dissolves.

3

Increase the heat and add the remaining ingredients. Bring to a simmer, stirring the mixture occasionally. Remove from the heat. Discard the bay leaf and pour the mixture into the ovenproof dish.

4

Bake for 30 minutes. Then remove, stir, and sprinkle with nutmeg. Bake for another hour–1 hour 10 minutes. Remove from the heat and serve hot. You can store the pudding in an airtight container in the fridge for 2–3 days.

50–55 mins plus chilling   **SERVES 4**   Also great **COLD**

RICE PUDDING
coconut and lime

This sumptuous dessert, delicately flavored with lime and coconut, makes the perfect finale to a meal inspired by Asian flavors.

1 Lightly crack **2 cardamom pods** and place them in a large saucepan. Add **1 small, halved cinnamon stick** and place the saucepan over medium heat. Toast lightly for 30–45 seconds, until fragrant.

2 Add **1 x 14oz (400ml) can coconut milk**, **¾ cup whole milk**, **⅓ cup brown sugar**, and **⅛ tsp salt** to the saucepan. Bring the mixture to a boil, stirring until the sugar dissolves, then reduce the heat to low.

3 Add **1 cup cooked plain, long-grain rice** and **grated zest of ½ lime** to the saucepan. Cook for 40 minutes, stirring occasionally, until thick. Remove from the heat and take out the cardamom pods and cinnamon stick.

4 Divide the pudding between four ramekins. Decorate with **toasted coconut** and **lime zest** to serve. You can also chill it for 30 minutes and serve cold. You can store the pudding in an airtight container in the fridge for 4–5 days, although it will become very thick.

50–55 mins plus cooling   **SERVES 4**   Also great **COLD**

ARROZ con leche

Popular all over South America, arroz con leche is a delicious vanilla-infused sweet rice pudding. The use of three kinds of milk provides the creamy texture.

1 Split **1 vanilla bean** and place both the seeds and the bean in a saucepan. Add **1 small, halved cinnamon stick** and place the saucepan over medium heat. Toast lightly for 30–45 seconds, until fragrant.

2 Add **1½ cups evaporated milk**, **1 cup whole milk**, **¾ cup condensed milk**, and **⅛ tsp salt**. Bring to a boil, stirring frequently, then reduce the heat to a simmer.

3 Add **1 cup cooked plain, long-grain rice** to the pan. Cook for 40 minutes, stirring frequently, until thick. Remove from the heat and take out the vanilla bean and cinnamon stick. Let cool slightly.

4 Divide the pudding between four ramekins, sprinkle with **ground cinnamon**, and serve warm. You can keep the pudding in an airtight container in the fridge for 4–5 days, although it will become very thick.

Coconut and lime

Arroz con leche

⏰ **30 mins**
plus chilling and cooling　　🍴 **SERVES 4–6**　　🌡 Also great **COLD**

RICE PUDDING Swedish with berry sauce

Traditionally made at Christmas in Sweden, this cold dessert is served with a warm and sharp berry sauce for a contrast in flavor and texture.

1 Boil **3 cups whole milk**, **1½ cups long-grain rice**, and **¼ cup granulated sugar** in a large, heavy-bottomed saucepan, stirring frequently. Then reduce the heat to a simmer and cook for 15 minutes, stirring frequently, until the rice is soft. Remove, let cool, then transfer to a large bowl.

2 Whisk **1¼ cups heavy cream** in a bowl to form soft peaks and fold into the rice. Then fold in **1 cup blanched, toasted, and finely chopped almonds**, **1 tbsp sherry**, and **1 tsp vanilla extract**. Chill the pudding for 3–4 hours.

3 For the sauce, place **¼ cup granulated sugar**, **1 tbsp water**, and **10oz (300g) mixed raspberries**, **blackberries**, and **cranberries** in a large saucepan. Cook over low heat for 3–4 minutes, until cooked through. Remove from the heat.

4 Use an immersion blender to blend the mixture to a puree, then strain it into a small bowl. Serve the chilled pudding with the warm sauce poured over the top. You can store it in an airtight container in the fridge for up to 3 days.

⏰ **50 mins**
plus cooling　　🍴 **SERVES 4**　　🌡 Also great **COLD**

RICE PUDDING Arborio

Rice pudding is traditionally made with a short-grain pudding rice. Italian Arborio rice is starchier and produces an even creamier finish.

1 Lightly crack **4 cardamom pods** and place them in a large saucepan. Add **1 large, halved cinnamon stick** and **4 whole cloves** and place the pan over medium heat. Toast lightly for 30–45 seconds, until fragrant.

2 Add **4 cups whole milk**, **¼ cup heavy cream**, **¼ tsp grated nutmeg**, **⅓ cup dark brown sugar**, and **½ cup Arborio rice**. Bring to a boil, stirring until the sugar dissolves.

3 Reduce the heat to a low simmer and cook the pudding for 40–45 minutes, stirring frequently, until the rice has cooked through. Remove from the heat and take out the cardamom pods and cinnamon stick.

4 Add **½ tsp vanilla bean paste** or **vanilla extract** and stir to combine. Divide the pudding between four bowls and top each with **5 blackberries**. Serve immediately. You can store it in an airtight container in the fridge for 4–5 days, although it will become very thick.

Swedish with berry sauce

Arborio

🕐 **1 hr** 🍴 **SERVES 4** 🌡 Also great **COLD**

BAKED APPLES with cinnamon sugar

Of all fruits, apples are the easiest to bake. For a luscious no-fuss dessert, they just need sweetening with sugar, flavoring with a little spice, and a long, gentle baking time. Serve with bowls of good-quality ice cream for a winning hot-cold combination.

INGREDIENTS

½ tsp ground cinnamon, plus extra for dusting

¼ cup light brown sugar

¼ tsp ground allspice

4 sweet apples, such as Braeburn

2 tbsp unsalted butter

vanilla ice cream, to serve

Preheat the oven to 375°F (190°C). Place the cinnamon, sugar, and allspice in a bowl and mix well to combine.

1

Core each apple, leaving about ¾in (2cm) of the bottom intact. Fill the center of each apple with a quarter of the sugar mixture.

2

Pour ½ cup water into a shallow baking dish. Place the apples in the dish and top them with equal quantities of the butter.

3

Bake for 40–50 minutes, until tender. Remove from the heat. Top the apples with scoops of vanilla ice cream and dust with cinnamon. Serve warm. You can store them in an airtight container in the fridge for 1–2 days.

4

50 mins plus cooling   **SERVES 6**   Also great **COLD**

ROASTED PEACHES
with cardamom cream

Use ripe and juicy peaches for this recipe, because natural sugars in the juice concentrate as the fruit roasts.

INGREDIENTS
3 large peaches, halved and pitted
3 tbsp dark brown sugar
pinch of salt
2 tbsp unsalted butter, melted

For the cream
1 cup heavy cream
½ tsp ground cardamom
¼ tsp vanilla extract
3 tbsp confectioners' sugar

SPECIAL EQUIPMENT
2-quart baking dish

PLAN AHEAD
You can prepare and store the cream in an airtight container in the fridge up to 1 day ahead.

1 Preheat the oven to 400°F (200°C). Remove any rough fibers from the peaches and place them cut-side up in the baking dish. Whisk the brown sugar, salt, and butter in a small bowl and pour over the peaches.

2 Roast the peaches for 30–35 minutes or longer, depending on their size and ripeness, until tender when tested with a fork and lightly golden on top. Remove from the heat and let cool slightly.

3 For the cream, whisk all the ingredients in a large bowl to form medium peaks. Chill the mixture until cold. Serve the roasted peaches warm with the cream. You can store the peaches in an airtight container in the fridge for 1–2 days.

25 mins plus cooling   **SERVES 4**   Also great **COLD**

BANANAS FOSTER with orange and pecans

This decadent dessert is a quick and easy flourish at the end of a meal. You can whip it up in minutes with fresh bananas and a few pantry essentials.

INGREDIENTS
⅓ cup pecans, coarsely chopped
4 tbsp unsalted butter
4 heaping tbsp dark brown sugar
juice and grated zest of 1 orange
2 large underripe bananas, cut into ½in (1cm) pieces
¼ cup dark rum
4 slices brioche, thickly cut
4 large scoops good-quality vanilla ice cream

1 Toast the pecans in a large, dry, heavy-bottomed frying pan over medium heat for 3–4 minutes. Stir occasionally, until brown in places. Remove from the heat and let cool.

2 Place the butter, sugar, and orange juice in a large frying pan. Add the orange zest, reserving a little, and cook over medium heat, stirring until the sugar dissolves. Increase the heat to high and cook the sauce for another 2–3 minutes, until it reduces slightly and begins to look glossy.

3 Add the bananas and cook for another 2–3 minutes, until the sauce reduces and the banana pieces are just tender. Add the pecans and rum and cook for another 1 minute. Use a match to carefully light the alcohol—the pan will flare up for 1 minute. Remove from the heat.

4 Lightly toast the brioche slices and cut each into 2 x 2¾in (7cm) rounds. Place two rounds each on four serving plates. Top with a quarter of the banana mixture and one scoop of ice cream. Serve immediately topped with the reserved orange zest.

⏱ **20 mins** plus cooling   🍴 **SERVES 4**   🌡 Also great **COLD**

CARAMELIZED APRICOTS with almonds

Homemade caramel makes a wonderful sauce for sweet and ripe apricots.

INGREDIENTS

4–5 tbsp sliced almonds

2½ tbsp unsalted butter

pinch of salt

¼ cup dark brown sugar

8 apricots, halved and pitted

whipped cream, to serve

SPECIAL EQUIPMENT

9in (23cm) frying pan

1 Toast the almonds in a dry frying pan over medium heat, stirring constantly, until lightly colored and fragrant. Remove from the heat, transfer to a dish, and let cool completely.

2 Place the butter, salt, and sugar in the frying pan and cook over medium heat until smooth and bubbling. Carefully place the apricots, cut-side down, over the caramel. Increase the heat slightly.

3 Cook the apricots for 4–5 minutes, until the cut sides are caramelized and softened. Remove from the heat and let cool slightly. Sprinkle the almonds over the apricots. Serve warm with whipped cream. You can store the apricots in an airtight container in the fridge for 1–2 days.

⏱ **20–25 mins**   🍴 **SERVES 4**   🌡 Also great **COLD**

ROASTED FIGS with thyme and red wine

If you are lucky enough to have access to homegrown figs, you may find that they are not as sweet as their store-bought cousins. Roasting them like this can intensify their sweetness.

INGREDIENTS

3 tbsp red wine

¼ cup light brown sugar

¼ tsp vanilla extract

¼ tsp lemon juice

grated zest of ½ lemon

2–3 sprigs of thyme

8 fresh figs, halved lengthwise

plain yogurt, to serve

SPECIAL EQUIPMENT

2-quart baking dish

1 Preheat the oven to 400°F (200°C). Combine the wine, sugar, vanilla extract, and lemon juice and zest in a large bowl. Remove the leaves from the sprigs of thyme, add to the mixture, and mix. Add the figs and toss well to coat.

2 Place the figs, cut-side down, in a baking dish and pour in the wine mixture. Roast the figs in the oven for 10–15 minutes or longer, depending on their size and ripeness, until they are tender when pierced with a fork.

3 Remove and brush the cooking liquid over the figs to glaze. Transfer the figs to serving plates and drizzle with a little of the cooking liquid, if desired. Serve with a spoonful of plain yogurt. You can store the figs and the cooking liquid in an airtight container in the fridge for 2–3 days.

🕐 **45–55 mins**
plus cooling and chilling

🍴 **SERVES 4**

🌡 Also great
COLD

POACHED PEARS
in red wine

Taking on the rich purple hues of red wine, poached pears
are a simple and classic dessert. Here the pears are laced with
cinnamon, orange zest, and a little fresh thyme. The flavors
deepen the longer the pears are kept in the cooking liquid.

INGREDIENTS

2½ cups red wine
⅔ cup granulated sugar
1 cinnamon stick
peeled zest of 1 orange
1 sprig of thyme
4 just-ripe pears, peeled
whipped cream, to serve

PLAN AHEAD

You can prepare and store
the pears and cooking liquid,
covered in the fridge, up to
2 days ahead.

1 Place the wine, sugar,
cinnamon, orange zest,
and thyme in a heavy-
bottomed saucepan
with a lid. Bring to a
boil, stirring until the
sugar melts. Reduce the
heat to a low simmer.

2 Slice a disk off the bottom of each pear to
allow it to stand upright. Add them to the
pan, making sure they are submerged in the
wine. Cover and cook for 20–30 minutes, until
the pears are just soft when pierced the tip
of a sharp knife.

4 Strain ¾ cup of the cooking liquid into a heavy-bottomed saucepan. Bring to a boil, then reduce the heat to a simmer. Cook for 15 minutes, until slightly thickened. Let cool until just warm. Place the pears upright on serving plates and pour over a little of the sauce. Serve warm with whipped cream.

3 Remove and cool to room temperature. Transfer the pears and cooking liquid to a large dish and cover with plastic wrap. Chill until needed, or overnight to darken the color. Bring to room temperature before serving, then discard the cinnamon, orange zest, and thyme.

🕐 **30–35 mins**
plus steeping and cooling   🍴 **SERVES 4**   🌡 Also great
COLD

PLUMS in tea and star anise

Plums have a rich and deep flavor that intensifies as they cook. Add Earl Grey tea and pungent star anise for an exotic twist.

1 Place **2 Earl Grey teabags, 2 tbsp granulated sugar, 2 whole star anise**, and **1 cinnamon stick** in a large, heavy-bottomed saucepan with a lid. Pour in **2 cups boiling water**, cover, and steep for 10 minutes.

2 Remove the teabags and stir to ensure that the sugar has melted. Add **8 large, just-ripe, halved plums**, cut-side up, and bring to a boil, then reduce the heat to a low simmer. Cook for 8–10 minutes, until the plums are soft when pierced with a knife.

3 Transfer the plums, cut-side up, to four serving bowls. Set aside to cool. Return the pan to the heat and bring the liquid to a boil, then reduce the heat to a low simmer and cook for 15 minutes, until the liquid has reduced and thickened slightly.

4 Remove and cool until just warm. Take out the spices and pour the juice over the plums. Top with **1 scoop softened vanilla ice cream** and serve immediately. You can chill the fruit and liquid for up to 3 days. Bring to room temperature to serve.

🕐 **40 mins**
plus cooling   🍴 **SERVES 4**   🌡 Also great
COLD

APRICOTS with wine and lemon thyme

Perfect to serve when apricots are in season, this simple, fragrant dessert makes the ideal finish to any summertime meal.

1 Place **2 cups dry white wine, 3 tbsp honey, 1 sprig of lemon thyme**, and **zest and juice of 1 large lemon** in a large, heavy-bottomed saucepan. Bring to a boil, stirring, until the honey has melted.

2 Remove from the heat. Add **8 large, just-ripe, halved and pitted apricots** to the pan, cut-side up, and bring to a boil over medium heat. Reduce the heat to a low simmer and cook for 5 minutes, until the apricots are just soft when pierced with a knife.

3 Transfer the apricots, cut-side up, to four serving bowls. Set aside to cool. Remove the thyme and lemon zest and return the pan to the heat. Bring the liquid to a boil, then reduce the heat to a low simmer.

4 Add **1 tbsp granulated sugar** and cook for 20–25 minutes, until the liquid has reduced and thickened. Remove and let cool until just warm, then pour over the apricots. Serve with **crème fraîche**. You can chill the fruit and liquid for up to 3 days. Bring to room temperature to serve.

Plums in tea
and star anise

🕐 **25–30 mins**
plus cooling   🍴 **SERVES 4–6**   🌡 Also great
COLD

FRUIT COMPOTE with yogurt and pistachios

Even when seasonal fruit is scarce, whip up a fruity dessert using the dried fruit in your pantry. Save any leftovers to serve with breakfast.

1 Heat **2 cups water, ¼ cup light brown sugar, zest and juice of 1 large orange**, and **1 cinnamon stick** in a heavy-bottomed, saucepan with a lid. Stir frequently to dissolve the sugar.

2 Add **2½ cups assorted chopped dried fruit** such as cherries, figs, prunes, apricots, and cranberries. Bring to a boil, then reduce the heat to a low simmer. Cook for 20–25 minutes, covered, until the fruit is soft and plump. Remove from the heat and take out the cinnamon stick.

3 Pour the compote into four serving bowls and cool to room temperature. To serve, add **1 tbsp Greek yogurt** to each bowl and top with **¼ cup coarsely chopped, unsalted, and shelled pistachios**. You can chill the fruit and liquid for up to 3 days. Bring to room temperature to serve.

Apricots with wine and lemon thyme

Fruit compote with yogurt and pistachios

COLD

Patisserie ▪ Trifles and layered cakes
Puddings ▪ Cakes and tortes ▪ Bars
and cookies

INGREDIENTS

4 large egg whites,
   at room temperature

¼ tsp salt

¼ tsp cream of tartar

1 cup superfine sugar

2 tsp vanilla extract

1½ cups heavy cream

2 tsp confectioners' sugar,
   plus extra for dusting
   (optional)

strawberries and
   raspberries, to
   serve (optional)

SPECIAL EQUIPMENT

piping bag fitted with
a ½in (1cm) nozzle

PLAN AHEAD

You can store the
unfilled meringues in
an airtight container
for up to 1 week ahead.

🕐 **3 hrs 15 mins**
plus cooling

🍴 **MAKES 30**

MERINGUES with cream

Light, crisp, and creamy white in color, meringues are
a versatile dessert staple. For faultless results, use eggs
at room temperature, a scrupulously clean mixing bowl,
and a low and slow cooking time.

1 Preheat the oven to
225°F (110°C) and line
two baking sheets
with parchment paper.
Set aside. Beat the
egg whites and salt
in a large bowl with
a handheld mixer
until foamy.

2 Add the cream of tartar and beat until soft peaks
form. Then add the superfine sugar, a tablespoon
at a time, and beat after each addition until the
mixture is well combined and forms stiff peaks.

3

Add the vanilla extract to the mixture and fold it in gently with a spatula, so that you lose as little air as possible. Once evenly combined, transfer the mixture to the piping bag.

Pipe 30 even-sized meringues onto each baking sheet. Bake for 3 hours until crisp. Turn off the heat and let cool completely in the oven. Beat the cream and confectioners' sugar until thick and use to sandwich the meringues. Serve immediately with strawberries, raspberries, and a dusting of confectioners' sugar, if desired.

4

Make sure the meringues are spaced well apart.

🕐 **45 mins**
plus infusing and chilling

🍴 **SERVES 4**

ÎLES flottantes

This French classic features just-poached meringues served over crème anglaise, a delicious vanilla custard.

INGREDIENTS

1¼ cups heavy cream

1 vanilla bean

¾ cup + 2 tsp granulated sugar

2 cups whole milk

2 tsp cornstarch

4 egg yolks

1 tsp pure vanilla extract

3 egg whites

2 tbsp grated chocolate, to serve

PLAN AHEAD

You can cover the custard with plastic wrap and store it in the fridge for up to 2 days ahead.

1 Place the cream, vanilla bean, 2 teaspoons of sugar, and half the milk in a saucepan. Bring to a simmer, then remove from the heat. Leave to infuse for 30 minutes, before removing the vanilla bean.

2 Place the cornstarch in a bowl and stir in a little cold milk. Pour the mixture into the infused milk and stir to combine. Bring the mixture to a boil, stirring constantly. Reduce the heat to a simmer, cook for 2 minutes, and remove. Beat the egg yolks in a separate bowl until smooth.

3 Gradually add the egg yolks to the milk mixture and beat to combine. Mix the custard until it is thick enough to coat the back of a spoon, making sure it does not curdle. Stir in the vanilla extract. Pour the custard into a large bowl and cover its surface with dampened plastic wrap. Chill until needed.

4 In a large bowl, beat the egg whites to stiff peaks. Gradually mix in the sugar until combined. Boil the remaining milk and 1¼ cups water in a deep-sided frying pan. Then reduce the heat to a simmer and carefully add 3–4 tablespoons of the mixture to the pan.

5 Cook the meringues in the hot liquid for 1 minute, turning them over once, until they double in size. Remove with a slotted spoon and drain on a plate lined with paper towels. Divide the custard between 4 bowls and top with the meringues. Sprinkle with chocolate to serve immediately.

🕐 **1 hr 50 mins**
plus cooling

🍴 **MAKES 12**

MINI PAVLOVAS tropical fruit

These pavlovas are great if you need to cater for large numbers. Make sure you press small indents in the mixture before baking, so the filling can nestle in place.

INGREDIENTS

1¼ cups superfine sugar

1¾ tsp cornstarch

5 egg whites, at room temperature

pinch of salt

1 tsp white wine vinegar

¼ tsp vanilla extract

¼ tsp orange blossom extract

For the filling

1¼ cups heavy cream, whipped

5–6 kiwis, halved and thinly sliced

3–4 passion fruits, pulped

PLAN AHEAD

You can prepare and store the unfilled pavlovas in an airtight container for up to 1 week ahead.

1 Preheat the oven to 275°F (140°C). Trace 12 circles, each measuring 3in (7.5cm) in diameter, on a sheet of parchment paper. Flip the sheet over and use it to line a large baking sheet. Combine the sugar and cornstarch in a bowl.

2 In a large bowl, beat the egg whites and salt until foamy. Gradually mix in the sugar mixture to form stiff peaks. Add the white wine vinegar, vanilla extract, and orange blossom extract, folding gently so that you lose as little air as possible.

3 Divide the mixture between the circles on the parchment paper, creating swirls with a palette knife. Make small indents in the center. Reduce the oven temperature to 225°F (120°C) and bake for 1 hour, until the pavlovas are hard and hollow when tapped.

4 Turn off the heat and leave the pavlovas in the oven to cool completely before removing them. Top the pavlovas with equal quantities of whipped cream, kiwi, and passion fruit. Serve immediately.

1 hr 50 mins plus cooling   **SERVES 6–8**

PAVLOVA chocolate, apple, and pear

Light, airy pavlovas are often associated with summertime, but fall fruits can work beautifully with a cocoa-infused meringue base. Added warmth comes from a little sprinkled cardamom and cinnamon in the cream filling.

INGREDIENTS

4 egg whites, at room temperature

pinch of salt

¼ tsp cream of tartar

1 cup superfine sugar

½ tsp vanilla extract

2 tbsp cocoa powder, plus extra for dusting

For the filling

¼ tsp cinnamon

1½ tsp confectioners' sugar

¼ tsp cardamom

3oz (85g) green apple, thinly sliced

3oz (85g) pear, thinly sliced

1 cup heavy cream, whipped

PLAN AHEAD

You can prepare and store the unfilled pavlova in an airtight container for up to 1 week ahead.

1 Preheat the oven to 275°F (140°C). Line a baking sheet with parchment paper and set aside. Beat the egg whites and salt in a bowl until foamy. Add the cream of tartar and beat to form soft peaks. Then gradually add the superfine sugar and beat to form stiff peaks.

2 Add the vanilla extract and cocoa powder and mix well to combine. Use a palette knife to spread the mixture on the baking sheet to a circle about 2in (5cm) thick and 8in (20cm) wide. Create neat swirls as you spread the mixture and make a small indent in the center.

3 Reduce the oven temperature to 250°F (130°C) and bake the pavlova for 1 hour and 20 minutes, until it is hard. Turn off the heat and let it cool completely in the oven before removing.

4 For the filling, combine the cinnamon, confectioners' sugar, and cardamom in a bowl. Add the fruit, toss to coat, and leave for 5–10 minutes. Spread the whipped cream on the pavlova. Arrange the fruit on top, sprinkle with cocoa powder, and serve immediately.

50–55 mins
plus resting and cooling

MAKES 20

MACARONS buttercream

Light and delicate creations, macarons are tricky to get right. If the humidity or heat in your kitchen is too harsh, or if you do not rest the mixture for long enough, you can get unexpected results. Follow this recipe closely for impressive results.

INGREDIENTS
¾ cup confectioners' sugar
½ cup ground almonds
2 large egg whites,
at room temperature
¼ cup granulated sugar

For the filling
4 tbsp unsalted butter,
softened
1 cup confectioners' sugar
½ tsp vanilla extract

SPECIAL EQUIPMENT
piping bag fitted with a
1in (3cm) plain nozzle
piping bag fitted with a
½in (1cm) plain nozzle

PLAN AHEAD
You can prepare and store the unfilled macaron shells in an airtight container up to 3 days ahead.

1

Preheat the oven to 300°F (150°C). Use the 1in (3cm) nozzle to trace 20 well-spaced circles each on two sheets of parchment paper. Turn the sheets over and place on two baking sheets.

2

Pulse the confectioners' sugar and almonds in a food processor to a fine powder. Beat the egg whites in a bowl to form soft peaks, then beat in the granulated sugar, a little at a time, until the mixture is stiff and well combined, but still glossy.

3

Gently fold the almond and sugar mixture into the egg mixture, gradually, so that you lose as little air as possible. Be careful not to overmix. Place the piping bag with the 1¼in (3cm) nozzle in a glass and carefully transfer the macaron mixture into it.

The mixture should be shiny, with a thick, ribbon-like consistency.

4

Using the traced guidelines, pipe the macaron mixture into the center of each circle, holding the piping bag vertically. Keep the circles even in volume, as the mixture will spread very slightly. Lightly bang the baking sheets on a work surface. Let rest at room temperature for 30 minutes.

KNOW-HOW It is important to bang the pans, as it levels any peaks that may stay when baked. You can also dampen the end of your finger and push peaks down gently.

5

Bake on the top rack of the oven for 20–25 minutes, until the surface of the shells are set but delicate. Remove and let rest on the baking sheets for 15–20 minutes, then transfer to a wire rack to cool completely.

6

For the filling, beat the ingredients in a bowl until soft and creamy. Place the second piping bag in a glass and spoon in the filling. Pipe a small amount of the filling onto the flat side of 10 macaron shells and gently sandwich them with the remaining shells. Serve immediately. You can store filled macarons for 2–3 days in an airtight container.

🕐 **50–55 mins**
plus resting and cooling

🍴 **MAKES 20**

MACARONS raspberry

Pretty as a picture, these macarons are stuffed with fresh raspberries and mascarpone and look fantastic served on a dessert platter.

1 Preheat the oven to 300°F (150°C). Trace 20 circles each on two sheets of parchment paper. Turn them over, use to line two baking sheets, and set aside. Pulse ⅔ **cup ground almonds** and ¾ **cup confectioners' sugar** in a food processor to a fine powder. Strain to discard large lumps and set aside.

2 Beat **2 large egg whites** with a handheld mixer in a large bowl to form stiff peaks. Add ¼ **cup granulated sugar**, a little at a time, beating well after each addition until the mixture is stiff and glossy. Add ¼ **tsp red food coloring paste** and beat until you achieve the desired shade of pink.

3 Use a silicone spatula to gently fold half the dry ingredients into the egg white mixture until combined. Add the remaining dry ingredients and mix until you reach a shiny mixture with a thick, ribbon-like consistency. Transfer the mixture to a **piping bag** fitted with a ½**in (1cm) plain nozzle.**

4 Pipe the mixture in the center of each traced circle. Lightly bang the sheets on a work surface and let rest for 30 minutes. Bake in the oven for 20–25 minutes, until the surface is firm. Rest on the baking sheets for 10 minutes, then transfer to a wire rack to cool completely.

5 Beat **5½oz (150g) mascarpone, 2 tbsp heavy cream,** and **2 tbsp confectioners' sugar** in a bowl and transfer to a piping bag. Halve **30 raspberries** lengthwise. Pipe a little of the cream filling onto 10 shells and top with 3 raspberry slices, arranged cut-side down in a star shape. Pipe the filling onto the remaining shells and place on top of the raspberries. Serve immediately.

🕐 **50–55 mins**
plus resting, cooling, and chilling

🍴 **MAKES 20**

MACARONS pistachio

It is important to use raw, unsalted pistachios for this melt-in-the-mouth recipe—rub off the skin with a clean paper towel before grinding them.

1 Preheat the oven to 300°F (150°C). Prepare two baking sheets (see Raspberry macarons, step 1) and set aside. Pulse ½ **cup unsalted, shelled, peeled whole pistachios** in a food processor to a coarse powder. Add ¾ **cup confectioners' sugar** and ¼ **cup ground almonds** and pulse to a very fine powder. Strain to discard large lumps and set aside.

2 Beat **2 large egg whites** with a handheld mixer in a large bowl to form stiff peaks. Add ¼ **cup sugar**, a little at a time, beating after each addition until the mixture is stiff and glossy. Add ¼ **tsp green food coloring paste** and beat until you achieve the desired shade.

3 Use a silicone spatula to fold the dry ingredients into the egg white mixture in two stages (see Raspberry macarons, step 3). Transfer the mixture to a **piping bag** fitted with a ½**in (1cm) plain nozzle**. Pipe, rest, and bake the macaron shells (see Raspberry macarons, step 4). Rest the baked shells on the baking sheets for 10 minutes, then transfer to a wire rack to cool.

4 Melt **4½oz (125g) finely chopped white chocolate, 3 tbsp heavy cream,** and **1 tsp unsalted butter** in a heatproof bowl over a saucepan of simmering water, making sure it does not touch the bowl. Beat the mixture with a wooden spoon until thick and shiny. Transfer to a piping bag and chill until cool, but not stiff.

5 To serve, pipe a little of the chocolate ganache onto 10 shells and sandwich with the remaining shells. You can store them in an airtight container, chilled, for up to 1 day.

Raspberry

Pistachio

🕐 **50–55 mins**
plus resting, cooling, and chilling

🍴 **MAKES 20**

MACARONS chocolate

A ganache is one of the basic recipes all dessert enthusiasts should have at their fingertips—here it makes a perfect filling for dark chocolate macarons.

1 Preheat the oven to 300°F (150°C). Prepare two baking sheets (see Raspberry macarons, step 1) and set aside. Pulse **½ cup ground almonds**, **¼ cup cocoa powder**, and **¾ cup confectioners' sugar** in a food processor until well combined.

2 Beat **2 large egg whites** with a handheld mixer in a large bowl to form stiff peaks. Add **¼ cup sugar**, a little at a time, Beating after each addition until the mixture is stiff and glossy. Use a silicone spatula to fold the dry ingredients into the egg white mixture in two stages (see Raspberry macarons, step 3).

3 Transfer the mixture to a **piping bag** fitted with a **½in (1cm) plain nozzle**. Pipe, rest, and bake the macaron shells (see Raspberry macarons, step 4). Rest the baked shells on the baking sheets for 10 minutes, then transfer to a wire rack to cool.

4 Heat **⅓ cup heavy cream** in a heavy-bottomed saucepan until hot, but not boiling. Remove from the heat and add **3½oz (100g) finely chopped dark chocolate**. Let melt, then combine with a wooden spoon. Transfer to a piping bag and chill until cool, but not stiff.

5 To serve, pipe a little of the chocolate ganache onto 10 shells and sandwich with the remaining shells. You can store them in an airtight container, chilled, for up to 1 day.

Chocolate

Simple alternatives

This array of macaron recipes adapts the classic recipe on pages 104–105. Make sure you use food coloring paste, as liquid varieties may loosen the mixture.

Rosewater and raspberry Add ¼ tsp red food coloring paste to the macaron mixture (see p105, step 3) and combine well. For the filling, combine 2oz (60g) crushed raspberries, 4½oz (125g) mascarpone, and ¼ tsp rosewater.

Orange flower Add ¼ tsp orange food coloring paste to the macaron mixture (see p105, step 3). Add 1 tsp finely grated orange zest and 1 tsp orange flower water to the buttercream filling (see p105, step 6).

Mocha Add 1 tbsp instant coffee powder to the ground almonds and sugar before pulsing (see p105, step 2). Sandwich the macaron shells with the chocolate ganache filling (see Chocolate macarons, steps 4–5).

Hazelnut Replace ¼ cup of the ground almonds with skinned and finely ground hazelnuts (see p105, step 2). Sandwich with the buttercream filling (see p105, step 6) and roll the edges of the filled macarons in very finely chopped hazelnuts.

Lime and dark chocolate Add ¼ tsp green food coloring paste to the macaron mixture (see p105, step 3) and 1 tsp finely grated lime zest to the chocolate ganache filling (see Chocolate macarons, steps 4–5).

Tangerine Add 1 tsp grated tangerine zest to the ground almonds and sugar (see p105, step 2). Add ¼ tsp orange food coloring paste to the macaron mixture (see p105, step 3). Add 1 tsp grated tangerine zest to the buttercream filling (see p105, step 6).

Lavender Add ¼ tsp purple food coloring to the macaron mixture (see p105, step 3). Add ¼ tsp finely chopped culinary lavender to the buttercream filling (see p105, step 6).

Chocolate orange Make the chocolate macaron shells (see Chocolate macarons, steps 1–4). For the filling, add 1 tsp finely grated orange zest to the buttercream filling (see p105, step 6).

45 mins
plus cooling and chilling

MAKES 26–30

TRUFFLES dark chocolate

In their simplest form, truffles are a mixture of good-quality chocolate and cream. It is difficult to achieve a chocolatier-style finish, but this simple method of dipping, dusting, and brushing gives them an attractive and appetizing look.

INGREDIENTS
⅔ cup heavy cream
12oz (350g) good-quality dark chocolate, finely grated
2–3 tbsp cocoa powder

SPECIAL EQUIPMENT
2 disposable piping bags

1

Heat the cream in a saucepan over medium heat until hot, but not boiling. Place 8oz (225g) of the chocolate in a heatproof bowl, pour in the cream, and let it melt. Whisk the mixture until smooth and glossy. Let cool for 30 minutes.

2

Spoon the ganache into the piping bags and snip off the ends. Line a large baking sheet with parchment paper. Pipe walnut-sized balls of the ganache onto the sheet, spaced well apart. Chill for 30 minutes, until hardened.

3

Roll each ball gently between your palms, until smooth. Place the truffles back on the sheet and chill for another 30 minutes.

4

Melt the remaining chocolate in a heatproof bowl over a pan of simmering water, making sure it does not touch the water. Stir until smooth. Place the cocoa powder in a small bowl.

5

Place a truffle on a spoon and dip it into the melted chocolate. Remove, allow any excess to drip back into the bowl, and place gently in the bowl of cocoa powder to coat. Transfer the coated truffle to a clean, lined baking sheet.

6

Repeat for the remaining truffles. Gently brush off any excess cocoa powder and chill for at least 1 hour before serving. You can store the truffles in an airtight container in the fridge for up to 1 week.

Chocolate, chile, and cinnamon

Pistachio and white chocolate

🕐 **50 mins**
plus cooling and chilling

🍴 **MAKES 26–30**

TRUFFLES chocolate, chile, and cinnamon

Mixing chile and cinnamon is an unusual but inspired idea, as it brings a gentle heat to the truffles. For a pronounced warmth, you can increase the quantity of both spices by ¼ teaspoon.

1 Heat **⅔ cup heavy cream** in a saucepan over medium heat until hot, but not boiling. Place **8oz (225g) finely grated good-quality dark chocolate** in a heatproof bowl, pour the cream over the top, and let melt. Whisk the mixture until smooth and glossy. Stir in **½ tsp ground cinnamon** and **½ tsp ground cayenne pepper**. Let the ganache cool for 30 minutes.

2 Line a baking sheet with parchment paper. Spoon the ganache into **2 piping bags** and snip off the ends. Pipe small, walnut-sized balls of the ganache onto the baking sheet, spaced apart. Chill for 30 minutes, until hardened. Roll each ball gently between your palms until smooth, place back on the sheet, and chill for another 30 minutes.

3 Line a baking sheet with parchment paper. Melt **4oz (115g) finely grated good-quality dark chocolate** in a small, heatproof bowl over a saucepan of barely simmering water, making sure it does not touch the water.

4 Place a truffle on a spoon and carefully dip it into the melted chocolate to coat. Remove, allow any excess to drip back into the bowl, and place gently onto the lined sheet. Repeat for the remaining truffles.

5 Melt **1¾oz (50g) finely grated good-quality white chocolate** in a small heatproof bowl (see step 3), then let cool slightly. Use a teaspoon to drizzle the chocolate over the truffles in a zigzag design. Chill them for at least 1 hour and then serve. You can store the truffles in an airtight container in the fridge for up to 1 week.

45 mins
plus cooling and chilling   MAKES 26–30

TRUFFLES pistachio and white chocolate

These creamy treats are a delight to eat and to look at. A specialty baking ingredient, pistachio paste provides a wonderfully intense flavor and smooth texture.

1 Heat **⅔ cup heavy cream** and melt **8oz (225g) finely grated good-quality dark chocolate** (see Chocolate, chile, and cinnamon truffles, step 1). Combine the two ingredients and whisk until smooth and glossy. Stir in **2 tbsp pistachio paste** and let cool for 30 minutes.

2 Line a baking sheet with parchment paper. Spoon the ganache into **2 piping bags**, pipe it onto the baking sheet, and let chill for 30 minutes (see Chocolate, chile, and cinnamon truffles, step 2). Roll each ball gently between your palms, until smooth. Place the truffles back on the sheet and chill for another 30 minutes.

3 Melt **5¾oz (165g) finely grated good-quality white chocolate** in a small, heatproof bowl over a saucepan of barely simmering water, making sure it does not touch the water. Line a baking sheet with parchment paper. Coat the truffles with the chocolate (see Chocolate, chile, and cinnamon truffles, step 4), then place them gently onto the lined sheet.

4 Sprinkle with **¼ cup finely ground unsalted and skinned pistachios**. Chill for at least 1 hour before serving. You can store the truffles in an airtight container in the fridge for up to 1 week.

45 mins
plus cooling and chilling   MAKES 26–30

TRUFFLES raspberry and sea salt

Freeze-dried raspberries bring bright color and a concentrated raspberry flavor to these truffles. They also complement dark chocolate very well.

1 Heat **⅔ cup heavy cream** and melt **8oz (225g) finely grated good-quality dark chocolate** (see Chocolate, chile, and cinnamon truffles, step 1). Combine the two ingredients and whisk until smooth and glossy. Stir in **2 tbsp freeze-dried raspberries** and **½ tsp raspberry extract**. Cool for 30 minutes.

2 Line a baking sheet with parchment paper. Spoon the ganache into **2 piping bags**, pipe it onto the baking sheet, and let chill for 30 minutes (see Chocolate, chile, and cinnamon truffles, step 2). Roll each ball gently between your palms, until smooth. Place the truffles back on the sheet and chill for another 30 minutes.

3 Melt **4oz (115g) finely grated good-quality dark chocolate** (see Chocolate, chile, and cinnamon truffles, step 3). Line a baking sheet with parchment paper. Coat the truffles with the chocolate (see Chocolate, chile, and cinnamon truffles, step 4), then place gently onto the lined sheet. Repeat for the remaining truffles.

4 Sprinkle half the truffles with **1 tsp sea salt flakes**. Sprinkle the remaining truffles with **1 tbsp freeze-dried raspberries**. Chill them for at least 1 hour before serving. You can store the truffles in an airtight container in the fridge for up to 1 week.

Raspberry and sea salt

 **1 hr 20 mins**
plus cooling and chilling

MAKES 4

MILLE-FEUILLES
vanilla

This French dessert is perfection in pastry form. To get ultra-thin, golden brown layers, sandwich the pastry between two baking sheets halfway through cooking—this presses out any bubbles.

INGREDIENTS

1¾ cups all-purpose flour, plus extra for dusting

18 tbsp unsalted butter, chilled and grated

½ tsp fine salt

1 egg, beaten to glaze

1¼ cups confectioners' sugar

1 heaping tsp cocoa powder

For the crème pâtissière

1⅔ cups whole milk

¼ cup cornstarch

¼ cup granulated sugar

3 large egg yolks, at room temperature

PLAN AHEAD

You can prepare and chill the crème pâtissière up to 1 day ahead. Beat it well before use.

Fold the pastry
into thirds, roll, and
repeat three times.

1 Sift the flour into a large bowl. Stir in the butter with a
butter knife and add the salt. Rub the mixture together
until it resembles bread crumbs. Add 5–6 tablespoons of
ice water and bring the mixture together to form a dough.
Wrap the dough in plastic wrap and chill for 20 minutes.

2 On a floured surface, roll out the dough to a large, ¼in (5mm)
thick rectangle. Fold over one-third of the dough. Fold the
other third over the top, then flip it over and roll. Repeat
three times. Wrap in plastic wrap and chill for 20 minutes.
Preheat the oven to 375°F (190°C).

The slices should be
3in (7.5cm) wide
and 6in (15cm) long.

3 Roll out the dough on a lightly floured surface to a thin
rectangle, about 12 x 16½in (30 x 42cm). Cut the dough
into 12 smaller, even-sized slices. Trim the edges and
transfer them to two large baking sheets sprinkled with
a little water. Brush them lightly with the beaten egg.

4 Bake on the top rack of the oven for 7–10 minutes, until the
slices are puffed up and lightly golden. Place a baking pan
on top of the slices and press them down carefully. Bake for
another 7–10 minutes, until the slices are flat, crisp, and
golden brown. Let cool.

The crème pâtissière thickens as you whisk it on the heat.

KNOW-HOW Use a damp piece of parchment paper or plastic wrap to cover the crème pâtissière in the fridge—this keeps a skin from forming.

5 For the crème pâtissière, heat three-quarters of the milk for 3–5 minutes. Whisk the remaining ingredients in a heatproof bowl. Whisk in the hot milk until the sugar dissolves. Place in a clean pan and whisk over low heat for 4–5 minutes. Pour into a bowl and cool. Cover and chill.

6 Combine the confectioners' sugar with a little water to form a smooth paste. In a separate bowl, combine 1 tablespoon of the paste with the cocoa powder until smooth, adding a little water if needed. Spread an even layer of the icing over four pastry slices.

You may need to beat the cooled crème pâtissière a little before using it.

7 Drizzle thin horizontal lines of the cocoa frosting over the icing and drag a skewer through to create a feathered pattern. Work quickly to decorate the icing before it sets. Set the four pastry slices aside to dry.

8 Spread the remaining eight pastry slices with equal amounts of the crème pâtissière. Carefully stack two slices together to form four mille-feuilles, pressing down gently to keep them in place. Place one frosted pastry slice over each mille-feuilles and serve immediately.

⏱ **1 hr 10 mins**
plus cooling and chilling   🍴 **MAKES 4**

MILLE-FEUILLES
pear and hazelnut

This is a great way to use extra poached pears. If poached in red wine (see Poached pears, pp94–95), fold them into the cream at the last minute to make the best of the vivid color contrast.

INGREDIENTS

½ cup white wine

2 tbsp granulated sugar

½ tsp vanilla extract

2 pears, peeled, cored, and diced into ½in (1cm) pieces

2 sheets store-bought puff pastry, about 8 x 12in (20 x 30cm)

flour, for dusting

1 egg, lightly beaten

⅓ cup blanched hazelnuts, chopped finely

½ cup mascarpone cheese

½ cup heavy whipping cream, whisked to form soft peaks

1 tbsp confectioners' sugar, plus extra to dust

PLAN AHEAD

You can cook, strain, and store the pears in an airtight container in the fridge up to 3 days ahead.

1 Heat the wine, granulated sugar, vanilla extract, and ½ cup water in a saucepan over medium heat until the sugar dissolves. Bring to a boil, then reduce the heat to a low simmer.

2 Add the pears to the liquid and cook them for 15–20 minutes, until soft. Drain and discard the liquid. Place the pears in a bowl and let cool completely before chilling. Preheat the oven to 375°F (190°C).

3 Unroll the pastry sheets on a lightly floured surface. Cut each sheet into 6 x 5in (12cm) long and 2½in (6cm) wide slices. Trim the edges, place them on baking sheets, and brush with the beaten egg.

4 Sprinkle four pastry slices with a few hazelnuts and press down gently. Bake on the top rack of the oven for 5–7 minutes, until lightly golden and puffed up. Then press them down gently with a baking sheet, and leave it on top. Bake for another 7–10 minutes, until flat, crisp, and golden. Let cool completely on a wire rack.

5 For the filling, beat the mascarpone in a bowl until light and fluffy. Fold in the whipped cream, poached pears, confectioners' sugar, and the remaining hazelnuts until evenly combined.

6 Spread one-eighth of the filling over each of the plain pastry slices. Stack two slices together to form four mille-feuilles, pressing down gently to keep them in place. Top each mille-feuille with a nut-topped slice, dust with confectioners' sugar, and serve immediately.

⏱ **30 mins**
plus cooling and chilling   🍴 **MAKES 4**

MILHOJAS

Popular in South America, these crisp pastries are sandwiched with another favorite of the region—dulce de leche.

INGREDIENTS

½ cup dulce de leche (see p76)

⅔ cup heavy cream

2 egg yolks

all-purpose flour, for dusting

2 sheets store-bought puff pastry, about 8 x 12in (20 x 30cm)

1 egg, beaten to glaze

confectioners' sugar, to dust

PLAN AHEAD

You can prepare and store the filling in an airtight container in the fridge up to 3 days ahead.

1 Whisk the dulce de leche and cream in a small, heavy-bottomed saucepan. Heat the mixture over low heat until hot, stirring constantly to ensure that it does not burn. Whisk the egg yolks in a small heatproof bowl.

2 Gently pour the hot cream mixture over the egg yolks, whisking constantly to combine. Pour the custard back into the saucepan and heat gently, stirring constantly, until it thickens. Pour it into a shallow bowl. Cool completely, cover the surface with plastic wrap, and chill for 2 hours.

3 Preheat the oven to 375°F (190°C). Unroll the pastry sheets on a lightly floured surface. Cut each into six slices, trim the edges, and spread out on a baking sheet (see Pear and hazelnut mille-feuilles, step 3). Brush them with the beaten egg.

4 Score diagonal stripes on the slices, being careful not to cut through. Bake all the slices until flat, crisp, and golden (see Pear and hazelnut mille-feuilles, step 4). Place on a wire rack to cool completely.

5 Then spread one-eighth of the filling over eight pastry slices. Stack them to form four mille-feuilles (see Pear and hazelnut mille-feuilles, step 6). Top with the remaining slices, dust with confectioners' sugar, and serve immediately.

🕐 **2 hrs 30 mins**
plus cooling and chilling   🍴 **SERVES 8**

MILLE-FEUILLES summer fruit

A large mille-feuille is a great dessert to serve at a party—it looks fantastic and is far simpler to make than several smaller pastries. Use whichever berries are in season, or for a quick fix, fill with good-quality canned fruit, diced into small pieces.

INGREDIENTS

2 x 14oz (375g) packages store-bought puff pastry

14oz (400g) mixed berries, such as blueberries, raspberries, and hulled and diced strawberries

confectioners' sugar, to dust

For the cream filling

1½ cups whole milk

4 egg yolks

¼ cup granulated sugar

¼ cup all-purpose flour, sifted, plus extra for dusting

1 cup heavy cream

1 For the filling, bring the milk to a boil in a large saucepan over medium heat. Let cool. Whisk the egg yolks and granulated sugar in a heatproof bowl for 2–3 minutes, until thick. Whisk in the flour until combined, then gradually whisk in the milk until smooth.

2 Bring the mixture to a boil in a clean pan, whisking, until thickened. Then reduce the heat to low and whisk for another 2 minutes. Remove and whisk until smooth, if needed. Transfer to a bowl and cool completely. Cover with plastic wrap and chill for 1 hour.

3 Preheat the oven to 400°F (200°C). Sprinkle two large baking sheets with water. On a floured surface, roll out the pastry sheets to two rectangles slightly larger than the baking sheets and about ⅛in (3mm) thick. Transfer to the baking sheets, press down, and chill for 15 minutes.

4 Prick both sheets of pastry with a fork and bake for 15–20 minutes, until just beginning to brown. Then press them down with another two baking sheets and bake for another 10 minutes, until well-browned.

5 While the pastry sheets are still warm, trim the edges and cut into three 6 x 10in (5 x 25cm) strips. Let cool. Whisk the cream until stiff and fold it into the filling. Spread half the cream filling over two of the pastry strips. Scatter with half of the fruit.

6 Add another layer of pastry, filling, and fruit. Top with the last pastry strip and press down gently. Dust generously with confectioners' sugar and serve. You can store the mille-feuilles in the fridge for up to 6 hours.

32 mins plus cooling   **SERVES 4**

PROFITEROLES classic

Freshly prepared profiteroles should be golden, light, bursting with thick cream, and drenched in a dark-chocolate ganache. Make sure that once cooked, you prick the choux buns to allow the steam to escape—this ensures a crisp, delicate pastry.

INGREDIENTS

½ cup all-purpose flour
4 tbsp unsalted butter
2 eggs, beaten

For the filling and topping

1¾ cups heavy cream
7oz (200g) good-quality dark chocolate, broken into pieces
2 tbsp corn syrup
2 tbsp unsalted butter

SPECIAL EQUIPMENT

piping bag with a ½in (1cm) plain nozzle
piping bag with a ¼in (5mm) star nozzle

PLAN AHEAD

You can store the unfilled buns in an airtight container up to 2 days ahead, or freeze them up to 12 weeks ahead.

1

Preheat the oven to 425°F (220°C). Line two large baking sheets with parchment paper. Sift the flour into a large bowl, holding the strainer high to help aerate it.

2

Melt the butter and ⅔ cup water in a saucepan over gentle heat. Bring to a boil and remove from the heat. Add the flour and beat the mixture until it is smooth and forms a ball. Let cool for 10 minutes.

3

Gradually add the eggs, beating well after each addition to form a stiff, smooth, and shiny batter. Spoon the batter into the piping bag fitted with the plain nozzle.

4

Use a knife to make a hole in each bun—this allows steam to escape.

Pipe 16 walnut-sized rounds of the batter onto the baking sheets. Bake for 20 minutes, until risen and golden. Remove and make a hole on one side of each bun. Return to the oven for 2 minutes to crisp up. Transfer them to a wire rack to cool completely.

5

Whisk 1¼ cups of the cream in a large bowl to form soft peaks. Gently heat the chocolate, corn syrup, butter, and remaining cream in a pan, stirring, until melted and smooth.

6

Spoon the whipped cream into the piping bag with the star nozzle and pipe into the buns. Place them on a serving plate, drizzle the chocolate sauce over the top, and serve immediately.

🕐 **2 hrs 40 mins**
plus chilling and cooling   🍴 **SERVES 8**

PARIS-BREST

This praline and choux pastry dessert is complex, but worthy of a special occasion. To simplify the recipe, make the filling the day before you bake the pastry.

INGREDIENTS

3 large egg yolks
1 cup whole milk
2 tbsp cornstarch
⅛ tsp salt
⅔ cup granulated sugar
1 tbsp unsalted butter
1½ tsp vanilla extract
1 cup hazelnuts, skinned
1 tsp powdered gelatin
1 cup heavy cream, beaten
  to form stiff peaks
confectioners' sugar, to dust

For the dough

1 cup all-purpose flour
¼ tsp salt
¼ cup 1% milk
8 tbsp unsalted butter
4 large eggs, lightly
  beaten, plus 1 large egg,
  lightly beaten, for glazing
½ cup sliced almonds

SPECIAL EQUIPMENT

piping bag fitted with a
¾in (2cm) plain round
nozzle

PLAN AHEAD

You can store the unfilled ring in an airtight container up to 1 day ahead. You may wish to crisp it up in a medium oven for 5 minutes before you fill it. You can prepare the filling and store it in an airtight container in the fridge up to 1 day ahead.

1 Whisk the egg yolks and half the milk in a heatproof bowl. Whisk in the cornstarch until smooth. Combine the remaining milk, salt, and ⅓ cup granulated sugar in a saucepan and bring to a boil. Remove from the heat and whisk it into the egg yolk mixture, until combined. Strain the mixture into a clean pan and bring to a boil over medium heat, stirring, until thick. Cook for 30 seconds, pour it into a bowl, and stir in the butter and vanilla extract. Cover with plastic wrap and chill for 1 hour.

2 In a separate pan, boil the remaining granulated sugar and 2 tablespoons of water over gentle heat. Cook for 7 minutes, until golden. Spread the nuts on a lined baking sheet, pour over the caramel, and let cool. Crush and pulse the brittle to fine crumbs in a food processor and stir into the pastry cream. Whisk the gelatin and 1 tablespoon water in a pan and leave for 3–4 minutes to thicken. Cook it over low heat for 20–30 seconds, then fold it into the pastry cream along with the whipped cream. Chill for at least 1 hour.

3 Preheat the oven to 425°F (220°C). Draw an 8in (20cm) circle on the parchment paper, flip it over, and use it to line a baking sheet. For the dough, combine the flour and salt in a bowl. In a pan, gently boil the

milk, butter, and 1 cup water. Remove from the heat and whisk in the flour mixture until smooth. Whisk the dough for another 1–2 minutes until shiny, smooth, and pulling away from the edges. Stir in half the beaten eggs until smooth. Then stir in the remaining beaten eggs until combined.

4 Spoon one-third of the mixture into the piping bag and pipe a large 1in (2.5cm) thick ring along the inside of the traced circle on the parchment. Add a third more of the dough to the bag and pipe another ring along the outer edge of the first, touching it. Pipe a third ring with the rest of the dough, along the point at which the two rings meet. Brush the top with the beaten egg and sprinkle with the almonds. Bake for 15 minutes.

5 Reduce the heat to 375°F (190°C) and bake for 25 minutes. Remove from the oven and turn off the heat. Cut a few slits on top of the dough and place it back in the oven for 20 minutes, leaving the oven door ajar. Remove and place on a wire rack to cool completely, then use a serrated knife to slice the wreath in half lengthwise and pipe the filling on the bottom half. Top with the other half, dust with confectioners' sugar, and serve immediately. Best served on the same day.

🕐 **55 mins–1 hr** plus cooling 🍴 **SERVES 4**

ECLAIRS chocolate

These lovely pastries are also members of the choux family. You can fill them with pastry cream (see pp112–15).

INGREDIENTS
4 tbsp unsalted butter

¾ cup all-purpose flour, sifted

2 eggs, lightly beaten

1 cup heavy cream or whipping cream

3½oz (100g) good-quality dark chocolate, broken into pieces

SPECIAL EQUIPMENT
piping bag fitted with a ¾in (1.5cm) plain nozzle

PLAN AHEAD
You can store the eclair buns in an airtight container up to 2 days ahead, or freeze them up to 12 weeks ahead.

1 Preheat the oven to 400°F (200°C). Melt the butter in a pan with ⅔ cup cold water. Bring to a boil, then remove from the heat and stir in the flour. Beat with a wooden spoon until well combined.

2 Gradually add the eggs to the flour and butter mixture, whisking constantly to combine. Continue whisking until the mixture is shiny and smooth (see Paris-brest, step 3). Transfer to the piping bag.

3 Line two baking sheets with parchment paper. Pipe 8 lengths of the eclair mixture, each about 5in (12cm) long, onto the sheets, using a wet knife to cut each length. Bake for 20–25 minutes, until golden brown. Remove and cut a slit down the side of each bun.

4 Return the buns to the oven for another 5 minutes, until cooked through. Then remove and let cool completely. Beat the cream in a bowl with a handheld mixer to form soft peaks and spoon it into each eclair.

5 Melt the chocolate in a heatproof bowl over a pan of simmering water, making sure it does not touch the water. Spoon it over the top of each eclair and let set. Serve immediately. Best served on the same day.

🕐 **1 hr 25–30 mins** plus cooling 🍴 **SERVES 4**

PROFITEROLES salted caramel

Sweet and salty, crisp and creamy—this recipe provides a riot of flavor and texture. Place the buns in the center of the table, pour over the topping, and ask your guests to help themselves.

INGREDIENTS
12–15 unfilled profiterole buns (see p119, steps 1–4)

For the caramel

½ cup granulated sugar

1½ cups heavy cream

1 tbsp unsalted butter

¾ tsp vanilla extract

¼ tsp salt

For the topping

½ cup heavy cream

7oz (200g) good-quality dark chocolate, broken into pieces

2 tbsp unsalted butter

2 tbsp corn syrup

pinch of salt

SPECIAL EQUIPMENT
piping bag fitted with a ¼in (5mm) round nozzle

1 For the caramel, place the sugar and 2 tablespoons of water in a saucepan. Bring to a boil over medium-high heat. As the caramel is cooking, dip a pastry brush in a little water and brush down the sides of the saucepan to prevent crystallization.

2 Cook the sugar for about 5 minutes, until patches of color appear. Swirl the pan to ensure it cooks evenly. Remove from the heat once the caramel reaches a medium-amber color. Slowly add ½ cup cream and the butter, vanilla, and salt to the pan and combine well with a wooden spoon.

3 Place back on a medium–low heat to melt any parts that may have hardened, transfer to a bowl, and cool to room temperature. In a separate bowl, beat the remaining cream to form soft peaks, then fold in the caramel, beating until stiff peaks form. Place the salted caramel cream in the piping bag and fill each profiterole bun with cream.

4 For the topping, melt all the ingredients in a heatproof bowl over a saucepan of gently simmering water, making sure it does not touch the water. Remove from the heat and let cool for 1–2 minutes. Then drizzle the topping over the profiteroles and serve immediately. Best served on the same day.

🕐 **1 hr 30 mins**
plus chilling and cooling

🍴 **SERVES 8**

🌡 Also great
HOT

TARTE au citron

There are two types of lemon tarts—those filled with cooked curd, and French-style tarts that are filled to the brim with lemon custard and baked in the oven. This custard-style tart is light, delicate, and very lemony.

INGREDIENTS

1½ cups all-purpose flour, plus extra for dusting
2 tbsp granulated sugar
7 tbsp unsalted butter, chilled and diced
1 egg, beaten
half-and-half, to serve
raspberries, to serve

For the filling
⅔ cup heavy cream
¾ cup granulated sugar

juice and zest of 2 lemons
4 eggs, plus 1 egg yolk

SPECIAL EQUIPMENT
9in (23cm) loose-bottomed fluted tart pan
baking beans

PLAN AHEAD
You can store the blind-baked tart crust in an airtight container up to 3 days ahead.

Combine the flour and sugar in a bowl. Rub in the butter until the mixture resembles bread crumbs. Add the egg and bring together to form a dough, adding a little ice water if it seems dry. Knead it briefly on a floured surface until smooth. Wrap in plastic wrap and chill for 1 hour.

1

Preheat the oven to 350°F (180°C). On a floured surface, roll out the dough to a large circle, ⅛in (3mm) thick. Use it to line the pan, leaving an overhang of ¾in (2cm). Knead the dough briefly if it crumbles. Prick the dough, line with parchment paper, and fill with baking beans.

2

Place the tart crust on a baking sheet and bake for 20–25 minutes. Then remove the beans and paper and bake the crust for another 5 minutes, until golden. Trim the tart crust. For the filling, whisk all the ingredients in a bowl until well combined.

3

KNOW-HOW It is important to trim the overhang while the crust is still warm, because it hardens as it cools, making it difficult to cut.

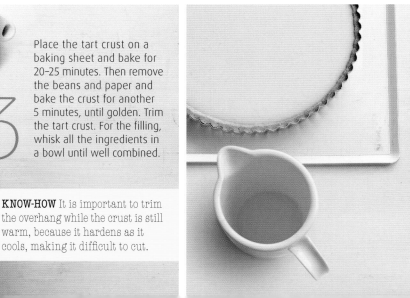

4

Place the tart crust on a baking sheet, pour in the filling, and slide it into the oven. Bake for 40–45 minutes, until just set. Remove from the heat, transfer to a wire rack, and cool to room temperature. Serve with half-and-half and raspberries. You can store the tart, covered in the fridge, for up to 2 days.

TART lime and coconut

Substitute coconut milk for cream and lime for lemon and you're left with an exciting take on the French classic.

INGREDIENTS

1¼ cups all-purpose flour, plus extra for dusting

2 tbsp granulated sugar

7 tbsp unsalted butter, softened

1 egg yolk, beaten with 2 tbsp water

confectioners' sugar, to dust

For the filling

¾ cup thick coconut milk or coconut cream

1 cup granulated sugar

5 eggs

grated zest of 2 limes

juice of 4 limes

SPECIAL EQUIPMENT

9in (23cm) loose-bottomed fluted tart pan

baking beans

PLAN AHEAD

You can store the blind-baked tart crust in an airtight container up to 3 days ahead.

1 Combine the flour and granulated sugar in a bowl. Rub in the butter until the mixture resembles fine bread crumbs. Add the beaten egg yolk and bring together to form a soft dough, adding a little water if it seems dry. Wrap in plastic wrap and chill for 30 minutes.

2 Preheat the oven to 350°F (180°C). On a floured surface, roll out the dough to a large circle, ¼in (5mm) thick. Use it to line the tart pan, leaving a ½in (1cm) overhang. Prick the dough, line with parchment paper, and fill with baking beans.

3 Place the pan on a baking sheet. Blind bake the tart for 20 minutes, then remove the beans and paper and bake for another 5 minutes if the center looks uncooked. Trim while it is still warm and set aside.

4 For the filling, whisk all the ingredients in a large bowl until well combined. Pour into a pitcher and let rest for 5 minutes. Then put the tart crust on a baking sheet placed on an oven rack. Pour the filling in evenly.

5 Carefully slide the rack into the oven and bake for 20–25 minutes, until the filling is just set. Remove and let cool completely. Dust with confectioners' sugar and serve cold. You can store the tart, covered in the fridge, for up to 2 days.

🕐 **1 hr 30 mins**
plus chilling and cooling

🍴 **SERVES 6**

🌡 Also great
HOT

TART brown sugar

Also known as sugar cream pie, this delicious dessert has very few ingredients, and as such makes a great last-minute dessert. The filling has a rich, toffee-like flavor and soft texture.

INGREDIENTS

1½ cups all-purpose flour, plus extra for dusting

2 tbsp granulated sugar

8 tbsp unsalted butter, chilled and diced

1 egg yolk, beaten with 2 tbsp ice water

whipped cream, to serve

For the filling

¾ cup light brown sugar, plus extra for dusting

2 tbsp all-purpose flour

1¾ cups heavy cream

1 tsp vanilla extract

pinch of salt

SPECIAL EQUIPMENT

9in (23cm) loose-bottomed fluted tart pan

baking beans

PLAN AHEAD

You can store the blind-baked tart crust in an airtight container up to 3 days ahead.

1 Combine the flour and granulated sugar in a bowl. Rub in the butter, add the egg yolk, and make the dough (see Lime and coconut tart, step 1). Knead it briefly on a floured surface until smooth and even. Wrap it in plastic wrap and chill for 1 hour.

2 Preheat the oven to 350°F (180°C). On a floured surface, roll out the dough to a large circle, ⅛in (2mm) thick. Use it to line the pan, leaving a ½in (1cm) overhang. Make sure the dough has no cracks, pinching out any that appear. Prick the dough, line with parchment paper, and fill with baking beans.

3 Blind bake the tart crust for 20–25 minutes (see Lime and coconut tart, step 3). Trim the overhang and place on a baking sheet. For the filling, whisk the brown sugar and flour in a bowl. Then whisk in the cream, vanilla extract, and salt until combined, and pour into a large pitcher.

4 Place the baking sheet on an oven rack. Pour the filling into the tart crust and slide the rack into the oven. Bake for 40 minutes, until just set. Remove and cool to room temperature, then remove the tart from the pan. Sprinkle with brown sugar and serve with whipped cream. You can store the tart, covered in the fridge, for up to 2 days.

1 hr
plus chilling

MAKES 4

TARTLETS raspberry and pastry cream

These tartlets look stunning enough to have come from a bakery, but are incredibly simple to make at home. The pie crusts and pastry cream are easy to make ahead, so you can assemble the tarts at the last minute.

INGREDIENTS
1¼ cups all-purpose flour, plus extra for dusting
2 tbsp granulated sugar
7 tbsp unsalted butter, chilled and diced
1 egg, beaten with 1 tbsp ice water
half-and-half, to serve, (optional)

For the pastry cream
1 cup whole milk
2 egg yolks
¼ cup granulated sugar
1 tbsp cornstarch
1 tsp vanilla extract

For the topping
3 tbsp apricot jam, strained
9oz (250g) raspberries

SPECIAL EQUIPMENT
4 x 4in (10cm) loose-bottomed tart pans
baking beans

PLAN AHEAD
You can prepare and store the pastry cream in an airtight container in the fridge up to 2 days ahead. You can wrap and store the blind-baked pie crusts in the fridge up to 3 days ahead.

Preheat the oven to 350°F (180°C). Combine the flour and sugar in a bowl. Stir in the butter until the mixture resembles fine bread crumbs. Add the beaten egg and bring together to form a dough, adding a little extra ice water if it seems too dry. Knead it briefly, wrap in plastic wrap, and chill for 30 minutes.

1

Divide the dough into four equal portions. On a lightly floured surface, roll out each portion to an ⅛in (3mm) circle and use to line the tartlet cases, leaving an overhang of at least ½in (1cm).

Trim any excess dough once it is in the tartlet cases.

2

Prick the dough, line with parchment paper, and fill with baking beans. Bake for 15 minutes, then remove the beans and paper and bake for 5–10 minutes, until crisp. Remove from the heat and trim the overhang. Cool them completely in the pans before transferring to a wire rack.

3

For the pastry cream, heat the milk in a small, heavy-bottomed saucepan until hot, but not boiling. In a heatproof bowl, whisk the egg yolks, sugar, cornstarch, and vanilla extract, and little by little, pour in the hot milk.

Whisk the mixture constantly until the sugar dissolves.

4

5

Pour the custard into a clean saucepan. Cook over medium heat for 2–3 minutes, stirring until just thickened. Reduce the heat to low and cook for another 2–3 minutes, whisking constantly. Transfer to a bowl, cover with plastic wrap, and chill until cold.

Heat the jam and 1 tablespoon water in a saucepan over low heat, stirring until smooth. Remove and let cool. Divide the pastry cream between the crusts, beating it gently if it is thick. Top each with the raspberries, then add a little of the apricot glaze. Chill for 1 hour. Serve with cream, if desired. Best served on the same day.

6

🕐 **1 hr 20 mins**
plus chilling and cooling   🍴 **MAKES 6**

TARTLETS mocha

The filling in these little tarts is intense and chocolaty—perfect in small doses.

1 Combine **1 cup all-purpose flour**, **2 tbsp granulated sugar**, and **¼ cup good-quality cocoa powder** in a bowl. Rub in **7 tbsp chilled and diced unsalted butter**, until the mixture resembles bread crumbs.

2 Add **3 tbsp cooled strong black coffee** to the bowl. Bring together to form a dough, adding a little chilled water if it seems dry. Knead it briefly until smooth, wrap in plastic wrap, and chill for 30 minutes. Preheat the oven to 350°F (180°C).

3 On a lightly floured surface, divide and roll out the dough to four rounds, each ⅛in (3mm) thick. Use them to line **6 x 4in (10cm) loose-bottomed tart pans**, leaving a ½in (1cm) overhang. Prick the bottom of the dough.

4 Line the tart pans with parchment paper and fill with **baking beans**. Place them on a baking sheet and bake for 15 minutes. If they look uncooked, remove the beans and paper and bake for another 5 minutes. Remove, trim, and let cool. Reduce the temperature to 325°F (160°C).

5 Heat **1¼ cups heavy cream** in a heavy-bottomed saucepan until steaming. Remove and stir in **9oz (250g) chopped good-quality dark chocolate**, until melted. Beat until smooth, transfer to a bowl, and let cool. Gradually whisk in **2 eggs** and stir in **1 tsp vanilla extract**.

6 Pour the filling into the tartlet crusts. Bake in the oven for 20 minutes, until just set. Let cool in the pans, then remove and serve immediately.

PLAN AHEAD
You can store the blind-baked tart crusts in an airtight container in the freezer up to 3 months ahead.

🕐 **35–45 mins**
plus infusing and cooling   🍴 **MAKES 6**

TARTLETS custard

You can freeze store-bought phyllo dough, making it a great standby for tartlet crusts.

1 Preheat the oven to 375° (190ºC). Heat **1 cup whole milk**, **⅔ cup heavy cream**, and **6 crushed cardamom pods** in a heavy-bottomed saucepan until steaming. Remove from the heat and let infuse. Melt **2 tbsp unsalted butter** in a saucepan over medium heat.

2 Roll out **3 sheets of phyllo dough** and cover with a paper towel. On a floured surface, spread out one sheet and brush it with a little of the melted butter. Cover with another sheet, brush with butter, and top with the final sheet. Cut the dough into six equal-sized pieces.

3 Grease a **deep six-hole, 2½in (6cm) wide muffin pan**. Use the dough pieces to line the molds, pushing them into the sides until they stick up in places. Brush the edges with any remaining butter and cover the pan with a damp paper towel.

4 Reheat the milk mixture over gentle heat, but do not boil. Whisk **2 eggs** and **2 tbsp granulated sugar** in a large bowl. Strain the milk mixture into the egg mixture, discarding the cardamom. Whisk the custard until smooth, transfer to a pitcher, and pour evenly into the tart crusts.

5 Bake the tartlets for 15–20 minutes, until they are crisp and just set in the center. Cool in the pan for 10 minutes, then remove and let cool completely. Serve immediately.

Custard

Mocha

🕐 **55 mins**
plus chilling and cooling   🍴 **MAKES 6**

TARTLETS banana and Nutella

These tartlets are a sure-fire hit with children and adults alike. Serve them with cream or vanilla ice cream.

1 Combine **1¼ cups all-purpose flour** and **2 tbsp granulated sugar** in a bowl. Rub in **7 tbsp softened, unsalted butter** until the mixture resembles bread crumbs. Beat **1 egg yolk** with **2 tbsp water** in a bowl. Add to the flour mixture, bring together to form a dough, then wrap and chill the dough (see Mocha tartlets, step 2).

2 Preheat the oven to 350°F (180°C). On a lightly floured surface, roll out the dough into six rounds, each ⅛in (3mm) thick. Use them to line **6 x 4in (10cm) loose-bottomed tart pans**, leaving a ½in (1cm) overhang. Prick the bottom of the dough.

3 Line with parchment paper and fill with **baking beans**. Blind-bake the tartlet crusts (see Mocha tartlets, step 3–4). Remove, trim, and let cool. Increase the temperature to 400°F (200°C).

4 Combine ⅓ **cup unsweetened, dried coconut flakes**, **¼ cup all-purpose flour**, and **2 tbsp light brown sugar** in a bowl. Rub in **2 tbsp softened, unsalted butter**, until the mixture resembles coarse bread crumbs.

5 Line the tartlet crusts with **2–3 bananas, cut into ½in (1cm) rounds**. Spread **1 tbsp Nutella** over the bananas in each tartlet and sprinkle loosely with the coconut topping. Bake for 15 minutes, until lightly brown on top. Let cool in the pans, then remove and serve.

PLAN AHEAD
You can store the blind-baked tartlet crusts in an airtight container in the freezer up to 3 months ahead.

Simple alternatives

Raspberries and pastry cream make the ultimate summer filling for a tartlet (see pp126–27), but there are many fabulous ingredient substitutions you can try.

Summer berry Follow the method for the classic tartlets and top them with a mixture of raspberries, blueberries, and hulled and diced strawberries.

Strawberry Replace the raspberries with 9oz (250g) strawberries, chopped into thick slices or halved if small.

Chocolate and kiwi Add 2 tbsp cocoa powder to the pastry cream mixture (p127, step 4). Replace the raspberries with 4 thinly sliced kiwis.

Peach In place of the raspberries, use 3 thinly sliced peaches and arrange them over the pastry cream in a circular pattern.

Caramelized apricot Use 4 ripe halved, pitted, and thinly sliced apricots in place of the raspberries. Use a small kitchen blowtorch to caramelize the glaze for a few seconds just before serving.

Blueberry A layer of ripe blueberries is an easy substitute for the raspberries. Use 9oz (250g) blueberries and a raspberry or blueberry jam to glaze the topping.

Coconut and mango Follow the classic recipe, but add 2 tsp unsweetened, dried coconut flakes to the cold milk in step 4. Top the tartlets with 2 thinly sliced mangoes instead of the raspberries.

Banana and Nutella

 **1 hr 25 mins**
plus chilling and cooling

 SERVES 8

Also great
HOT

LINZERTORTE almond and raspberry

A speciality of Vienna in Austria, linzertorte is sure to delight. It consists of a flaky almond pie crust that is filled with a tart-yet-sweet raspberry reduction and topped with a decorative lattice topping.

INGREDIENTS

¾ cup all-purpose flour, plus extra for dusting
pinch of ground cloves
½ tsp ground cinnamon
1¾ cups ground almonds
9 tbsp unsalted butter, softened and diced, plus extra for greasing
1 egg yolk
½ cup granulated sugar
¼ tsp salt
finely grated zest of 1 lemon
juice of ½ lemon
1–2 tbsp confectioners' sugar, to dust

For the filling

½ cup granulated sugar
13oz (375g) raspberries

SPECIAL EQUIPMENT

9in (23cm) loose-bottomed tart pan
fluted pastry wheel

PLAN AHEAD

You can prepare and store the dough covered in plastic wrap in the fridge up to 2 days ahead. Bring the dough to room temperature before rolling out.

1 Sift the flour into a large bowl. Add the cloves, cinnamon, and almonds. Mix well to combine, then make a well in the center. Combine the butter, egg yolk, granulated sugar, salt, and lemon zest and juice in a separate bowl.

2 Pour the wet mixture into the well in the center of the dry ingredients. Use a wooden spoon to mix well, then bring the mixture together to form a dough.

Be careful not to overwork the dough, kneading it until just smooth.

Cook the filling until the sugar dissolves and the raspberries burst.

3 On a lightly floured surface, shape the dough into a ball and knead for 1–2 minutes, until well combined and smooth. Wrap it in plastic wrap and chill for 1–2 hours.

4 Preheat the oven to 375°F (190°C). Grease the pan and set aside. For the filling, cook the ingredients in a large saucepan over medium heat for 10–12 minutes, until thickened. Remove and let cool.

 Strain half of the raspberry mixture into a bowl, using the back of a wooden spoon to press the fruit pulp through. Then pour the remaining raspberry mixture into the bowl and mix well.

On a lightly floured surface, roll out two-thirds of the dough to an 11in (28cm) round and use to line the pan. Trim and reserve any overhanging dough. Spread the filling in the pie crust evenly.

Use the overhang to line the edge of the pie crust.

 Roll out the remaining dough to a 6 x 12in (15 x 30cm) rectangle. Use a fluted wheel to cut 5 x ½in (12 x 1cm) strips and create a lattice top over the filling, trimming the strips to the correct length as you go. Chill for 15 minutes.

Bake for 15 minutes, then reduce the temperature to 350°F (180°C) and bake for another 25–30 minutes. Cool the tart in the pan for 5–10 minutes, then remove and cool for 30 minutes. Dust with confectioners' sugar and serve. You can store the tart in an airtight container for up to 2 days.

🕐 **1 hr 20 mins**
plus chilling and cooling 🍴 **SERVES 8** 🌡 Also great **HOT**

CROSTATA di marmellata

This classic Italian recipe is a large jam tart with a beautifully latticed top. Replace the apricot jam with any variety you wish.

INGREDIENTS

1¼ cups all-purpose flour, plus extra for dusting

7 tbsp unsalted butter, chilled and diced

¼ cup granulated sugar

1 egg yolk

2 tbsp whole milk, plus extra if needed

½ tsp vanilla extract

1½ cups good-quality apricot or cherry jam

1 egg, beaten to glaze

SPECIAL EQUIPMENT

9in (23cm) loose-bottomed tart pan

baking beans

PLAN AHEAD

You can store the blind-baked pie crust in an airtight container in the freezer up to 1 month ahead.

1 Place the flour in a bowl and rub in the butter until the mixture resembles fine bread crumbs. Stir in the sugar. Beat the egg yolk, milk, and vanilla extract in a separate bowl and add to the dry ingredients. Bring the mixture together to form a dough, adding more milk if it seems dry. Wrap in plastic wrap and chill for 1 hour.

2 Preheat the oven to 350°F (180°C). On a floured surface, roll out the dough to a ⅛in (3mm) thick circle. If it crumbles, knead it gently and roll out again. Line the pan with the dough, leaving an overhang of ¾in (2cm). Roll the trimmings, rewrap, and chill for later.

3 Prick the pie crust, line with parchment paper, and fill with the baking beans. Place it on a baking sheet and bake for 20 minutes. If the center looks uncooked, remove the beans and paper and bake for another 5 minutes. Remove from the heat and trim the overhang. Increase the oven temperature to 400°F (200°C).

4 Spread the jam in the pie crust in a ½–¾in (1–2cm) thick layer. Roll out the reserved dough to a ⅛in (3mm) thick square just larger than the tart. Cut out 12 x ½in (1cm) wide strips and create a lattice top over the filling.

5 Brush the top and edges of the tart with the beaten egg and bake for 20–25 minutes until golden brown. Remove and cool for 10 minutes in the pan, then remove the tart from the pan and cool completely before serving. You can store it in an airtight container in the fridge for up to 2 days.

🕐 **2 hrs 10 mins**
plus chilling 🍴 **SERVES 8** 🌡 Also great **HOT**

JALOUSIE apple

The French word *jalousie* translates as a slatted shutter, and refers to the beautiful decorative slashes in the pastry.

INGREDIENTS

1¾ cups all-purpose flour, plus extra for dusting

1 tsp salt

18 tbsp unsalted butter, chilled and coarsely grated

1 tsp lemon juice

1in (2.5cm) piece of fresh ginger, finely chopped

½ cup granulated sugar

1 egg white, beaten, to glaze

For the filling

1 tbsp unsalted butter

2¼lb (1kg) tart apples, peeled, cored, and diced

1 Sift the flour and salt into a bowl. Rub in the butter until it resembles bread crumbs. Add the lemon juice and ½ cup water and bring together to form a dough. Knead it on a floured surface, flatten slightly, and place in a plastic bag. Chill for 20 minutes.

2 On a floured surface, roll out the dough to a long rectangle, short sides 10in (25cm). Fold over one-third of the dough, then fold the other third over the top. Flip it over and roll out to a similar size as the original rectangle, making sure the seams are sealed. Repeat the folding, turning, and rolling. Chill for 20 minutes.

3 Roll, fold, and turn the dough twice more, then chill for 20 minutes. Melt the butter in a saucepan over low heat. Add the apples, ginger, and the sugar, reserving 2 tablespoons. Sauté for 15–20 minutes, until the apples are tender and caramelized. Let cool.

4 Roll out the dough on a floured surface to 11 x 13in (28 x 33cm). Halve lengthwise. Fold one of the halves in half again, and slash the fold at ¼in (5mm) gaps, leaving the edge intact. Place the other half on a nonstick baking sheet and spread over the filling. Open up the cut dough and place over the filling.

5 Chill for 15 minutes and preheat the oven to 425°F (220°C). Bake for 20–25 minutes. Brush with the egg white and sprinkle with the remaining sugar. Return to the oven and continue baking for 10–15 minutes. Remove and cool completely before serving. Best served on the same day.

⏱ **50 mins**
plus chilling and cooling

🍴 **MAKES 12**

🌡 Also great
HOT

LATTICE-TOPPED TARTS mincemeat

The perfect sweet treat around Christmastime, mincemeat tarts benefit from a lattice top—it looks very attractive and keeps them light. Serve with custard, if desired.

INGREDIENTS

1½ cups all-purpose flour, plus extra for dusting

2 tbsp granulated sugar

7 tbsp unsalted butter, chilled and diced

grated zest of 1 orange

1 egg, beaten, plus 1 egg extra, for glazing

For the filling

10oz (300g) good-quality mincemeat

1 tbsp brandy

zest of 1 orange

1 small apple, peeled and coarsely grated

¼ cup almonds, coarsely chopped

SPECIAL EQUIPMENT

12-hole shallow bun pan

2¾in (7cm) fluted pastry cutter

PLAN AHEAD

You can prepare and chill the unbaked pies in the pan 1–2 days ahead. Add 5–10 minutes to the baking time.

1 For the filling, combine all the ingredients in a large airtight container. Cover and chill for at least 12 hours, or preferably overnight.

2 Place the flour and sugar in a bowl. Rub in the butter until the mixture resembles bread crumbs. Add the orange zest and egg and bring together to form a smooth dough. Wrap in plastic wrap and chill for 30 minutes.

3 Preheat the oven to 350°F (180°C). On a floured surface, roll out the dough to a large circle, ⅛in (3mm) thick. Cut out 12 rounds with the pastry cutter and use to line the pan. Divide the filling between them, patting it down slightly.

4 Roll out the dough off-cuts and cut out 36 strips, each at least 5in (12cm) long and ½in (1cm) wide. Cut the strips in half to get a total of 72 strips. Brush the edges of the tarts with the beaten egg and use the strips to create a lattice top over each tart.

5 Brush the tarts with a little egg glaze and bake for 20 minutes until golden brown. Cool in the pan for 5 minutes before removing to a wire rack to cool completely before serving. You can store the tarts in an airtight container up to 3 days ahead.

🕐 **1 hr 20 mins**
plus chilling and cooling

🍴 **SERVES 8**

MERINGUE PIE lemon

The meringue topping on a classic meringue pie is softer and more delicate than a traditional meringue, to contrast with the flaky crust. If you like a crispier texture, leave the pie in the oven for an additional 15 minutes, watching the color carefully.

INGREDIENTS
8 tbsp unsalted butter, chilled and grated, plus extra for greasing
1¼ cups all-purpose flour, plus extra for dusting
1 tbsp granulated sugar
½ tsp salt
1 tsp apple cider vinegar, whisked with ¼ cup cold water

For the filling
¼ tsp salt
¼ cup cornstarch
3 tbsp all-purpose flour
1 cup granulated sugar
5 large egg yolks, beaten
1 tbsp unsalted butter
grated zest of 2 lemons
½ cup lemon juice

For the meringue
4 egg whites
⅛ tsp salt
¼ tsp cream of tartar
½ cup granulated sugar
1 tbsp cornstarch

SPECIAL EQUIPMENT
9in (23cm) fluted tart dish or pan, about 2in (5cm) deep
baking beans

PLAN AHEAD
You can store the blind-baked pie crust in an airtight container in the fridge 2–3 days ahead.

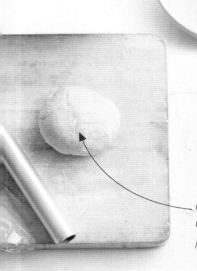

Grease the dish. Combine the flour, sugar, salt, and butter in a large bowl. Sprinkle the vinegar mixture over the top and use two forks to fluff the mixture until it forms clumps. Add a little cold water if it seems dry. Knead the dough, wrap it in plastic wrap, and chill for 30 minutes.

Knead the dough very gently until it just comes together.

1

Preheat the oven to 375°F (190°C). On a floured surface, roll out the dough to a 12in (30cm) circle, ⅛in (3mm) thick. Use to line the dish, leaving an overhang of ½in (1cm). Prick the dough and chill for 30 minutes. Then line it with parchment paper, fill with baking beans, and bake for 25 minutes. Remove the beans and paper and return to the oven, until golden. Let cool.

2

Remove the beans and paper and bake the pie crust for 6–10 minutes, until golden.

3

Reduce the temperature to 350°F (180°C). For the filling, mix the dry ingredients in a saucepan. Whisk in 1¼ cups water gradually, until smooth. Cook for 5–6 minutes over medium heat, stirring, until thick. Bring to a boil, then reduce the heat. Cook for another minute, then whisk a small amount of the mixture into the yolks.

The mixture may clump at first, but will come together toward the end.

4

Stir a little more hot mixture into the yolk mixture and pour the yolk mixture into the pan. Bring to a boil over medium-low heat, stirring frequently. Reduce the heat and cook for 1 minute. Remove from the heat and whisk in the remaining filling ingredients, until combined. Cover and keep warm.

5

For the meringue, whisk the egg whites and salt in a bowl until foamy, then whisk in the cream of tartar to form soft peaks. Combine the sugar and cornstarch in a small bowl and gradually whisk into the egg white mixture to form stiff, glossy peaks.

Pour the filling into the pie crust. Spoon the meringue in a circle around the inside edge of the pie, then top the whole pie. Bake for 15 minutes, until lightly browned. Cool completely on a wire rack before serving. Best served on the same day.

6

MERINGUE PIE
chocolate

Using both milk chocolate and dark chocolate in the filling for this pie gives an added complexity to its rich flavor.

INGREDIENTS

3 large egg yolks
⅓ cup condensed milk
2 cups whole milk
¼ cup cornstarch
¼ tsp salt
¾ tsp vanilla extract
1 tbsp unsalted butter, diced
4½oz (125g) good-quality very dark chocolate, finely chopped
3oz (85g) good-quality milk chocolate, finely chopped

1 sweet shortcrust pie crust (see p137, steps 1-2)

For the meringue
½ cup granulated sugar
1 tbsp cornstarch
4 egg whites
⅛ tsp salt
¼ tsp cream of tartar

SPECIAL EQUIPMENT

9in (23cm) fluted tart pan, about 2in (5cm) deep

1 Preheat the oven to 350°F (180°C). Whisk the egg yolks, condensed milk, and 1 cup whole milk in a bowl. Whisk the cornstarch, salt, and remaining milk in a saucepan with a lid until smooth. Cook over medium heat for 4–5 minutes, until steaming. Remove and whisk a small amount into the yolk mixture to combine.

2 Stir a little more of the hot mixture into the yolk mixture. Pour the yolk mixture into the pan. Cook over medium–low heat, stirring constantly, until thick. Bring to a boil, then reduce the heat and cook for 30 seconds. Remove from the heat and whisk in the vanilla extract, butter, and both types of chocolate, until fully incorporated. Cover to keep warm.

3 For the meringue, combine the sugar and cornstarch in a bowl. In a separate bowl, whisk the eggs whites and salt until foamy. Whisk in the cream of tartar to form soft peaks. Add the sugar mixture to the egg white mixture, a tablespoon at a time, whisking well after each addition. Whisk the mixture until it is glossy and forms stiff peaks.

4 Pour the chocolate filling into the pie crust. Spoon the meringue in a circle around the inside edge of the pie, then top the whole pie. Bake for 15 minutes, until the meringue is lightly browned. Place on a wire rack to cool completely, then chill for at least 5 hours, until the filling has set, before serving. Best served on the same day.

🕐 **1 hr 40 mins** plus cooling   🍴 **SERVES 8**

MERINGUE PIE grapefruit

Grapefruit can offset the sweetness of meringue with a welcome tartness—however, if you find normal grapefruit a little too tart, try a sweeter pink variety instead.

INGREDIENTS

5 large egg yolks

¼ tsp salt

¼ cup cornstarch

3 tbsp all-purpose flour

¾ cup granulated sugar

1 tbsp unsalted butter

½ tsp lemon zest

1 tbsp grated grapefruit zest

1 tbsp lemon juice

½ cup grapefruit juice

1 sweet shortcrust pie crust (see p137, steps 1–2)

For the meringue

4 egg whites

⅛ tsp salt

¼ tsp cream of tartar

1 tbsp cornstarch

½ cup granulated sugar

SPECIAL EQUIPMENT

9in (23cm) fluted tart pan, about 2in (5cm) deep

1 Preheat the oven to 350°F (180°C). Whisk the egg yolks in a heatproof bowl. Combine the salt, cornstarch, flour, and sugar in a saucepan with a lid.

2 Pour in 50ml 3 tablespoons water and whisk until smooth. Stir 1 cup water into the cornstarch mixture. Bring to a boil over medium heat, stirring, until thick.

3 Reduce the heat to medium–low and cook for 1 minute. Remove from the heat and pour a small amount into the yolk mixture. Whisk well to combine, then stir a little more of the hot mixture into the yolk mixture. Pour the yolk mixture into the pan.

4 Bring to a boil over medium–low heat, stirring frequently. Reduce the heat to low and cook for 1 minute. Remove and whisk in the butter and both types of zest.

5 Whisk in the lemon juice and grapefruit juice until fully incorporated. Cover the yolk mixture and keep warm. Prepare the meringue (see Chocolate meringue pie, step 3).

6 Pour the grapefruit filling into the pie crust. Top with the meringue (see Chocolate meringue pie, step 4). Bake for 10 minutes, until lightly browned. Cool the pie completely on a wire rack before serving. Best served on the same day.

 **1 hr 30 mins**
plus chilling and cooling

SERVES 8

PIE banana cream

Banana and custard are old-fashioned favorites that work fabulously when combined in a crisp and buttery pie crust. Smother the pie with billowy whipped cream for a truly decadent dessert.

INGREDIENTS

1¼ cups all-purpose flour, plus extra for dusting

1 tbsp granulated sugar

½ tsp salt

8 tbsp unsalted butter, chilled and diced

1 tsp apple cider vinegar

2–4 bananas, sliced, plus extra for topping

For the filling

½ cup granulated sugar

½ tsp salt

3 tbsp cornstarch

2 cups whole milk

3 large egg yolks

1 tbsp unsalted butter

1 tsp vanilla extract

For the topping

¾ cup heavy cream

2 tsp confectioners' sugar

SPECIAL EQUIPMENT

9in (23cm) pie dish, about 2in (5cm) deep

baking beans

PLAN AHEAD

You can prepare and store the dough, covered in the fridge, up to 2 days ahead. You can store the blind-baked pie crust in an airtight container up to 2 days ahead.

Rub in the butter with the flour mixture until it resembles bread crumbs.

1   Place the flour, granulated sugar, and salt in a large bowl and mix well to combine Rub in the butter with your fingertips until the mixture resembles bread crumbs. Place the vinegar in a separate bowl. Pour in ½ cup cold water and mix well to combine.

2   Gradually add ¼ cup of the liquid mixture to the flour mixture, using two forks to fluff and stir them together until clumps form. Add a little more of the liquid mixture if it seems too dry, making sure you do not add too much, as it can toughen the pastry.

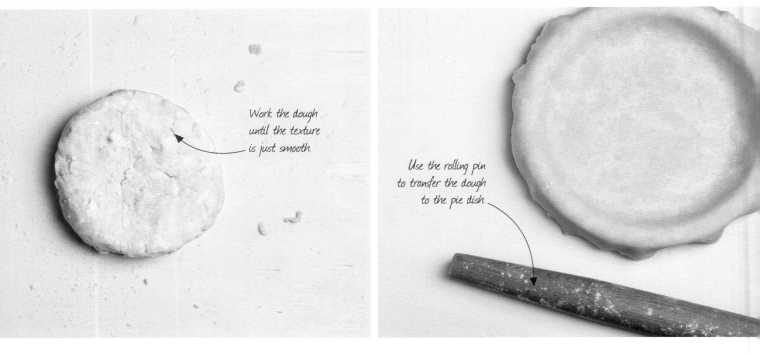

Work the dough until the texture is just smooth.

Use the rolling pin to transfer the dough to the pie dish.

3   On a lightly floured work surface, turn out the mixture and knead it gently for 3–6 minutes to form a dough. Cover the dough with plastic wrap and chill in the fridge for about 30 minutes, or preferably overnight.

4   On a floured surface, roll out the dough to a 12–13in (30–33cm) circle, about ⅛in (3mm) thick. Use the circle to line the pie dish, leaving a ½in (1cm) overhang. Crimp the edges of the dough and chill the for 30 minutes. Preheat the oven to 375°F (190°C).

5 Prick the pie crust. Line with a sheet of parchment paper and fill with baking beans. Bake for 25 minutes, until the edges are slightly brown, then remove the parchment and beans and bake for another 6–10 minutes, until the pie crust is golden brown. Remove and let cool.

6 For the filling, combine the granulated sugar, salt, and cornstarch in a saucepan. Add the milk, gradually, whisking until smooth. Heat the mixture over medium-high heat until steaming. Remove and whisk 2 tablespoons of the mixture with the egg yolks in a small bowl.

7 Pour the egg and milk mixture back into the pan and bring to a boil over medium heat. Stir well and remove from the heat. Beat in the butter and vanilla extract until well combined. Transfer to a large bowl, cover with plastic wrap, and chill for 30 minutes.

8 Layer half the banana slices in the pie crust. Top with the filling, cover with plastic wrap, and chill for 2 hours. Beat the heavy cream and confectioners' sugar to form stiff peaks. Top the pie with the remaining bananas and the cream, and serve. You can store the pie, covered, for up to 3 days in the fridge.

Pro piping

For patisserie-style decorative results, give your pie a piped cream topping. All you need is a large piping bag and a variety of tips.

Circular rosettes To decorate a Banana cream pie (see pp140–43), pipe medium-sized rosettes around the edge of the pie, and follow with a central circle of smaller rosettes. Insert upright slices of banana between each rosette. Serve immediately.

Stars Use a medium open-star tip to pipe stars tightly over your cream pie. For an even finish, start at the outside edge of the pie, and pipe concentric circles of stars, working toward the center of the pie. Serve immediately.

Shells Top the Mascarpone and berry cream pie (see opposite), with cream and berries. Beat ¾ cup heavy cream with 1 tsp confectioners' sugar, and pipe large shells of the mixture over the pie using an open-star tip. Allow the cream to fan as you drag and drop each shell. Decorate with berries.

Roses Use a large drop flower tip to pipe large roses. Start with the center of each rose and pipe in a counterclockwise direction, applying an even pressure. Pipe a ring of roses around the edge of the pie, finishing with one in the center. For the Coconut cream pie (see right), sprinkle with coconut.

🕐 **1 hr 30 mins**
plus chilling and setting

🍴 **SERVES 8**

CREAM PIE coconut cream

Three types of coconut are used to maximize the flavor of this pie. Using coconut milk as the custard base is an easy way to impart extra flavor to the filling.

INGREDIENTS

8 tbsp unsalted butter, chilled and diced, plus extra for greasing
1¼ cups all-purpose flour, plus extra for dusting
1 tbsp granulated sugar
½ tsp salt
1 tsp apple cider vinegar

For the filling

3 large egg yolks
¾ cup granulated sugar
½ tsp salt
¼ cup cornstarch
2 cups coconut milk
½ cup whole milk
1 tbsp unsalted butter
¼ tsp vanilla extract
1 cup unsweetened, dried coconut flakes

For the topping

¼ cup unsweetened, dried coconut flakes
¾ cup heavy cream
1 tsp sugar

SPECIAL EQUIPMENT

9in (23cm) round pie dish, about 2in (5cm) deep
baking beans

PLAN AHEAD

You can store the blind-baked crust in an airtight container up to 3 days ahead.

1 Grease the pie dish and set aside. Combine the flour, sugar, and salt in a bowl. Rub in the butter and mix until the mixture resembles bread crumbs. Combine the vinegar with ½ cup cold water in a separate bowl and gradually add ¼ cup of it to the flour mixture.

2 Use two forks to fluff the flour mixture to form loose crumbs, adding more water if it is dry. On a floured surface, knead the dough until just smooth. Wrap it in plastic wrap and chill for 30 minutes.

3 Roll out the dough on a floured surface to an 11in (28cm) circle, at least ⅛in (3mm) thick. Use to line the pie dish, leaving a ¾in (2cm) overhang. Crimp the edges and chill the dough for 30 minutes. Preheat the oven to 375°F (190°C).

4 Prick the dough, line with parchment paper, and fill with baking beans. Bake for 25 minutes, until the edges are slightly brown. Remove the beans and paper, and bake for another 6–10 minutes, until golden brown. Remove and let cool.

5 For the filling, place the egg yolks in a heatproof bowl. Combine the sugar, salt, and cornstarch in a large saucepan. Slowly whisk in both types of milk until smooth and well combined. Cook the mixture over medium heat until steaming. Remove from the heat.

6 Pour a little of the milk mixture into the egg yolks, whisking constantly until combined. Add the egg mixture to the pan, whisking continuously to combine. Cook over medium heat until thick, then bring to a boil, stir well, and remove from the heat.

7 Add the butter, vanilla extract, and unsweetened, dried coconut flakes to the cream filling. Mix well and pour the filling into the crust. Cover in plastic wrap and chill for 2–3 hours, until set.

8 For the topping, toast the coconut in a frying pan over medium heat until lightly brown. Beat the cream and sugar in a bowl to form stiff peaks. Top the pie with the cream, sprinkle with the toasted coconut, and serve. You can store the pie, covered in the fridge, for 1–2 days.

🕐 **30 mins** plus chilling   🍴 **SERVES 8**

CREAM PIE
chocolate and cinnamon

Adding a little cinnamon to the chocolate gives a warm and spicy flavor to this pie, and contrasts well with the cream topping.

INGREDIENTS

1 tbsp unsalted butter, plus extra for greasing

1 recipe pie dough (see Coconut cream pie, steps 1–2)

3 large egg yolks

½ cup light brown sugar

½ tsp salt

¼ cup cornstarch

2½ cups whole milk

1 tsp ground cinnamon, plus extra for dusting

½ tsp vanilla extract

¼ tsp almond extract

5oz (140g) good-quality dark chocolate, finely chopped

3oz (85g) good-quality milk chocolate, finely chopped

For the topping

¾ cup heavy cream

2 tsp confectioners' sugar

SPECIAL EQUIPMENT

9in (23cm) round pie dish

baking beans

1 Preheat the oven to 375°F (190°C) and grease the pie dish. Roll out the dough, use to line the pie dish, and blind bake it (see Coconut cream pie, steps 3–4). Beat the egg yolks in a heatproof bowl and set aside.

2 Combine the brown sugar, salt, and cornstarch in a saucepan. Slowly whisk in the milk until smooth and cook over medium heat until steaming. Remove from the heat and pour a little of the milk mixture into the egg yolks, whisking constantly until combined.

3 Pour the egg mixture into the pan. Cook over medium heat, whisking constantly, until thick. Then bring to a boil, stir well, and remove from the heat.

4 Add the butter, cinnamon, vanilla extract, almond extract, and both types of chocolate to the cream filling. Mix well and pour into the crust. Wrap the pie in plastic wrap and chill for 5–6 hours, until set.

5 For the topping, beat the ingredients in a bowl to form stiff peaks and spoon over the filling. Dust lightly with cinnamon and serve. You can store the pie, covered in the fridge, for 2–3 days.

🕐 **30 mins** plus chilling and setting   🍴 **SERVES 8**

CREAM PIE
mascarpone and berry

Mix mascarpone with citrus-infused whipped cream to make a quick and easy filling for a pie. If you use a store-bought pie crust, it can be rustled up in minutes.

INGREDIENTS

1 recipe pie dough (see Coconut cream pie, steps 1–2)

12oz (350g) mascarpone cheese

¾ cup whipping cream

⅓ cup granulated sugar, plus 2 tbsp extra

¼ tsp salt

¾ tsp vanilla extract

grated zest of 2 lemons

4½oz (125g) blueberries

4½oz (125g) blackberries

SPECIAL EQUIPMENT

9in (23cm) round pie dish

baking beans

1 Preheat the oven to 375°F (190°C). Roll out the dough, use to line the pie dish, and blind bake it (see Coconut cream pie, steps 3–4). Place the mascarpone in a bowl and fold gently to soften. In a separate bowl, beat the cream, sugar, salt, and vanilla extract to form stiff peaks.

2 Add in a small amount of the cream mixture to the mascarpone and mix well. Fold in the remaining cream mixture until well combined. Fold in the lemon zest until evenly incorporated.

3 Pour the filling into the crust. Top with the blueberries and blackberries. Wrap the pie with plastic wrap and chill for at least 1 hour, until set. Serve chilled. You can store the pie, covered in the fridge, for up to 2 days.

45–50 mins
plus chilling and cooling

SERVES 10

MUD PIE Mississippi

A chocolate lover's delight, this all-American dessert is a crowd-pleaser no matter the occasion—especially if children are involved. Serve the pie in small slices; it is rich and a little goes a long way.

INGREDIENTS

6 tbsp unsalted butter, melted, plus extra for greasing

10oz (300g) Oreos, finely crushed

For the filling

8 tbsp unsalted butter

1oz (30g) unsweetened chocolate

3oz (85g) good-quality dark chocolate

3 tbsp all-purpose flour

1 tsp instant espresso powder

pinch of salt

¾ cup dark brown sugar

¼ cup granulated sugar

½ tsp vanilla extract

3 large eggs

For the topping

¾ cup heavy cream

1½ tsp confectioners' sugar

¼ cup chopped pecans

SPECIAL EQUIPMENT

9in (23cm) pie dish, about 2in (5cm) deep

PLAN AHEAD

You can prepare and store the unfilled cookie crust in an airtight container in the fridge up to 1 week ahead.

1 Grease the pie dish. Place the butter and cookie crumbs in a large bowl. Mix well to combine.

2 Spread the mixture evenly in the pie dish, pressing it firmly into the bottom and sides to form a smooth base. Chill for 45 minutes, until firm.

3 Preheat the oven to 375°F (190°C). For the filling, melt the butter and both types of chocolate in a saucepan over medium–low heat. Remove from the heat. Add the flour, espresso powder, salt, and both types of sugar. Whisk until well combined.

4 Gradually whisk the vanilla extract and the eggs into the chocolate mixture until combined and smooth. Pour the filling into the cookie crust.

5 Bake the pie for 30–35 minutes, until the filling is just set. Remove from the heat. Let cool for 1–2 hours, until the filling sinks a little.

6 For the topping, beat the cream and confectioners' sugar in a bowl to form soft peaks and spread over the pie. Sprinkle with the pecans and serve. You can store the pie covered in the fridge for up to 2 days.

🕐 **15–20 mins**
plus chilling

🍴 **SERVES 10**

MUD PIE peanut butter

Dark chocolate, peanut butter, and whipped cream combine together to make an intense filling for this rich, sweet dessert. If peanut butter cups are not available, try a handful of chopped salted peanuts.

1 Grease a **9in (23cm) pie dish**. Combine **10oz (300g) finely crushed Oreos** and **6 tbsp melted, unsalted butter** in a bowl and spread the mixture evenly in the dish. Press it into the bottom and sides to form a smooth crust and chill for 45 minutes until firm.

2 For the filling, beat **8oz (225g) cream cheese**, **1¼ cups creamy peanut butter**, and **¾ cup confectioners' sugar** in a bowl until combined. Stir in **¼ cup heavy cream** and mix until smooth. In a separate bowl, whisk **½ cup heavy cream** to form stiff peaks.

3 Gradually fold the cream into the peanut butter mixture until well combined. Pour the filling over the cookie crust evenly. For the topping, beat **¾ cup heavy cream**, **½ tsp vanilla extract**, **2 tsp granulated sugar**, and a **pinch of salt** in a bowl to form stiff peaks.

4 Spread the topping over the filling. Top with **3 large crushed peanut butter cups** and cover with plastic wrap. Chill for at least 1 hour, until firm, before serving. You can store the pie covered in the fridge for 3–4 days.

PLAN AHEAD
You can prepare and store the unfilled cookie crust in an airtight container in the fridge 2–3 days ahead.

Peanut butter

⏱ **35 mins**
plus cooling and chilling

🍴 **SERVES 10**

MUD PIE mocha

Chocolate and coffee are a classic flavor pairing. This recipe combines the best of both ingredients to produce a rich pie. Instant coffee can be used instead of espresso powder—simply double the amount.

1 Grease a **9in (23cm) pie dish**. Combine **10oz (300g) finely crushed Oreos** and **6 tbsp melted, unsalted butter** in a large bowl. Spread it in the dish and chill for 45 minutes (see Peanut butter mud pie, step 1).

2 Melt and combine **6oz (175g) finely chopped dark chocolate, 4 tbsp unsalted butter, 3 tbsp water**, and **1 tbsp instant espresso powder** in a heatproof bowl over a saucepan of simmering water, making sure it does not touch the water. Let cool.

3 Beat **1 cup whipping cream, ½ tsp vanilla extract, ⅛ tsp salt**, and **2 tbsp granulated sugar** in a bowl to form stiff peaks. Chill until needed. Whisk **3 large egg yolks** and **2 tbsp granulated sugar** in a separate heatproof bowl.

4 Place the bowl of whisked egg yolks over a pan of simmering water, making sure it does not touch the water. Whisk the mixture vigorously for 3 minutes, until it turns pale and almost triples in volume. Remove and cool for 1–2 minutes, then add it to the chocolate mixture and combine well.

5 Gradually fold the chilled cream mixture into the chocolate mixture, until it is evenly incorporated and no streaks remain. Pour the filling over the cookie crust and cover with plastic wrap. Chill for 2–3 hours, until set.

6 For the topping, beat **1 cup heavy cream** and **1 tbsp granulated sugar** in a large bowl to form stiff peaks. Spread it over the pie and sprinkle with some **grated chocolate** to serve. You can store the pie covered in the fridge for up to 2 days.

PLAN AHEAD
You can prepare and store the unfilled cookie crust in an airtight container in the fridge 2–3 days ahead.

Mocha

INGREDIENTS

1¾ cups graham crackers, crushed

5 tbsp unsalted butter, melted

For the filling

1 large egg, plus 1 yolk

1 tbsp grated lime zest, plus extra to decorate

1 x 14oz (400g) can condensed milk

1 cup lime juice

pinch of salt

For the topping

¾ cup heavy cream

2 tsp confectioners' sugar

SPECIAL EQUIPMENT

9in (23cm) pie dish, about 2in (5cm) deep

PLAN AHEAD

You can store the blind-baked graham cracker crust in an airtight container in the fridge up to 1 day ahead.

🕐 **40–45 mins** plus cooling 🍴 **SERVES 8**

PIE key lime

This dessert takes its name from the small limes that grow in the Florida Keys, where the recipe originated—although it is now popular throughout the United States. A graham cracker crust is a simple and easy alternative to a pie crust.

1

Preheat the oven to 350°F (180°C). Pulse the graham crackers in a food processor to a fine powder and place in a bowl. Add the butter and mix well to combine.

2

Spread the mixture in the pie dish, pressing it evenly into the bottom and sides for a firm crust. Bake the graham cracker crust for 8–10 minutes, until golden. Set aside to cool.

3

For the filling, whisk the egg, yolk, and lime zest in a bowl for 2 minutes. Then whisk in the milk, lime juice, and salt until smooth. Pour the filling mixture over the crust. Bake the pie for 25–30 minutes, until the filling is set.

4

Remove from the heat and let cool completely. Chill for 1–2 hours. For the topping, beat the cream and sugar in a bowl to form stiff peaks. Spread it over the filling and decorate with lime zest to serve. You can store the pie, covered in the fridge, for up to 2 days.

PIE peach and sour cream

🕐 50–55 mins plus cooling   🍴 SERVES 8

Using sour cream in this pie filling gives it a rich, tangy flavor that complements the sweet peaches.

INGREDIENTS
6oz (175g) graham crackers, finely crushed

5 tbsp unsalted butter, melted

For the filling

12oz (350g) peaches, pitted and sliced

½ cup granulated sugar

1 cup sour cream

½ tsp vanilla extract

¼ tsp salt

grated zest of 1 lemon

1 large egg

1 tbsp all-purpose flour

SPECIAL EQUIPMENT
9in (23cm) pie dish, about 2in (5cm) deep

PLAN AHEAD
You can store the blind-baked graham cracker crust in an airtight container in the fridge up to 1 day ahead.

1 Preheat the oven to 350°F (180°C). Combine the graham crackers and butter in a large bowl. Spread the mixture in the pie dish and bake in the oven (see Orange pie, step 1). Set aside to cool.

2 For the filling, combine the peaches and 1 tablespoon of the sugar in a large bowl and leave to macerate. In a separate bowl, place the sour cream, vanilla extract, salt, lemon zest, and remaining sugar. Whisk well until the sugar dissolves.

3 Whisk in the egg, then stir in the flour and whisk well to combine. Use a slotted spoon to transfer the peaches to the cream mixture and fold them in until evenly combined.

4 Pour the filling evenly into the graham cracker crust. Bake the pie for 30–35 minutes, until the filling is set. Remove from the heat and cool to room temperature before serving. You can store the pie in an airtight container in the fridge for up to 1 day.

🕐 30–35 mins plus cooling and chilling   🍴 SERVES 8

PIE orange

Sweet orange juice and zest bring a bright flavor to this pie. Substitute blood oranges for a bolder color and deeper flavor.

INGREDIENTS
6oz (175g) graham crackers, finely crushed

5 tbsp unsalted butter, melted

For the filling

1 large egg, plus 1 yolk

grated zest of 1 orange, plus extra to decorate

1 x 14oz (400g) can condensed milk

¾ cup orange juice

¼ cup lemon juice

pinch of salt

For the topping

⅔ cup heavy cream

2 tsp confectioners' sugar

SPECIAL EQUIPMENT
9in (23cm) pie dish, about 2in (5cm) deep

PLAN AHEAD
You can store the blind-baked graham cracker crust in an airtight container in the fridge up to 1 day ahead.

1 Preheat the oven to 350°F (180°C). Combine the graham crackers and butter in a large bowl. Spread the mixture evenly in the pie dish, pressing it down into the bottom and sides to form a smooth crust. Bake for 8–10 minutes, until golden. Set aside to cool.

2 For the filling, whisk the egg, yolk, and orange zest for 2 minutes in a large bowl. Whisk in the milk until well combined. Then whisk in the orange juice, lemon juice, and salt until smooth.

3 Pour the filling evenly into the graham cracker crust. Bake the pie for 15–20 minutes, until the center is set. Remove from the heat and cool to room temperature, then chill the pie for 1–2 hours.

4 For the topping, beat the cream and sugar in a large bowl to form stiff peaks. Spread the mixture in the center of the filling and decorate with orange zest to serve. You can store the pie in an airtight container in the fridge for up to 1 day.

🕐 **20 mins**
plus chilling 🍴 **SERVES 8–10**

PIE banoffee

This modern classic is incredibly rich and sweet, just as it should be. It is great for a party, because a little goes a long way. Allow the chilled caramel and pie crust to rest out of the fridge in advance of serving so that it can soften.

INGREDIENTS

9oz (250g) graham crackers, crushed

7 tbsp unsalted butter, melted and cooled

For the caramel

4 tbsp unsalted butter

⅓ cup light brown sugar

1 x 14oz (400g) can condensed milk

For the topping

2 large, ripe bananas, sliced into ¼in (5mm) thick rounds

1 cup heavy cream, whipped

1oz (30g) good-quality dark chocolate, to decorate

SPECIAL EQUIPMENT

9in (23cm) round springform cake pan

PLAN AHEAD

You can store the blind-baked graham cracker crust in an airtight container in the fridge up to 1 day ahead.

1 Line the pan with parchment paper. Combine the graham crackers and butter in a large bowl until well combined. Spread the mixture evenly in the pie dish, pressing it down firmly to form a smooth crust. Cover and chill.

2 For the caramel, melt the butter and sugar in a small, heavy-bottomed saucepan over medium heat. Stir in the milk and bring to a boil. Reduce the heat to a simmer and cook for 2–3 minutes, stirring constantly, until thick and golden.

3 Pour the caramel evenly over the graham cracker crust. Chill for 30 minutes, until set. Transfer to a large serving plate 30 minutes before serving. Cover the caramel with a layer of the bananas and spread the cream evenly over the top.

4 Shave half the chocolate to form short ribbons. Grate the remaining chocolate and sprinkle both forms of chocolate over the pie. Serve immediately. You can store it in an airtight container in the fridge for up to 2 days.

🕐 **35 mins**
plus chilling and cooling

🍴 **SERVES 6–8**

TRIFLE summer fruit

A well-prepared trifle is a wonderful thing—soft and gently yielding with a creamy texture and subtle flavors. It is best to use frozen berries for this recipe, because they are softer than fresh ones and so complement the texture of the trifle.

INGREDIENTS

1 tbsp butter, melted, for brushing

¼ cup all-purpose flour, plus extra for dusting

2 eggs, separated

¼ cup granulated sugar

7oz (200g) frozen mixed berries, thawed

⅔ cup heavy cream, whipped to soft peaks

1 heaping tbsp finely chopped unsalted and skinned pistachios

For the custard

1 cup half-and-half

1 cup whole milk

4 egg yolks

¼ cup granulated sugar

1 tsp vanilla extract

1 tbsp cornstarch

SPECIAL EQUIPMENT

8 x 12in (20 x 30cm) jelly roll pan

9in (23cm) deep-sided glass bowl

PLAN AHEAD

You can prepare and store the custard, covered in plastic wrap, in the fridge up to 2 days ahead.

1

Preheat the oven to 425°F (220°C). Line the pan with parchment paper, brush it lightly with butter, and chill for 5 minutes. Dust the sheet lightly with flour and pour off any excess.

2

Beat the egg yolks and 3 tbsp sugar in a bowl with a handheld mixer until light and fluffy. Whisk the egg whites in a large bowl to form stiff peaks, then whisk in the remaining sugar until glossy. Fold the egg yolk mixture and flour into the egg white mixture until combined.

3

Pour the batter into the pan to form a thin, even layer. Bake for 7–10 minutes, until it is risen, and an inserted toothpick comes out clean. Cool in the pan for 2 minutes before transferring to a wire rack to cool completely. Cut into small pieces.

4

For the custard, heat the cream and milk in a heavy-bottomed saucepan until hot, but not boiling. Whisk the remaining ingredients in a heatproof bowl until smooth. Gradually whisk in the cream mixture until the sugar dissolves.

5

Pour the mixture into a clean, heavy-bottomed pan and bring to a boil over medium heat, stirring constantly. Reduce the heat to a simmer and cook for 3–4 minutes, stirring until it is thick enough to coat the back of the spoon. Pour the custard into a dish and cover its surface with plastic wrap. Chill for 1 hour.

6

Line the bowl with cake pieces. Top with the fruit, pouring in any juices. Spread the custard over, and then the cream. Sprinkle with the pistachios. Chill for 4 hours before serving. You can store the trifle in the fridge for up to 1 day.

Spread out the fruit in an even layer.

🕐 **10 mins**
plus chilling   🍴 **MAKES 4**

MINI TRIFLES peach, lemon, and Amaretti

This quick and easy recipe requires simple pantry ingredients, making it the ideal choice for last-minute entertaining. Use any jam jars you have on hand.

INGREDIENTS
⅔ cup good-quality lemon curd

1 cup good-quality store-bought custard

5½oz (150g) Amaretti cookies, plus extra to decorate

1 x 14oz can peaches in natural juice, drained and coarsely chopped

½ cup heavy cream, whipped to form soft peaks

SPECIAL EQUIPMENT
4 x 11fl oz (320ml) wide-mouthed jars

1 Whisk the lemon curd with 1 tablespoon of the custard in a bowl until combined. Fold in the remaining custard until well combined and smooth.

2 Line the bottom of the jam jars with the cookies, breaking them a little to fill any gaps if necessary. Spread a thin layer of the peaches over the cookies.

3 Top the peaches with a layer of the custard mixture. Repeat the process to get another layer each of the cookies, peaches, and custard.

4 Top the trifles with a layer of the whipped cream and chill them for at least 4 hours. Then top with some cookie crumbs and serve immediately. Best served on the same day.

🕐 **20 mins**
plus cooling and chilling   🍴 **SERVES 6–8**

TRIFLE sherry and raspberry

Tangy raspberries, sliced almonds, and homemade custard give this sherry trifle a modern makeover.

INGREDIENTS
4oz (115g) ladyfingers

¼ cup sherry

6oz (175g) raspberries

⅔ cup heavy cream, whipped to form soft peaks

1 heaping tbsp sliced almonds, toasted

For the custard

4 egg yolks

2 tbsp granulated sugar

1 tsp vanilla extract

1 tbsp cornstarch

1 cup whole milk

1 cup half-and-half

SPECIAL EQUIPMENT
9in (23cm) deep-sided glass bowl

PLAN AHEAD
You can prepare and store the custard, covered in the fridge, up to 2 days ahead.

1 For the custard, beat the egg yolks, sugar, vanilla extract, and cornstarch in a large bowl until well combined and smooth. Heat the milk and cream in a heavy-bottomed saucepan until hot, but not boiling.

2 Gradually pour the milk mixture over the egg yolk mixture, whisking constantly, until the sugar dissolves. Pour the custard mixture into a clean pan. Bring to a boil over medium heat, stirring constantly.

3 Cook the custard over a low simmer for 3–4 minutes, stirring constantly, until it is thick enough to coat the back of a spoon. Remove from the heat and pour into a shallow dish. Cover the surface of the custard with plastic wrap, let cool completely, then chill for 1 hour.

4 Cut one-third of the ladyfingers in half. Place them around the sides of the bowl, finished sides facing outward. Fill the center of the ring with the remaining ladyfingers, breaking and pushing them down to form a firm, single layer.

5 Sprinkle the sherry over the ladyfingers and scatter with the raspberries. Beat the custard gently until smooth and spread it out over the raspberries in an even layer. Top with the whipped cream and sprinkle with the almonds. Chill for 4 hours before serving. You can store the trifle in the fridge for up to 1 day.

🕐 **35 mins**
plus cooling and chilling   🍴 **SERVES 6–8**

TRIFLE black forest

This is a grown-up version of a traditional trifle. It celebrates the well-loved flavor combination of chocolate and cherries, using both chocolate sponge cake and creamy chocolate custard to enhance the richness.

INGREDIENTS

1 tbsp melted butter

⅓ cup cocoa powder, plus extra for dusting

5 eggs, separated

⅔ cup granulated sugar, plus 1 tbsp extra

1 tbsp all-purpose flour

10oz (300g) frozen black cherries

¼ cup Kirsch

¾ cup heavy cream, whipped to form soft peaks

shaved or grated dark chocolate, to decorate

For the custard

4 egg yolks

2 tbsp granulated sugar

2 tbsp cocoa powder

1 tbsp cornstarch

1 cup whole milk

1 cup half-and-half

SPECIAL EQUIPMENT

12 x 15in (30 x 37cm) jelly roll pan

9in (23cm) deep-sided glass bowl

PLAN AHEAD

You can prepare and store the custard, covered in the fridge, up to 2 days ahead.

1 Preheat the oven to 425°F (220°C). Line the pan with parchment paper and brush lightly with the butter. Chill for 5 minutes. Then dust it with 1 teaspoon of cocoa powder, pouring off any excess.

2 Beat the egg yolks with ½ cup of the sugar in a bowl until light and fluffy. In a separate bowl, beat the egg whites to form stiff peaks, then beat in the remaining sugar until glossy.

3 Sift the cocoa powder and flour into a bowl. Gently fold the cocoa mixture and egg white mixture into the egg yolk mixture, in batches, so that you lose as little air as possible. Pour the batter into the pan evenly.

4 Bake the cake for 7–10 minutes, until it is well-risen and an inserted toothpick comes out clean. Remove from the heat and cool in the pan for 2 minutes before transferring to a wire rack to cool completely.

5 For the custard, whisk the egg yolks, sugar, cocoa powder, and cornstarch in a large bowl until smooth.

Heat the milk and cream in a heavy-bottomed saucepan and gradually pour in the egg yolk mixture (see Sherry and raspberry trifle, steps 1–2).

6 Pour the custard mixture into a clean pan and bring to a boil. Reduce the heat and cook for 3–4 minutes, stirring, until thick (see Sherry and raspberry trifle, steps 2–3). Transfer to a shallow bowl, cover, cool, then chill (see Sherry and raspberry trifle, steps 2–3).

7 Combine the cherries and 1 tablespoon of sugar in a bowl. Let thaw, then chop into pieces and reserve the liquid. Cut the cake into pieces and spread half of it in a single layer in the bowl. Sprinkle with half of the Kirsch and top with a single layer of the cherries.

8 Spread over half of the cold custard and half of the whipped cream. Repeat to add another layer each of the cake, Kirsch, cherries, custard, and cream. Sprinkle with the chocolate and chill for at least 4 hours before serving. You can store it in the fridge for up to 1 day.

INGREDIENTS
¾ cup self-rising flour

1½ tsp baking powder

3 eggs

12 tbsp unsalted butter, softened

⅔ cup granulated sugar

¼ cup whole milk

½ cup cocoa powder

1 tbsp red food coloring paste

1 tsp vanilla extract

For the frosting

2oz (60g) cream cheese, at room temperature

4 tbsp unsalted butter, at room temperature

1¾ cups confectioners' sugar

1 tbsp whole milk

1 tsp vanilla extract

For the compote

7oz (200g) blueberries

2 tbsp granulated sugar

For decorating

40 blueberries

2 tbsp candied violets

2 tbsp freeze-dried raspberries

2 tbsp finely chopped unsalted and skinned pistachios

SPECIAL EQUIPMENT
9 x 13in (23 x 33cm) jelly roll pan

2in (5cm) round cutter

6 x 5½fl oz (160ml) glass jars, each 2 x 3in (5 x 7.5cm)

disposable piping bag

PLAN AHEAD
You can store the sponge cake in an airtight container up to 2 days ahead. You can prepare and store the compote in an airtight container in the fridge up to 3 days ahead.

🕐 **1 hr 5 mins**
plus cooling and chilling

🍴 **MAKES 6**

CAKE CUPS red velvet and blueberry

Modern mini trifles, cake cups are fun to make, look great, and taste divine. These cups offer layers of delicate sponge cake, fluffy frosting, and juicy berry compote in every mouthful. For best results, use 5½fl oz (160ml) jars with wide openings.

1

Preheat the oven to 350°F (180°C). Line the pan with parchment paper. Sift the flour and baking powder into a bowl and add the eggs, butter, sugar, and milk.

2

Beat the ingredients until smooth and combined, then fold in the cocoa powder, food coloring, and vanilla extract.

Fold it all in until no streaks remain.

3

Pour the mixture evenly into the pan and bake for 20 minutes. Remove and let cool in the pan, then use the cutter to cut out 18 rounds and place one in each jar.

4

For the frosting, beat all the ingredients together until light and creamy. Transfer to a piping bag, snipping off the end.

A piping bag gives you a precise finish.

5

For the compote, place the blueberries, sugar, and 1 tablespoon water in a heavy-bottomed saucepan with a lid over low heat. Cook, covered, for 5 minutes, then uncover and cook for another 5 minutes, until thick. Cool completely. Pipe a little of the frosting on top of each cake round.

Smooth out the frosting to create an even layer.

6

Top the frosting with 2 teaspoons of the compote. Repeat the process until you reach the third layer of cake. Pipe over some frosting, cover, and chill for 1–4 hours. To serve, decorate the cake cups with the blueberries and flavorings.

🕐 **1 hr 25 mins**
plus cooling

🍴 **MAKES 6**

CUPS fruity meringue

Deconstructed mini pavlovas, these melt in the mouth. You can use store-bought meringues.

1 Preheat the oven to 300°F (150°C). Line a baking sheet with parchment paper. Whisk **1 egg white** in a bowl to form soft peaks. Gradually beat in **¼ cup granulated sugar** until the mixture is thick, glossy, and forms stiff peaks.

2 Spread the mixture out in a ½in (1cm) layer on the baking sheet. Bake the meringue for 1 hour, until hard. Remove from the heat and cool completely, then break it into small pieces.

3 Whisk **½ cup heavy cream** in a bowl until smooth. Fold in **½ cup Greek yogurt** and set aside. Dice **3 ripe kiwi**, and chop **1 x 7oz (200g) can drained peaches** into thin slices. Set aside one-third of each fruit.

4 Place a layer of meringue in **6 x 5½fl oz (160ml) glass jars**. Top with one layer each of the kiwi, cream, and peach. Then add another layer of meringue, top with cream, and decorate with the reserved fruit. Serve immediately.

PLAN AHEAD
You can bake and store the meringue in an airtight container up to 5 days ahead.

🕐 **40–50 mins**
plus cooling and chilling

🍴 **MAKES 6**

CAKE CUPS lemon and fig

Pretty and full of fresh flavors, these cups could make the perfect finale to a Mediterranean meal.

1 Preheat the oven to 350°F (180°C). Line a **9 x 13in (23 x 33cm) cake pan** with parchment paper. Sift **1¼ cups self-rising flour** and **1½ tsp baking powder** into a large bowl. Add **12 tbsp soft unsalted butter**, **⅔ cup granulated sugar**, **3 eggs**, and **¼ cup whole milk**. Beat for 2 minutes.

2 Stir in the **juice and zest of 1 lemon** and **1 tbsp poppy seeds**. Pour the mixture into the pan and spread it out evenly. Bake for 20 minutes. Remove and cool completely in the pan. Use a **2in (5cm) cutter** to cut out 18 rounds. Place one round each in **6 x 5½fl oz (160ml) glass jars**.

3 Place **¾ cup whipped heavy cream** in a bowl and fold in **1 tsp rose water**. Top each cake round with 1 tbsp of the mixture and smooth it out. Thinly slice **5 large ripe figs** and layer on top. Repeat until you reach the third layer of cake. Finish with a layer of cream and chill for 1–4 hours. Decorate with **pomegranate seeds** and serve immediately.

PLAN AHEAD
You can bake and store the sponge cake in an airtight container up to 5 days ahead.

Lemon and fig

Fruity
meringue

🕐 **10 mins**   🍴 MAKES 6

CUPS quick granola

These easy and nutritious layered desserts are the perfect choice for health-conscious guests.

1 Whisk **1¼ cups full-fat Greek yogurt** in a large bowl until smooth and set aside. Place **2 tsp good-quality store-bought granola** in each of **6 x 5½fl oz (160ml) glass jars**. Spread it out in an even layer.

2 Top the granola with 2 tsp of the whipped yogurt and spread it out to form an even, thin layer. Halve **1 cup raspberries**, vertically, and layer over the yogurt.

3 Repeat to add two more layers of granola, yogurt, and raspberries. Finish with another layer of granola and decorate with **1 tbsp mixed dried fruit**, such as blueberries, raisins, and apricots. Serve immediately.

Quick granola

🕐 **1 hr 10 mins**
plus cooling and chilling   🍴 MAKES 6

CAKE CUPS black forest

With cherries, chocolate cake, and mascarpone, these cake cups are like mini black forest gâteaux.

1 Preheat the oven to 350°F (180°C). Line a **9 x 13in (23 x 33cm) cake pan** with parchment paper. Sift **¾ cup self-rising flour**, **½ cup cocoa powder**, and **1½ tsp baking powder** into a large bowl.

2 Add **12 tbsp soft unsalted butter**, **⅔ cup granulated sugar**, **3 eggs**, and **¼ cup whole milk**. Beat until smooth and pour into the pan evenly. Bake for 15–20 minutes. Remove and cool completely in the pan. Use a **2in (5cm) cutter** to cut out 18 rounds.

3 Place **1 cup chopped cherries** and **3 tbsp raspberry liqueur** in a bowl and let macerate. Beat **1 cup mascarpone** in a separate bowl until fluffy, then beat in **⅔ cup heavy cream**.

4 Place one cake round each in **6 x 5½fl oz (160ml) glass jars**. Top with 2 tsp mascarpone and a layer of cherries. Repeat until you have 3 layers of cake. Top with the cream and chill for 1–4 hours. Serve immediately, sprinkled with **grated dark chocolate** and chopped cherries.

PLAN AHEAD
You can store the cake in an airtight container up to 2 days ahead.

Black forest

🕐 **35 mins**
plus chilling

🍴 **SERVES 12**

ICEBOX CAKE raspberry and white chocolate

This is an easy recipe that layers graham crackers, fruit, and cream. For a tasty alternative, you can use British digestive biscuits if you can find them—simply follow the directions for the Chocolate and almond icebox cake (see p164).

INGREDIENTS
3½ cups heavy cream
¾ cup confectioners' sugar
juice of ½ lemon
grated zest of 2 lemons
24 graham crackers
3oz (85g) white chocolate, finely grated
1½lb (675g) raspberries, hulled

1 Whisk the cream, sugar, and lemon juice, and zest in a large bowl to form stiff peaks.

2 Place six crackers on a large serving dish. Spread over one-quarter of the cream evenly.

3 Sprinkle one-quarter of the chocolate over the cream. Halve 1lb 2oz (500g) of the raspberries. Layer one-third of the fruit over the chocolate.

4 Repeat to add three more layers of each ingredient, using the reserved whole raspberries for the top. Cover with plastic wrap and chill for 3–4 hours, or until the graham crackers have softened. Serve chilled. You can store the cake, covered in the fridge, for 1–2 days.

🕐 **20 mins**
plus chilling   🍴 **SERVES 12**

ICEBOX CAKE chocolate and almond

A quick and simple alternative to a chilled cheesecake, this rich dessert can feed a large crowd. British cookies called digestive biscuits can be found in the international aisle of most grocery stores. If you can't find them, use graham crackers instead.

INGREDIENTS

3½ cups heavy cream

½ cup cocoa powder

pinch of salt

½ cup corn syrup

28 digestive biscuits or graham crackers

½ cup sliced almonds

2oz (60g) good-quality dark chocolate, finely chopped

4oz (115g) strawberries, hulled and halved, to serve

SPECIAL EQUIPMENT

9in (23cm) springform cake pan

1 Whisk the cream in a bowl until slightly thick. Sift over the cocoa powder and salt and stir in the corn syrup. Whisk the mixture to form stiff peaks. Line the bottom of the pan with seven biscuits.

2 Spread one-quarter of the cream mixture over the biscuit layer and sprinkle evenly with one-quarter of the almonds. Repeat to form three more layers each of biscuits, cream, and almonds. Cover with plastic wrap and chill for 3–4 hours, until the biscuits have softened.

3 Gently melt the chocolate in a small heatproof bowl over a saucepan of gently simmering water, making sure it does not touch the water. Stir until smooth and remove from the heat. Let cool.

4 Place the pan on a serving plate and carefully remove the sides. Drizzle the chocolate over the cake, top with the strawberries, and serve. You can store the cake, covered with plastic wrap, in the fridge for 1–2 days.

🕐 **1 hr 5 mins**
plus resting, cooling, and chilling   🍴 **SERVES 8–10**

CHARLOTTE CAKE strawberry

With a set strawberry filling and light sponge cake base, Charlotte cake
was invented by the great pastry chef Marie-Antoine Carême in the 1800s.
He named it after Princess Charlotte.

INGREDIENTS

2lb (900g) strawberries,
hulled and halved, plus
extra to serve

¼ cup granulated sugar

1 heaping tsp (7g)
powdered gelatin

1¾ cups heavy cream

1 x 8oz (225g) tub
mascarpone
cheese, at room
temperature

1½ tsp vanilla extract

¼ tsp salt

½ cup confectioners' sugar,
sifted (optional)

10oz (300g) ladyfingers

SPECIAL EQUIPMENT

9in (23cm) springform
cake pan

1 Heat the strawberries and granulated sugar in a
saucepan over low heat for 10–12 minutes, until the
fruit is soft and has released its juices. Remove from the
heat and blend the mixture with an immersion blender
to form a smooth puree.

2 Transfer the fruit puree to a large bowl set over an
ice bath. Stir until cool. Combine ½ cup of the puree
with the gelatin in a small saucepan and let rest for 3–4
minutes, until thick. Gently warm the mixture over low
heat until no longer firm.

3 Stir the gelatin mixture into the cooled puree and
combine well. Whisk the cream, mascarpone, vanilla
extract, and salt in a bowl to form stiff peaks. Gradually
fold it into the fruit and gelatin mixture, until combined.
Stir in the confectioners' sugar to taste, if needed.

4 Cut about 1in (2.5cm) from the edges of 28 ladyfingers.
Line the bottom of the pan with whole ladyfingers.
Place the trimmed ladyfingers along the sides of the
pan, cut-side down, pouring in a little of the cream
mixture to help secure them.

5 Pour the remaining cream mixture onto the sponge
cake, cover with plastic wrap, and chill overnight.
Place the pan on a serving plate and carefully remove
the sides. Decorate with strawberries and serve. You can
store the cake, covered with plastic wrap, in the fridge
for up to 2 days.

30 mins
plus cooling and chilling

SERVES 8

TIRAMISU classic

This beloved Italian dessert is a fairly recent invention dating back to the 1960s. It is classically a light, layered dessert of coffee-flavored ladyfingers and mascarpone, but coffee liqueur and Marsala wine are also popular additions.

INGREDIENTS

2 tbsp instant espresso powder

2 tsp granulated sugar

½ cup Marsala wine

For the filling

6 large egg yolks

1 cup confectioners' sugar, sifted

⅓ cup Marsala wine

2 tsp vanilla extract

1lb (450g) mascarpone cheese, at room temperature

2 cups heavy cream, chilled

14oz (400g) ladyfingers

unsweetened cocoa powder, for dusting

SPECIAL EQUIPMENT

13 x 9 x 2in (33 x 23 x 5cm) pan or dish

1
Bring 2 cups of water to a boil and cool for 5 minutes. Then combine the water with the espresso powder, granulated sugar, and Marsala in a bowl. Let infuse. For the filling, beat the egg yolks and confectioners' sugar in a heatproof bowl for 2–3 minutes, until thick and pale in color.

2
Place the bowl over a saucepan of gently simmering water, making sure it does not touch the water. Add the Marsala in a steady stream, mixing constantly to combine. Beat the mixture for 5 minutes, until thick and ribbon-like in texture. Remove from the heat, cover, and cool. Stir in the vanilla extract.

3
Place the mascarpone in a large bowl and fold gently with a spatula to soften the cheese. Then add the cooled egg yolk and Marsala mixture. Mix gently until well combined and smooth.

4
In a separate bowl, whisk the heavy cream to form stiff peaks. Fold a little of the cream into the mascarpone mixture and mix well. Then gently fold in the rest and mix until it is well combined.

Start with a little of the whipped cream, then add the rest.

5
Dip half of the ladyfingers into the coffee mixture briefly on each side, then use them to line the bottom of the serving dish. Cover with half of the cream filling and sift some cocoa powder on top.

6
Add another layer of ladyfingers and filling. Sprinkle generously with cocoa powder, wrap in plastic wrap, and chill for 4–6 hours. Remove the tiramisu from the fridge 15 minutes before serving. You can store it, covered in the fridge, for 1–2 days.

Beer

Cherry mocha

TIRAMISU beer

Give this Italian classic a modern twist with a rich, dark stout such as Guinness, which works well with traditional flavors.

1. Combine **2 tsp granulated sugar** and **1 cup stout beer** in a bowl and set aside. Whisk **1 cup whipping cream, 1 tsp instant espresso powder**, and **a pinch of salt** in a large bowl to form stiff peaks.

2. Use a spatula to combine **1lb (450g) mascarpone cheese, 2½ tsp vanilla extract**, and **1 cup sifted confectioners' sugar** in a large bowl. Fold in the cream and coffee mixture, a little at a time, until evenly combined.

3. Briefly dip **7oz (200g) ladyfingers** in the beer mixture on each side and use to line the bottom of a **7 x 9in (18 x 23cm) dish**. Cover with half of the cream mixture filling and sprinkle over some **unsweetened cocoa powder**.

4. Add another layer of the ladyfingers and filling. Dust the top generously with more cocoa powder, wrap with plastic wrap, and chill for at least 4–6 hours. Remove from the fridge 15 minutes before serving. You can store it, covered in the fridge, for up to 2 days.

TIRAMISU cherry mocha

Dark chocolate and cherries are often paired together in desserts, such as Black Forest gâteau. The cherries give welcome contrast to the rich and creamy filling.

1. Bring **2 cups water** to a boil and let cool for 5 minutes, then combine the water with **2 tbsp instant espresso powder, 4 tsp granulated sugar**, and **1½ tbsp unsweetened cocoa powder** in a small bowl and let cool. In a large bowl, whisk **2 cups whipping cream, 1 tsp instant espresso powder**, and **a pinch of salt** to form stiff peaks.

2. In a separate bowl, combine **1lb (450g) mascarpone cheese, 2 tsp pure vanilla extract, 3 tbsp cocoa powder**, and **1 cup sifted confectioners' sugar**. Fold in the cream and coffee mixture, a little at a time, until evenly combined.

3. Briefly dip **7oz (200g) ladyfingers** in the coffee mixture on each side. Use half of them to line the bottom of a **7 x 9in (18 x 23cm) dish**. Cover with half of the cream mixture and scatter over half of **350g (12oz) pitted and quartered black cherries**.

4. Sift over some **cocoa powder** and add another layer of the ladyfingers, filling, and cherries. Dust, wrap, and chill (see Beer tiramisu, step 4). Remove from the fridge 15 minutes before serving. You can store it, covered in the fridge, for up to 2 days.

🕐 **30 mins** plus chilling   🍴 **SERVES 6**

TIRAMISU Amaretto

Amaretto, an almond-based liqueur, is often used in Italian desserts. In this recipe, it helps to distribute the coffee flavor.

1 Bring **2 cups water** to a boil and cool for 5 minutes. Combine the water with **2 tbsp instant espresso powder**, **2 tsp granulated sugar**, and **½ cup Amaretto** in a bowl and let cool. Whisk **6 egg yolks** and **⅔ cup granulated sugar** in a heatproof bowl until thick and pale yellow in color.

2 Place the bowl of egg yolks over a saucepan of simmering water, making sure it does not touch the water. Add **2 tbsp Amaretto** and whisk the mixture vigorously for 5–6 minutes, until it is thick and forms ribbons when the whisk is lifted. Remove, cover, and cool to room temperature, then stir in **1 tsp vanilla extract**.

3 In a large bowl, whisk **1 cup chilled whipping cream** to form stiff peaks and chill until needed. In a separate bowl, fold and soften **1lb (450g) mascarpone cheese** with a spatula. Add the egg yolk mixture and beat to combine, then gradually add the whipped cream and whisk well to combine.

4 Briefly dip **7oz (200g) ladyfingers** in the coffee mixture on each side. Use them to line the bottom of a **7 x 9in (18 x 23cm) dish**. Cover with half of the cream mixture and sift some **unsweetened cocoa powder** over the top.

5 Add another layer of the ladyfingers and filling. Dust, wrap, and chill (see Beer tiramisu, step 4). Remove from the fridge 15 minutes before serving. You can store it, covered in the fridge, for up to 2 days.

Amaretto

🕐 **1 hr**
plus cooling, chilling, and resting

🍴 **MAKES 6**

CRÈME BRÛLÉE classic

Every home-cook needs to know how to make the perfect crème brûlée. For a contrast of texture and flavor, you can serve these caramelized custards with delicate cookies, such as these Pecan sablés (see p262).

INGREDIENTS

5 egg yolks
¼ cup granulated sugar, plus 3 tbsp extra
1 tsp vanilla extract
2 cups heavy cream
sablés, to serve (optional)

SPECIAL EQUIPMENT

6 x 5fl oz (150ml) ramekins
small kitchen blowtorch

PLAN AHEAD

You can prepare and store the uncaramelized custard in the fridge up to 3 days ahead.

1 Preheat the oven to 325°F (160°C). Whisk the egg yolks, sugar, and vanilla extract in a large bowl until combined. Heat the cream in a small saucepan over low heat until it is hot, but not boiling.

Remove the cream from the heat and pour it into the egg yolk mixture. Whisk until the sugar dissolves. Place the ramekins in a roasting pan and pour the custard mixture into them evenly.

2

3

Carefully pour hot water into the pan to come halfway up the sides of the ramekins. Bake for 30–40 minutes, until just set, but slightly wobbly in the center. Remove from the heat and cool to room temperature. Cover with plastic wrap and chill for 2 hours.

Sprinkle ½ tablespoon sugar over each custard and gently spread it out with the back of a spoon. Melt the sugar with the blowtorch, sweeping the flame over it gently. Let the crème brûlées rest for at least 5 minutes before serving with sablés, if desired.

4

🕐 **1 hr**
plus cooling, chilling, and resting   🍴 **MAKES 6**

CRÈME BRÛLÉE
white chocolate

Creamy white chocolate gives a subtle flavor to these custards. Use good-quality white chocolate, which is not oversweet.

1 Preheat the oven to 325°F (160°C). Whisk **4 egg yolks**, **¼ cup granulated sugar**, and **1 tsp vanilla extract** in a large bowl until well combined. Heat **1¾ cups heavy cream** in a large saucepan over low heat until hot, but not boiling.

2 Remove from the heat and add **3½oz (100g) finely chopped good-quality white chocolate**. Stir until the chocolate melts, and then pour into the egg yolk mixture, whisking well to combine. Place **6 x 5fl oz (150ml) ramekins** in a roasting pan.

3 Pour the custard into the ramekins. Carefully pour hot water into the pan to come halfway up the sides of the ramekins, making sure it does not splash. Bake for 30–40 minutes, until just set but wobbly in the center. Cool for 5 minutes, then cover with plastic wrap and chill for 2 hours.

4 Sprinkle **½ tbsp granulated sugar** over each custard and gently spread it out with the back of a spoon. Use a **kitchen blowtorch** to caramelize the sugar, sweeping it over gently. Let rest for 5 minutes before serving.

PLAN AHEAD
You can prepare and store the uncaramelized custard in the fridge up to 3 days ahead.

White chocolate

Lavender

🕐 **1 hr 10 mins**
plus cooling, chilling, and resting   🍴 **MAKES 6**

CRÈME BRÛLÉE
lavender

Gently steeping dried lavender in heavy cream gives the most beautifully fragrant flavor to the finished dish.

1 Preheat the oven to 325°F (160°C). Heat **2 cups heavy cream** and **1 tbsp dried culinary lavender** in a large saucepan over low heat until hot, but not boiling. Remove from the heat, cover, and let steep for 15 minutes.

2 Whisk **5 egg yolks** and **¼ cup granulated sugar** in a large bowl until well combined. Strain the infused cream into the egg yolk mixture and whisk well to combine. Discard the lavender. Place **6 x 5fl oz (150ml) ramekins** in a roasting pan.

3 Pour the custard into the ramekins and carefully pour hot water into the pan (see White chocolate crème brûlée, step 3). Bake for 30–40 minutes, until just set but wobbly in the center. Cool, cover, and chill for 2 hours (see White chocolate crème brûlée, step 3).

4 Spread **½ tbsp granulated sugar** over each custard and use a **kitchen blowtorch** to caramelize (see White chocolate crème brûlée, step 4). Let rest for 5 minutes before serving.

PLAN AHEAD
You can prepare and store the uncaramelized custard in the fridge up to 3 days ahead.

CRÈME BRÛLÉE
Earl Grey

🕐 **1 hr 10 mins**
plus cooling, chilling, and resting   🍴 **MAKES 6**

Earl Grey tea's strong flavor is mixed with the gentle flavors of this custard base, imparting its characteristic citrus–floral notes.

1. Preheat the oven to 325°F (160°C). Heat **2 cups heavy cream** in a large saucepan over low heat until hot, but not boiling. Remove from the heat and add **4 Earl Grey teabags**. Cover and let steep for 10 minutes.

2. Whisk **5 egg yolks** and **¼ cup granulated sugar** in a large bowl. Strain the infused cream into the egg yolk mixture, pressing down on the teabags to extract the flavor. Discard the teabags. Whisk the mixture well to combine. Place **6 x 5fl oz (150ml) ramekins** in a roasting pan.

3. Pour the custard into the ramekins and carefully pour hot water into the pan (see White chocolate crème brûlée, step 3). Bake for 30–40 minutes, until just set but wobbly in the center. Cool, cover, and chill for 2 hours (see White chocolate crème brûlée, step 3).

4. Spread **½ tbsp light brown sugar** over each custard and gently spread it out with the back of a spoon. Use a **kitchen blowtorch** to caramelize (see White chocolate crème brûlée, step 4). Let rest for 5 minutes before serving.

PLAN AHEAD
You can prepare and store the uncaramelized custard in the fridge up to 3 days ahead.

Crèma Catalana

🕐 **40 mins**
plus steeping, cooling, and chilling   🍴 **MAKES 6**

CRÈMA CATALANA

This recipe originates from Catalonia, Spain. It is incredibly simple to make—you don't need to bake it in the oven or in a bainmarie.

1. Cut the **zest of 1 small lemon** into strips. Place it with **2 cups whole milk** and **1 cinnamon stick** in a heavy-bottomed saucepan. Cook over low heat until hot, but not boiling. Remove from the heat, cover, and let steep for 15 minutes.

2. Whisk **4 egg yolks**, **¼ cup granulated sugar**, and **1½ tbsp cornstarch** in a large bowl until combined. Strain the infused milk into the egg yolk mixture and whisk until the sugar has melted. Discard the cinnamon stick and lemon zest. Return the custard to the pan.

3. Cook over gentle heat, stirring until the custard begins to thicken. Reduce the heat to low and cook for 2 minutes, whisking constantly. Pour it into **6 x 5fl oz (150ml) ramekins**. Let cool completely, then cover with plastic wrap and chill for at least 3 hours.

4. Spread **½ tbsp granulated sugar** over each custard and use a **kitchen blowtorch** to caramelize (see White chocolate crème brûlée, step 4). Chill the crème brûlée for about 10 minutes before serving.

PLAN AHEAD
You can prepare and store the uncaramelized custard in the fridge up to 3 days ahead.

Earl Grey

20 mins
plus chilling   **SERVES 4**

VANILLA PUDDING
with raspberries

This simple pudding is nothing more than a smooth and silky chilled vanilla custard. Serve it with raspberries for a sweet-sharp flavor contrast. You can also prepare the pudding and chill it in individual glasses, or layer it with seasonal fruit.

INGREDIENTS

½ cup granulated sugar

3 tbsp cornstarch

3 large egg yolks

½ tsp salt

2 cups whole milk

1 tbsp unsalted butter

3 tsp vanilla extract

30–40 raspberries, to serve

1

Place the sugar, cornstarch, egg yolks, and salt in a large bowl. Pour in half the milk and whisk until well combined and smooth.

2

Heat the remaining milk in a saucepan over medium–low heat, until steaming. Pour half the hot milk into the yolk mixture, in a steady stream, whisking constantly to combine. Then pour the yolk and milk mixture back into the pan and mix well to combine.

3

Increase the heat to medium and bring to a boil, stirring constantly. Reduce the heat to a simmer and cook for another 1 minute, stirring, until the mixture has thickened. Remove and pour through a strainer into a large bowl.

4

Stir in the butter and vanilla extract until evenly combined. Cover with plastic wrap, making sure it touches the top of the pudding. Chill for at least 3–4 hours. Serve it with raspberries. You can store the pudding in an airtight container in the fridge for 2–3 days.

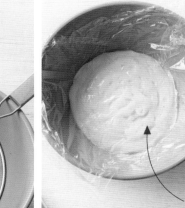

Covering the surface of the pudding with plastic wrap prevents a skin from forming.

20 mins plus chilling   **SERVES 8–10**

VANILLA PUDDING banana

Banana pudding, similar in style to a British trifle, is a classic Southern dessert, although you can now find it all over the United States. It is very quick to prepare and guaranteed to impress.

INGREDIENTS
6 large egg yolks
6 tbsp cornstarch
1 tsp salt
¾ cup granulated sugar
4 cups whole milk
2 tbsp butter
½ tsp vanilla extract
2½ tsp banana extract

For the topping
1 cup whipping cream
5½oz (150g) Nilla wafers
4 bananas, thinly sliced

1 Whisk the egg yolks, cornstarch, salt, sugar, and 1 cup milk in a large bowl until smooth. Heat the remaining milk in a saucepan over medium–low heat until steaming. Pour half the hot milk into the egg yolk mixture in a steady stream, whisking constantly to combine.

2 Pour the milk and egg yolk mixture back into the pan. Increase the heat to medium and bring to a boil, stirring constantly to prevent the mixture from sticking to the bottom of the pan. Reduce the heat and cook for another 1 minute, stirring, until it thickens.

3 Remove from the heat and pour the pudding through a fine strainer into a large bowl. Add the butter, vanilla extract, and banana extract, and whisk until smooth. Cover with plastic wrap, making sure it touches the surface of the pudding to prevent a skin from forming. Chill for 3–4 hours.

4 For the topping, place the cream in a large bowl and beat to form stiff peaks. Use half the Nilla wafers to line the bottom of a large serving bowl. Cover with half the pudding and top with a layer of the bananas.

5 Repeat to add one more layer of Nilla wafers and pudding. Top with the remaining bananas, then add the whipped cream. Cover with plastic wrap and chill for at least 1 hour before serving. You can store the pudding in the fridge for 1–2 days.

🕐 **15 mins**   🍴 **SERVES 4**   🌡 Also great **HOT**

VANILLA PUDDING zabaglione

Beat this Marsala-infused Italian dessert until it is light and frothy. The prolonged beating of the egg yolks over the indirect heat of a bainmarie ensures they are cooked through with a silky texture.

INGREDIENTS

3 large egg yolks
3 tbsp granulated sugar
¼ cup Marsala wine
¼ tsp vanilla extract
berries or other soft
  fruit, to serve

1 Beat the egg yolks and sugar in a large heatproof bowl with a handheld mixer for 3 minutes, until well combined and pale yellow in color. Place the bowl over a saucepan of gently simmering water, making sure it does not touch the water.

2 Pour the Marsala wine and vanilla extract into the bowl, in a steady stream, mixing constantly to bring the mixture together. Beat the mixture for

another 8–10 minutes, until it turns pale, triples in volume, and forms ribbons when the mixer is lifted.

3 Remove from the heat. Serve immediately, or at room temperature over berries or other soft fruit. Serve the pudding on the same day, as it will start to separate if chilled.

40 mins
plus chilling

MAKES 6

CRÈME CARAMEL classic

Making crème caramel is not as tricky as you might think. For best results, it is very important that you cook them gently in a bainmarie in the oven—this helps them to set without splitting.

INGREDIENTS
1 cup granulated sugar
2 eggs, plus 2 egg yolks
1 tsp vanilla extract
2 cups whole milk

SPECIAL EQUIPMENT
6 x 5fl oz (150ml) ramekins

1

Preheat the oven to 350°F (180°C). Place ⅔ cup of the sugar and 2 tablespoons of water in a small, heavy-bottomed saucepan. Cook over medium heat, without stirring, until the sugar dissolves and turns golden brown. Swirl the pan gently and occasionally to cook the sugar evenly.

2

Remove and distribute the caramel equally between the ramekins, swirling them to coat the bottom and a little way up the sides.

3

In a large heatproof bowl, whisk the eggs, egg yolks, vanilla extract, and the remaining sugar until well combined.

4

Place the milk in a saucepan over low heat until hot, but not boiling. Pour it over the egg mixture and whisk well. Chill the custard for 30 minutes.

5

Place the ramekins in a roasting pan and pour the custard into them evenly. Pour enough hot water into the pan to come halfway up the sides of the ramekins. Bake for 25–30 minutes, until the custard is just set, but still wobbly in the middle.

6

Remove and transfer the ramekins to a baking pan to cool, then chill them for 2 hours. To serve, run a knife around the insides of the ramekins and turn onto serving plates, scraping all the caramel on top. You can store them, covered with plastic wrap, in the fridge for up to 2 days. Bring to room temperature before serving.

🕐 **55 mins**
plus cooling and chilling   🍴 **MAKES 4**

CRÈME CARAMEL orange flower

Orange flower water is quickly becoming a popular ingredient in recipes for sweet treats. Its perfume-like fragrance is strong and heady, so a little goes a long way.

INGREDIENTS

1 cup granulated sugar

2 whole eggs, plus
   2 egg yolks

2 tsp orange flower water

2 cups whole milk

SPECIAL EQUIPMENT

4 x 7fl oz (200ml)
   ovenproof ramekins

1 Preheat the oven to 350°F (180°C). Cook ⅔ cup of the sugar in a heavy-bottomed saucepan over medium heat, until the sugar dissolves and turns golden. Swirl the pan gently and occasionally to ensure that the sugar cooks evenly.

2 Remove from the heat and distribute the caramel equally between the ramekins, swirling them to coat the bottom and a little way up the sides. In a large bowl, whisk the eggs, egg yolks, orange flower water, and remaining sugar, until combined.

3 Heat the milk in a saucepan over low heat, until hot but not boiling. Whisk the hot milk into the egg mixture until well combined. Chill the custard for 30 minutes, then pour into the ramekins.

4 Place the ramekins in a roasting pan. Pour enough hot water into the pan to come halfway up the sides of the ramekins. Bake for 35–40 minutes, until just set, but wobbling in the middle. Remove from the heat.

5 Cool to room temperature before chilling for 6 hours, or overnight. To serve, run a sharp knife around the insides of the ramekins and turn onto plates. Spoon the caramel on top.

🕐 **1 hr 15 mins**
plus cooling and chilling   🍴 **SERVES 6**

FLAN vanilla

Versions of this dessert hail from Spain, Mexico, and South America. This creamy variety is perfect for serving a crowd.

INGREDIENTS

unsalted butter,
   for greasing

¾ cup granulated sugar

3 eggs

1½ cups evaporated milk

⅔ cup heavy cream

1 tsp vanilla extract

SPECIAL EQUIPMENT

8in (20cm) deep-sided
   cake pan

1 Preheat the oven to 350°F (180°C). Grease the pan and set aside. Cook ⅔ cup of the sugar in a heavy-bottomed saucepan over medium heat, until the sugar dissolves and turns golden. Swirl the pan gently and occasionally to ensure that the sugar cooks evenly.

2 Remove from the heat and spread the caramel in the cake pan, swirling it to coat the bottom and a little way up the sides. In a large bowl, whisk the eggs and remaining sugar, until combined.

3 Add the evaporated milk, cream, and vanilla extract to the egg mixture and whisk until incorporated. Pour the custard into the cake pan in an even layer, cover with foil, and place in a roasting pan.

4 Pour enough hot water into the roasting pan to come halfway up the sides of the cake pan. Bake in the oven for 1 hour, until just set, but still wobbling in the middle. Remove from the heat.

5 Cool to room temperature before chilling for 6 hours, or overnight. To serve the flan, run a sharp knife around its sides to loosen it. Turn it onto a large serving dish and spoon the caramel on top.

⏱ **50 mins**
plus cooling and chilling　　🍴 **MAKES 4**

CRÈME CARAMEL coconut

This delicately flavored dessert makes the perfect end to an Asian feast. Easy to prepare in advance, you could serve it with a tropical fruit garnish.

INGREDIENTS

1 cup granulated sugar

2 whole eggs, plus
　2 egg yolks

1¾ cups coconut milk

½ cup whole milk

SPECIAL EQUIPMENT

4 x 7fl oz (200ml)
　ovenproof ramekins

1 Preheat the oven to 350°F (180°C). Cook ⅔ cup of the sugar in a heavy-bottomed saucepan over a medium heat, until the sugar dissolves and turns golden. Swirl the pan gently and occasionally to ensure that the sugar cooks evenly.

2 Remove from the heat and distribute the caramel between the ramekins (see Orange flower crème caramel, step 2). In a large bowl, whisk the eggs, egg yolks, and remaining sugar, until well combined.

3 Heat both types of milk in a saucepan over low heat, until hot, but not boiling. Add the hot milk mixture to the egg mixture and whisk until well combined. Chill the custard for 30 minutes.

4 Pour the custard into the ramekins and place them in a roasting pan. Pour hot water into the pan (see, Orange flower crème caramel, step 4). Bake for 30–40 minutes, until just set, but still wobbling in the middle. Remove from the heat.

5 Cool to room temperature before chilling for 6 hours, or overnight. To serve, run a sharp knife around the insides of the ramekins and turn onto plates. Spoon the caramel on top.

🕐 **40 mins**
plus chilling and cooling

🍴 **MAKES 6**

MOUSSE chocolate

This light and fluffy mousse is very simple to prepare, and endlessly adaptable. Depending on your preference, you can make it with dark or milk chocolate, and you can even flavor it with a splash of your favorite liqueur.

INGREDIENTS
½ cup whipping cream
1 tsp instant espresso powder
6oz (175g) good-quality dark chocolate, chopped
4 tbsp unsalted butter
3 large eggs, separated
¼ cup granulated sugar
pinch of salt
¼ tsp cream of tartar
chocolate shavings, to decorate

SPECIAL EQUIPMENT
6 x 7fl oz (200ml) cups

1 Beat the cream in a bowl to form stiff peaks and chill until needed. Combine the espresso powder with 2 tablespoons of hot water in a small bowl. Place the chocolate and butter in a large heatproof bowl. Pour in the coffee mixture and stir to mix.

2 *Stir until the chocolate has melted and is smooth.*

Melt the chocolate mixture over a saucepan of gently simmering water, making sure it does not touch the water. Stir well, remove from the heat, and let cool.

3 Beat the egg yolks and 2 tablespoons of sugar with a handheld mixer in a heatproof bowl until smooth. Then beat the mixture over a pan of simmering water for 2–3 minutes, until thick and pale. Let rest for 2 minutes, then combine with the chocolate mixture.

4 Beat the egg whites and salt in a separate bowl until fluffy. Add the cream of tartar and beat to form soft peaks. Gradually beat in the remaining sugar to form stiff peaks.

5 Stir a little of the egg white mixture into the chocolate mixture to lighten the texture. Then fold in the chilled cream and the remaining egg white mixture.

Fold gently until no streaks remain.

6 Divide the mixture evenly between the cups and chill for 2–3 hours, until set. You can keep the mousse, covered in the fridge, for up to 2 days. Remove from the fridge 10–15 minutes before serving and sprinkle with the chocolate shavings.

🕐 **30 mins**
plus chilling and setting   🍴 **MAKES 6**

MOUSSE Kahlúa-coffee

This is a wonderfully smooth chocolate and coffee combination. Although Kahlúa is used here, you can try any coffee liqueur.

1 Melt **4 tbsp unsalted butter**, **6oz (175g) finely chopped good-quality dark chocolate**, and **2½ tbsp Kahlúa** in a heatproof bowl over a saucepan of simmering water, making sure it does not touch the water. Stir well, remove from the heat, and let cool. Beat **½ cup whipping cream** in a bowl to form stiff peaks and chill until needed.

2 Beat **3 large egg yolks** and **2 tbsp granulated sugar** in a separate heatproof bowl until smooth. Place the bowl over a pan of simmering water, as before. Beat vigorously, adding **¼ cup strong coffee** in a steady stream. Beat for 3 minutes until the mixture is pale and has tripled in volume.

3 Remove from the heat, rest for 1 minute, then combine with the chocolate mixture. Beat the **3 large egg whites** and a **pinch of salt** in a bowl until frothy. Add **¼ tsp cream of tartar** and beat to form soft peaks. Then add **2 tbsp granulated sugar** and beat to form stiff peaks.

4 Gradually fold the egg white mixture and the whipped cream into the chocolate mixture, until no streaks remain. Pour it into **6 x 5¾fl oz (175ml) glasses** and chill for 2–3 hours, until set. You can keep the mousse, covered in the fridge, for 2–3 days. Remove from the fridge 10–15 minutes before serving and top with a little **whipped cream** and **grated dark chocolate**.

🕐 **35 mins**
plus chilling and setting   🍴 **MAKES 6**

MOUSSE butterscotch

This rich and silky mousse does not require beated egg whites to give it volume. Instead, butterscotch and cream provide the airy texture.

1 Melt **6oz (175g) butterscotch chips**, **4 tbsp unsalted butter**, and **2 tbsp heavy cream** in a heatproof bowl over a saucepan of simmering water, making sure it does not touch the water. Stir well, remove from the heat, and let cool.

2 Beat **1½ cups heavy cream** in a bowl to form stiff peaks. Chill until needed. In a heatproof bowl, beat **3 large egg yolks** and **2 tbsp granulated sugar**. Place the bowl over a pan of simmering water, as before. Beat vigorously for 3 minutes, until the mixture is pale and has tripled in volume.

3 Gradually fold the egg yolk mixture and whipped cream into the butterscotch mixture until no streaks remain. Pour the mixture into **6 x 4fl oz (120ml) glasses** and chill for 2–3 hours, until set. Cook **⅔ cup granulated sugar** in a heavy-bottomed saucepan over medium heat for 5 minutes.

4 Stir the sugar gently to form a light-colored caramel. Pour onto a lined baking sheet and let cool completely before breaking the caramel into small pieces. You can keep the mousse, covered in the fridge, for 2–3 days. Remove from the fridge 10–15 minutes before serving and top with the caramel.

Kahlúa–coffee

Butterscotch

🕐 **25 mins**
plus chilling, setting, and drying 🍴 **MAKES 6**

MOUSSE chocolate and mint

Evoke the flavor of after-dinner mints with this mousse. Add a flourish and additional flavor by decorating with frosted mint leaves.

1 Melt **6oz (175g) finely chopped dark chocolate**, **3 tbsp whipping cream**, and a **pinch of salt** in a heatproof bowl over a saucepan of simmering water, making sure it does not touch the water. Stir well, remove from the heat, and let cool. Beat **¾ cup whipping cream** in a bowl to form stiff peaks and chill until needed.

2 In a separate bowl, beat **2 egg whites** and a **pinch of salt** to form soft peaks. Add **2 tbsp granulated sugar**, one tablespoon at a time, and beat to form stiff peaks. Then gently stir in **½ tsp mint extract** until combined.

3 Mix a little of the egg whites into the chocolate mixture to lighten it. Gently fold in the rest along with the whipped cream until no streaks remain. Pour the mixture into **6 x 7fl oz (200ml) glasses** and chill for 2–3 hours, until set.

4 Brush **9 mint leaves** with **1 lightly beaten egg white**. Dip them in **granulated sugar** and let dry on parchment paper for 1 hour. You can keep the mousse, covered in the fridge, for 2–3 days. Remove from the fridge 10–15 minutes before serving and top with the crystallized mint leaves.

🕐 **40 mins**
plus chilling and setting 🍴 **MAKES 6**

MOUSSE strawberry lemonade

The flavor of lemon juice is quite distinct in this mousse, making it a little tart—just like pink lemonade.

1 Place **1lb (450g) hulled and quartered strawberries**, **¼ cup fresh lemon juice**, **½ cup granulated sugar**, and **a pinch of salt** in a saucepan. Simmer over low heat for 8–10 minutes until the strawberries have softened. Remove from the heat and use an immersion blender to blend until smooth.

2 Strain the puree and pour it back into the pan. Simmer the puree over medium-low heat for 5 minutes, then transfer to a heatproof bowl set over an ice bath and stir until cold. Transfer 2oz (60g) of the fruit puree to a small saucepan and stir in **1 tsp powdered gelatin**. Let thicken for 3–4 minutes.

3 Use a handheld mixer to beat **1 cup heavy cream** and **1 tsp vanilla extract** in a bowl to form stiff peaks. Heat the gelatin mixture over low heat until no longer firm. Add it to the reserved fruit puree and mix to combine. Gradually fold in the whipped cream, until no streaks remain.

4 Pour the mixture into **6 x 5¾fl oz (175ml) glasses** and chill for 2–3 hours until set. You can keep the mousse, covered in the fridge, for 2–3 days. Remove from the fridge 10–15 minutes before serving and top with **halved strawberries** and **lemon zest curls**.

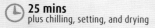

Chocolate and mint

Strawberry lemonade

🕐 **20 mins**
plus infusing, cooling, setting, and chilling

🍴 **MAKES 4**

PANNA COTTA
vanilla with raspberry coulis

Translated from Italian, *panna cotta* means "cooked cream."
Sweetened cream and milk are gently heated then set with
gelatin, providing a soft and delicate dessert that makes
a perfect foil for the raspberry coulis.

INGREDIENTS
1²/₃ cups whipping
  cream
1 cup whole milk
1 vanilla bean, split
  lengthwise
1 heaping tsp (7g)
  powdered gelatin
½ cup granulated sugar
1 tbsp sunflower oil,
  for greasing

For the coulis
7oz (200g) frozen
  raspberries
3 tbsp granulated sugar

SPECIAL EQUIPMENT
4 x 5fl oz (150ml) dariole
  molds or ramekins

1

Heat the cream, ¾ cup milk, and vanilla bean in a heavy-bottomed saucepan over low heat until steaming. Whisk the gelatin and reserved milk in a small bowl, then let it rest for about 5 minutes.

2

Remove from the heat, take out the vanilla bean, and scrape the seeds into the pan. Place the sugar in a heatproof bowl and pour the cream mixture over the top, whisking until the sugar dissolves. Whisk in the gelatin mixture.

3

Return the mixture to the pan and heat gently, stirring, for 2–3 minutes to ensure that the gelatin has dissolved. Do not boil or the gelatin will not set. Remove from the heat.

Lightly grease the ramekins and pour in the hot cream mixture evenly. Let them cool to room temperature. Cover with plastic wrap and chill for 4–6 hours, until set.

4

5

For the coulis, cook the raspberries, sugar, and 3 tablespoons of water in a pan over low heat for 2–3 minutes, until the fruit has broken down. Remove from the heat and puree the mixture with a handheld blender. Push through a strainer and chill until cold.

6

Carefully dip each ramekin in a bowl of hot water, run a knife around the edge, and invert onto a plate. Pour the coulis over to serve. You can store the panna cottas and coulis separately, covered in the fridge, for up to 2 days.

🕐 **20 mins**
plus cooling and chilling 🍴 **MAKES 4**

PANNA COTTA green tea

Vanilla panna cotta makes the perfect base for the delicate fragrance of green tea. Decorate with matcha powder to enhance the flavors further.

1 Place **3 tbsp whole milk** in a bowl, whisk in **1 heaping tsp (7g) powdered gelatin**, and let rest for 5 minutes. Meanwhile, place ¾ **cup whole milk**, **1⅔ cups whipping cream**, and **3 good-quality green teabags** in a heavy-bottomed saucepan over low heat. Heat for 5 minutes until steaming, but not boiling.

2 Remove the pan from the heat and take out the teabags, squeezing them to extract extra flavor, if desired. Place ½ **cup granulated sugar** in a heatproof bowl. Pour in the hot milk mixture and whisk well until the sugar dissolves. Then whisk in the gelatin mixture until combined.

3 Return the mixture to the pan and heat gently, stirring, for 3–4 minutes to ensure that the gelatin has dissolved. Do not boil or the gelatin will not set. Remove from the heat. Use **1 tbsp sunflower oil** to lightly grease **4 x 5fl oz (150ml) ramekins** and pour in the hot mixture evenly.

4 Let them cool to room temperature. Chill for 4–6 hours, or until set. Carefully dip the ramekins in a bowl of hot water, run a knife around the edges, and invert onto individual serving plates. Sprinkle with **matcha powder** and serve immediately. You can store the panna cottas, covered in the fridge, for up to 2 days.

🕐 **15 mins**
plus cooling and chilling 🍴 **MAKES 4**

PANNA COTTA lavender

Lavender has a heady perfume that lends a fabulously floral flavor to this dessert. Make sure you use culinary lavender.

1 Place **3 tbsp whole milk** in a bowl, whisk in **1 heaping tsp (7g) powdered gelatin**, and let rest for 5 minutes. Meanwhile, place ¾ **cup whole milk**, **1⅔ cups whipping cream**, and **1 tbsp dried culinary lavender flowers** in a heavy-bottomed saucepan over low heat. Heat for 5 minutes, until steaming, but not boiling.

2 Place ½ **cup granulated sugar** in a heatproof bowl. Strain the hot milk mixture into the bowl and whisk well until the sugar dissolves. Then whisk in the gelatin mixture until combined. Return the mixture to the pan and heat until the gelatin has dissolved (see Green tea panna cotta, step 3).

3 Remove from the heat. Use **1 tbsp sunflower oil** to lightly grease **4 x 5fl oz (150ml) ramekins** and pour in the hot mixture evenly. Cool to room temperature, then chill for 4–6 hours, until set.

4 Carefully turn out the panna cottas onto individual serving plates (see Green tea panna cotta, step 4). Serve immediately, with sablés, if desired (see p260). You can store the panna cottas, covered in the fridge, for up to 2 days.

Green tea

Lavender

Orange flower
and pomegranate

Yogurt and
pistachio

🕐 **15 mins**
plus cooling and chilling　　🍴 **MAKES 4**

PANNA COTTA
orange flower
and pomegranate

Orange flower water has a strong scent, so use it sparingly. A sprinkle of fresh pomegranate seeds enhances the Middle Eastern flavor.

1 Whisk **3 tbsp whole milk** and **1 heaping tsp (7g) powdered gelatin** in a bowl and let rest for 5 minutes. Meanwhile, place **¾ cup whole milk**, **1⅔ cups whipping cream**, **1½ tbsp orange flower water**, and **1 tsp finely grated orange zest** in a heavy-bottomed saucepan over low heat. Heat for 5 minutes, until steaming, but not boiling.

2 Place **½ cup granulated sugar** in a heatproof bowl. Strain the hot milk mixture into the bowl and whisk well until the sugar dissolves. Then whisk in the gelatin mixture until combined. Return the mixture to the pan and heat until the gelatin has dissolved (see Green tea panna cotta, step 3).

3 Remove from the heat. Use **1 tbsp sunflower oil** to lightly grease **4 x 5fl oz (150ml) ramekins** and pour in the hot mixture evenly. Cool to room temperature, then chill for 4–6 hours, until set.

4 Carefully turn out the panna cottas onto individual serving plates (see Green tea panna cotta, step 4). Serve sprinkled with the **seeds from 1 pomegranate.** You can store the panna cottas, covered in the fridge, for up to 2 days.

🕐 **15 mins**
plus cooling and chilling　　🍴 **MAKES 4**

PANNA COTTA yogurt
and pistachio

Almost like a fancy version of Greek yogurt and honey, this recipe is ideal to serve as a finale to a Mediterranean-inspired meal.

1 Whisk **¼ cup orange juice** and **1 heaping tsp (7g) powdered gelatin** in a bowl and let rest for 5 minutes. Place **1⅔ cups whipping cream** and **finely grated zest of 1 orange** in a heavy-bottomed saucepan over low heat. Heat for 5 minutes, until steaming, but not boiling.

2 Place **½ cup granulated sugar** in a heatproof bowl. Strain the cream milk mixture into the bowl and whisk until the sugar dissolves. Whisk in the gelatin mixture until combined. Return the mixture to the pan and heat until the gelatin has dissolved (see Green tea panna cotta, step 3).

3 Remove from the heat and stir in **9oz (250g) full-fat Greek yogurt**. Use **1 tbsp sunflower oil** to lightly grease **4 x 5fl oz (150ml) ramekins**, and pour in the hot mixture evenly. Cool completely, then chill for 3–4 hours, until set.

4 Carefully turn out the panna cottas onto individual serving plates (see Green tea panna cotta, step 4). Serve with a **drizzle of honey** and **chopped unsalted and skinned pistachios** sprinkled over the top. You can store the panna cottas, covered in the fridge, for up to 2 days.

🕐 **10 mins**
plus cooling and chilling

🍴 **MAKES 4**

POSSET lemon

A posset is a classic English dessert that dates back hundreds of years. It is egg free—lemon juice is used effectively to curdle and set hot cream and sugar. Serve alongside delicate, freshly baked sablés (see pp260–61).

INGREDIENTS

½ cup lemon juice

1¾ cups heavy cream

finely grated zest of
1 lemon, plus extra
to decorate

½ cup granulated sugar

sablés, to serve (optional)

SPECIAL EQUIPMENT

4 x 5fl oz (150ml) glasses

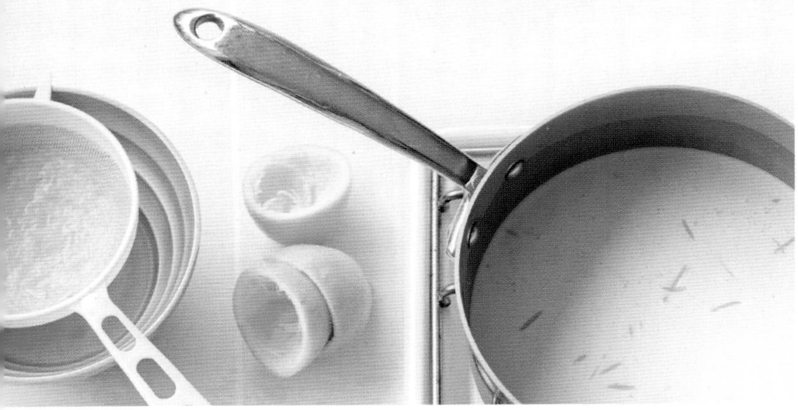

1 Strain the lemon juice into a heatproof bowl and set aside. Heat the cream, lemon zest, and sugar in a large heavy-bottomed saucepan over medium heat until just beginning to boil.

2 Reduce the heat to a low simmer and cook the mixture for 5 minutes, stirring occasionally, until slightly thickened.

3 Remove from the heat. Pour the mixture over the lemon juice, whisking constantly to combine. Let cool for 5 minutes.

4 Transfer the mixture to the glasses and chill for 6 hours, or overnight. Decorate with lemon zest and serve with sablés, if desired. You can store the possets, covered in the fridge, for up to 3 days.

POSSET blood orange

🕐 **1 hr 20 mins**
plus drying and chilling   🍴 **MAKES 4**

Blood orange juice gives this posset a bright color. Serve with candied citrus—for super-thin slices, freeze the fruit for 30 minutes and cut with a sharp knife.

INGREDIENTS
½ cup blood orange juice
3 tbsp lemon juice
1¾ cups heavy cream
finely grated zest of
 1 orange
½ cup granulated sugar
1 sprig of rosemary

For the candied citrus
1¼ cups granulated sugar
1 large, firm orange,
 thinly sliced
1 firm seedless lemon,
 thinly sliced
1 firm seedless lime,
 thinly sliced

SPECIAL EQUIPMENT
4 x 5fl oz (150ml) shallow
 bowls or glasses

PLAN AHEAD
You can prepare and store the candied fruit, in an open container to keep dry, up to 2 days ahead.

1 For the candied citrus, boil the sugar and 2 cups water in a large saucepan, stirring occasionally, until the sugar dissolves. Spread the citrus slices evenly in the pan and cover them with a sheet of parchment paper. Reduce the heat to a low simmer.

2 Cook for 1 hour, until the white parts of the slices are translucent. Carefully remove them from the pan and pat dry on a thick sheet of paper towels. Spread the slices on a wire rack and leave in a warm place for 1–2 days, turning them occasionally, until completely dry.

3 Strain both the juices into a heatproof bowl. Place the cream, orange zest, sugar, and rosemary in a heavy-bottomed saucepan and heat until just beginning to boil. Reduce the heat to a low simmer.

4 Cook the cream mixture for 5 minutes, stirring occasionally, until it thickens slightly. Remove from the heat and whisk into the juices in the bowl until well combined. Cool for 5 minutes, then discard the rosemary.

5 Transfer the mixture to the shallow bowls and chill for up to 6 hours, or overnight until set. Serve with the candied citrus slices. You can store the possets, covered in the fridge, for up to 3 days.

🕐 **30 mins**
plus cooling and chilling   🍴 **MAKES 4**

POSSET rhubarb and ginger

The sweet creaminess of this posset is offset by the pleasingly astringent rhubarb and a touch of warm spicy ginger.

INGREDIENTS
9oz (250g) rhubarb,
 washed, trimmed, and
 cut into 1in (3cm) pieces
1in (3cm) piece of fresh
 ginger, finely sliced
⅔ cup granulated sugar
1oz (30g) preserved ginger,
 finely chopped
juice of 2 lemons
juice of 1 large orange
1¾ cups heavy cream

finely grated zest of
 1 orange
1 tsp ground ginger

SPECIAL EQUIPMENT
4 x 5fl oz (150ml) shallow
 bowls or glasses

PLAN AHEAD
You can store the cooked rhubarb, covered in the fridge, up to 3 days ahead. Strain before use.

1 Place the rhubarb, sliced ginger, and ¼ cup of the sugar in a lidded heavy-bottomed saucepan. Add ¼ cup of water, cover, and bring to a boil. Reduce the heat to a low simmer and cook for another 5-7 minutes, until the rhubarb has softened and breaks down when stirred.

2 Remove the mixture from the heat, discard the ginger, and let cool completely. Strain to remove any excess liquid and stir in the preserved ginger. Chill the mixture for 2 hours, or until needed.

3 Strain both the juices into a heatproof bowl. Heat the cream, orange zest, ground ginger, and remaining sugar in a heavy-bottomed saucepan. Bring almost to a boil, then reduce the heat and cook for 5 minutes, stirring occasionally, until it thickens slightly.

4 Remove from the heat and whisk it into the juices in the bowl until well combined. Let cool. Drain any excess liquid from the rhubarb mixture and divide it evenly between the shallow bowls. Spread it out in a smooth layer and pour the cream mixture over evenly. Chill for up to 6 hours, or overnight, until set. Serve chilled. You can store the possets, covered in the fridge, for up to 3 days.

15 mins
plus cooling and chilling

MAKES 4

POSSET lime and coconut

You can use any acidic citrus juice to set possets. Here, lime juice and coconut combine to give this typically English dessert a tropical twist. Serve topped with toasted coconut, to add more texture.

INGREDIENTS

1¾ cups heavy cream

finely grated zest of 1 lime, plus extra for serving

½ cup granulated sugar

⅓ cup unsweetened, dried coconut flakes

½ cup lime juice

toasted coconut shavings, to decorate

SPECIAL EQUIPMENT

4 x 5fl oz (150ml) shallow cups or bowls

1 Heat the cream, lime zest, sugar, and coconut in a heavy-bottomed saucepan. Bring to a boil, then reduce the heat to a simmer. Cook for 5 minutes, stirring occasionally, until the cream thickens slightly.

2 Remove from the heat and let cool slightly. Use an immersion blender to blend the mixture until smooth. Return to the heat and bring to a simmer. Remove from the heat.

3 Strain the lime juice into a large heatproof bowl. Gradually pour the cream mixture over the top, whisking constantly until it is well combined. Let cool for about 5 minutes.

4 Transfer the mixture to the cups and chill for at least 6 hours, or overnight. Sprinkle with coconut shavings and lime zest before serving. You can store the possets, covered in the fridge, for up to 3 days.

10 mins plus chilling   🍴 **MAKES 4**

FOOL summer fruit

Traditionally, fruit fools contained only stewed fruit and custard. Modern fools feature fresh fruit puree and whipped cream to create a brighter flavor and fluffier texture—they have now become a classic in their own right.

INGREDIENTS

14oz (400g) mixed hulled strawberries, raspberries, and blueberries

2 tbsp granulated sugar, plus 1 tbsp extra

¾ cup heavy cream

⅔ cup full-fat Greek yogurt

½ tsp vanilla extract

SPECIAL EQUIPMENT

4 x 3½fl oz (100ml) glass jars or glasses

1 Slice the strawberries so that they are a similar size as the other fruit. Combine all the fruit with 1 tablespoon of sugar in a large bowl. Pulse two-thirds of the mixture in a food processor to form a puree.

2 Beat the cream in a bowl until fluffy. Add the yogurt, vanilla extract, and remaining sugar. Fold the mixture gently, so that you lose as little air as possible.

3 Gently fold the fruit puree into the cream mixture until no streaks remain.

The mixture should be well combined.

4 Fold the reserved fruit into the mixture. Divide the mixture between the jars, cover, and chill for 2 hours before serving. You can cover and store them in the fridge for up to 1 day.

 **30 mins**
plus cooling and chilling   **MAKES 4**

FOOL gooseberry and elderflower

This fool is perfect for a warm day. Enhance tart gooseberries with the floral flavors of elderflower cordial for a refreshing summertime twist to the fool.

1 Place **12oz (350g) trimmed gooseberries**, ½ **cup granulated sugar**, and **1 tbsp elderflower cordial** in a saucepan with a lid and stir to dissolve the sugar. Cover and cook over low heat for 5 minutes, until the gooseberries have released some water and have started to swell.

2 Uncover and cook for another 5 minutes, then remove from the heat and mash the gooseberries with a potato masher to break them up. Let cool completely before chilling until cold. In a large bowl, beat ¾ **cup heavy cream** to form stiff peaks.

3 Fold the fruit mixture into the cream. Then fold in **1 cup good-quality, store-bought custard** into the fruit and cream mixture. Mix well until light and fluffy and spoon the fool into **4 x 3½fl oz (100ml) glass jars**. Chill for at least 2 hours before serving. You can store them, covered in the fridge, for up to 1 day.

PLAN AHEAD
You can prepare and store the gooseberry puree, covered in the fridge, up to 3 days ahead.

Mango and passion fruit

Gooseberry and elderflower

10 mins
plus chilling MAKES 4

FOOL mango and passion fruit

Ripe mangoes puree easily, making them perfect for a smooth fool. Contrast their sweetness with tangy Greek yogurt and sharp, acidic passion fruit.

1 Finely chop **2 ripe mangoes** to form a pulp and chill until needed. Beat **¾ cup heavy cream** in a bowl to form peaks. Beat in **¼ cup confectioners' sugar** to form soft peaks.

2 Gently fold **1 cup full-fat Greek yogurt** and **½ tsp vanilla extract** into the cream mixture, so that you lose as little air as possible, until combined. Scoop out the pulp from **2 ripe passion fruit** and fold into the cream mixture.

3 Place a spoonful of the cream mixture in **4 x 3½fl oz (100ml) jars**. Top with a layer of the mango pulp. Repeat the process, finishing with a third layer of the cream mixture. Cover the fruit fool and chill for 2 hours.

4 Scoop out the pulp from **1 passion fruit** and use to top the fruit fools evenly. Sprinkle with some **finely chopped unsalted and skinned pistachios** and serve immediately. You can store them, covered in the fridge, for up to 1 day.

Rhubarb and custard

10 mins
plus chilling MAKES 4

FOOL rhubarb and custard

You can mellow sharp, spring rhubarb with a sweet homemade custard and whipped cream. Its pretty pink color is always a delight.

1 Place **14oz (400g) washed and trimmed rhubarb, cut into 1in (3cm) pieces** in a heavy-bottomed saucepan with a lid. Add **¼ cup granulated sugar** and **¼ cup water**, cover, and bring to a boil. Reduce the heat to a low simmer and cook for 3–5 minutes, until the rhubarb has softened. Increase the heat slightly and uncover.

2 Cook the rhubarb for another 2 minutes, stirring frequently, until it has broken down completely and the juices have reduced. Remove from the heat. Cool completely, drain any excess liquid, and chill the rhubarb for 2 hours.

3 Beat **2 egg yolks**, **1 tsp vanilla extract**, **1 tbsp cornstarch**, and **2 tbsp granulated sugar** in a heatproof bowl until smooth. Heat **½ cup whole milk** and **½ cup half-and-half** in a heavy-bottomed saucepan until hot, but not boiling. Pour it into the egg yolk mixture, whisking until the sugar dissolves.

4 Pour the mixture into a clean pan and bring to a boil over medium heat, stirring constantly. Reduce the heat to low. Cook for 3–4 minutes, stirring, until the custard is thick enough to coat the back of a spoon. Pour it into a shallow dish, cover the surface with plastic wrap, and let cool for at least 1 hour.

5 Beat the **½ cup heavy cream** in a bowl to form stiff peaks. Gently fold it into the custard. Then fold in the rhubarb until combined, yet a little streaky. Divide the fruit fool into **4 x 3½fl oz (100ml) jars**. Cover and chill for at least 2 hours before serving. You can store them, covered in the fridge, for up to 1 day.

PLAN AHEAD
You can prepare and store the custard, covered in the fridge, up to 1 day ahead.

 **30 mins**
plus chilling and setting

🍴 **SERVES 4**

JELLY strawberry

Store-bought Jell-O is rubbery and full of artificial colors and flavors. It is so easy to make your own—gently poach ripe, bright fruit to give you the flavor and color you need. Add fresh fruit to the mixture just before it sets for an elegant touch.

INGREDIENTS

2lb (900g) strawberries, hulled and quartered

½ cup granulated sugar, plus extra if needed

½ tsp vanilla extract

⅛ tsp salt

2 tbsp powdered gelatin

SPECIAL EQUIPMENT

4 x 7fl oz (200ml) serving bowls

1

Place the strawberry quarters in a saucepan, reserving 20. Add the sugar and 1 cup cold water. Simmer with a lid on over medium-low heat for 15 minutes.

2

Strain the liquid into a bowl. Do not press down on the fruit, as it will make the gelatin cloudy. Discard the fruit and return the liquid to the pan. Stir in the vanilla extract and salt. Taste and add more sugar, if needed.

3

Place ½ cup of cold water in a bowl. Stir in the gelatin and leave for 3–4 minutes, until it blooms and firms. Add it to the pan and cook the mixture over low heat, until dissolved.

4

Divide the mixture between the serving bowls and top with the reserved fruit. Cover and place in the fridge to chill and set for 2–3 hours, or overnight, before serving. You can store the gelatin, covered in the fridge, for up to 8 days.

🕐 **15 mins**
plus resting, chilling, and setting
🍴 **SERVES 4**

JELLY mango and milk

When milk is used to make jelly, the results are pudding-like and creamy—a rich and smooth dessert.

1 Place **½ cup milk** and **2 tbsp powdered gelatin** in a saucepan. Stir to combine and let rest for 5–10 minutes, until the gelatin blooms and thickens.

2 Add **2 cups mango juice or nectar**, **¼ cup whole milk**, **¼ cup granulated sugar**, and **a pinch of salt** to the pan. Cook over low heat, stirring frequently, until the sugar dissolves and the mixture is smooth. Do not boil the mixture. Remove from the heat.

3 Divide the mixture between **4 x 7fl oz (200ml) jars**. Cover with plastic wrap. Let chill and set in the fridge for 2–3 hours, or overnight, before serving. You can keep the jellies in the fridge for up to 5 days.

🕐 **15 mins**
plus resting, chilling, and setting
🍴 **SERVES 4**

JELLY Prosecco and raspberry

Serve these stylish jellies as a stunning climax to a celebratory meal.

1 Place **¼ cup water**, **¼ cup white grape juice**, and **2 tbsp powdered gelatin** in a saucepan. Stir to combine and let rest for 2–4 minutes, until the gelatin blooms and thickens.

2 Add **¼ cup granulated sugar** and **¾ cup white grape juice** to the pan. Cook over low heat, stirring frequently, until the sugar dissolves and the mixture is smooth. Do not boil the mixture. Remove from the heat and let cool for 3–4 minutes.

3 Gradually add **1¼ cups Prosecco** to the mixture, stirring gently to combine. Then divide the mixture between **4 x 7fl oz (200ml) jars**. Cover with plastic wrap and let chill and set in the fridge for 20–25 minutes.

4 Push **3–4 raspberries** into each jelly jar and chill them for another 2–3 hours, or overnight, until set and firm. Serve chilled. You can keep the jellies in the fridge for up to 7 days.

Prosecco and raspberry

Mango and milk

🕐 **20 mins**
plus steeping, chilling, and setting

🍴 **SERVES 4**

JELLY mulled red wine

These striking dark jellies make great additions to a festive dessert table. The recipe is also a great way to use up leftover mulled wine.

1 Place **1½ cups red wine**, **1 cinnamon stick**, **5 cloves**, and **grated zest of 1 orange** in a saucepan. Heat over medium-low heat until the mixture begins to simmer gently. Remove from the heat and let steep for 15–20 minutes.

2 Place **¾ cup apple juice** and **2 tbsp powdered gelatin** in a bowl. Stir to combine and leave for 3–4 minutes, until the gelatin blooms and thickens. Strain the wine mixture, discarding the spices, and place in a large pan.

3 Add **¼ cup granulated sugar** and the gelatin mixture to the pan. Warm over low heat, stirring until the sugar dissolves. Do not boil the mixture. Remove from the heat.

4 Divide the mixture between **4 x 7fl oz (200ml) jars** and cover with plastic wrap. Let chill and set in the fridge for 2–3 hours, or preferably overnight. Serve with a little **sweetened whipped cream**, if desired. You can keep the jellies in the fridge for up to 5 days.

Mulled red wine

Simple alternatives

Fruits with good color and high water content make the best choices for jellies. These recipes adapt the classic Strawberry jelly (see pp198–99).

Blackberry Ripe blackberries, known for their deeply colored juices, look and taste delicious when used in jelly. Use the same quantity of blackberries as the strawberries (see pp198–99).

Rhubarb Bright rhubarb gives jellies a beautifully pale pink color. Instead of the strawberries, stew 2lb (900g) rhubarb and the granulated sugar in 1 cup water for 15 minutes, Make sure you have about 2¾ cups liquid—discard any excess and continue with the recipe (see p198–99).

Gooseberry and elderflower Instead of stewing the strawberries, place 2lb (900g) gooseberries, the granulated sugar, and 1 cup water in a saucepan with a lid and cook over low heat for 15 minutes. Make sure you have about 2¾ cups liquid—discard any excess and continue with the recipe (see pp198–99).

Blood orange Instead of the strawberries and water, pour 2¾ cups freshly squeezed blood orange juice into a saucepan with a lid with the granulated sugar (see pp198–99). Cover and stew for 15 minutes. Drain 6oz (175g) canned mandarin orange segments, and use to top the jellies in the serving bowls before chilling.

Strawberry and mango For a twist on the flavor and added color, instead of the reserved strawberries, add 1 diced ripe mango to the jelly mixture and let it chill and set as normal (see pp198–99).

Raspberry Fresh raspberries make a delicious change from strawberries, especially when they are in season. Use the same quantity of raspberries as the strawberries (see pp198–99).

🕐 **20 mins**
plus cooling and chilling

🍴 **SERVES 4**

FRUIT SALAD with minted sugar syrup

A fruit salad is a refreshing and light dessert option. Cut the fruit into small pieces, so that it is easy to mix a few flavors in a single spoonful. This minted sugar syrup helps to bring out the flavor of the ingredients.

INGREDIENTS
1 ripe mango, peeled and cut into ½in (1cm) cubes
2 ripe kiwis, peeled and cut into ½in (1cm) cubes
3½oz (100g) ripe papaya, peeled and cut into ½in (1cm) cubes
3½oz (100g) pineapple, cut into ½in (1cm) cubes
seeds from 1 ripe pomegranate

For the syrup
¼ cup granulated sugar
1 tbsp lemon juice
10 large mint leaves

PLAN AHEAD
You can prepare and store the syrup in the fridge up to 1 week ahead.

1
For the syrup, place the ingredients in a small heavy-bottomed saucepan. Pour in ¼ cup cold water.

2
Bring to a boil, stirring frequently until the sugar dissolves. Remove from the heat, pour into a heatproof bowl, and let cool. Chill until needed.

3
Combine all the fruit in a large serving bowl, reserving one-quarter of the pomegranate seeds. Strain the syrup into a pitcher. Discard the mint.

4
Pour the syrup over the fruit and toss well to coat. Scatter with the reserved pomegranate seeds and serve. It is best served within 4 hours of preparation.

FRUIT SALAD
popsicles

Serve these healthy popsicles after a summer's meal. They are incredibly simple to prepare.

INGREDIENTS
9oz (250g) just-ripe mixed fruit, such as pineapple, kiwi, strawberries, blueberries, and mangoes
1¼ cups white grape juice

SPECIAL EQUIPMENT
6 x 3½fl oz (100ml) popsicle molds
6 popsicle sticks

1 Cut the fruit into small pieces, roughly the size of the blueberries. Place them in a large bowl and toss well to combine. Divide the fruit between the popsicle molds, packing them in loosely.

2 Pour the grape juice over the mixed fruit evenly, making sure you fill the molds just below the brim. Insert the sticks into the molds and transfer them to the freezer.

3 Freeze the molds for 4–6 hours, or until frozen solid. Place them briefly under hot running water to loosen and remove the popsicles. Serve immediately. You can store them in the freezer for up to 1 month.

🕐 **20 mins**
plus chilling 🍴 SERVES 4

FRUIT SALAD summer fruit
with balsamic glaze

Pairing strawberries with balsamic vinegar originated in Italy, and it is now popular internationally. Here, sweetened balsamic is used to glaze an array of summer fruits.

INGREDIENTS
2 tbsp good-quality balsamic vinegar
3 tbsp granulated sugar
10oz (300g) strawberries, hulled and quartered
3½oz (100g) blueberries
3½oz (100g) raspberries
2 ripe peaches, peeled, pitted, and diced to the size of the raspberries

1 Combine the vinegar, sugar, and 1 tablespoon water in a small heavy-bottomed saucepan. Bring to a boil, then reduce the heat to a low simmer. Cook, stirring, until the sugar melts.

2 Remove from the heat and cool to room temperature. Place the strawberries and blueberries in a large bowl. Pour in the balsamic glaze and toss gently to coat.

3 Chill the mixture for 30 minutes, then add the raspberries and peaches, toss gently to coat, and chill for another 30 minutes. Toss gently and serve immediately.

⏱ **25 mins** plus cooling   🍴 **SERVES 4**   🌡 Also great **HOT**

FRUIT SALAD *roasted winter fruit*

Whatever the weather outside, bring some heat to your dinner table with these roasted fruits and warming spices. Pecans add a welcome crunch that contrasts with the soft fruit.

INGREDIENTS

2 large apples, peeled, cored, and quartered

2 large just-ripe pears, peeled, cored, and quartered

5½oz (150g) blackberries

juice of 2 large oranges

½ tsp ground cinnamon

2 tbsp light brown sugar

⅓ cup pecans, coarsely chopped

For the yogurt

¾ cup full-fat Greek yogurt

1 tsp vanilla extract

1 tbsp confectioners' sugar

grated zest of 1 orange

1 Preheat the oven to 350°F (180°C). Slice the apple and pear pieces in half lengthwise. Place them in a large bowl and add the blackberries, orange juice, cinnamon, and brown sugar. Toss the fruit well to coat.

2 Transfer the mixture to a baking sheet and spread it out in an even layer. Scatter with the pecans and bake for 20 minutes, until the apples and pears are just soft when pierced with a knife. Remove from the heat and let cool for 5 minutes.

3 Place the yogurt, vanilla extract, confectioners' sugar, and orange zest in a large bowl and fold them well to combine. Serve the fruit salad warm with the yogurt, or let cool to room temperature. You can store the salad, covered in the fridge, for up to 2 days.

Sticks and skewers

You can skewer a variety of fruits. Dip, freeze, or grill them to create fun, healthy, and easy desserts—perfect for a summer's day.

Chocolate fondue Dice 1lb 2oz (500g) fresh fruit, such as mango, kiwi, and banana, into bite-sized pieces. Melt 3½oz (100g) good-quality dark chocolate and ½ cup heavy cream in a small bowl over just-simmering water. Remove from the heat and serve alongside the fruit for dipping.

Frozen bananas Trim the ends off 2 firm bananas and cut them in half. Insert a wooden popsicle stick into each banana half, and freeze them for 4 hours. Melt 7oz (200g) white chocolate (as above). Submerge each frozen banana in the chocolate, and let set. Melt 1¾oz (50g) dark chocolate, and drizzle it over the top. Serve immediately.

Pineapple kebabs Chop ½ large, ripe pineapple into chunks and marinate them in ¼ cup dark rum and ¼ cup brown sugar for 1–2 hours. Skewer the pineapple chunks and grill for 2–3 minutes each side, until caramelized and warm. Serve immediately.

Dipped strawberries Hull 20 firm, bite-sized strawberries. Gently push a lollipop stick into each one. Melt 3½oz (100g) white chocolate (see Chocolate fondue, above), and submerge each strawberry in the melted chocolate. Let set, then serve.

🕐 **1 hr 25 min–1 hr 35 mins**
plus cooling and setting

🍴 **SERVES 8**

SACHERTORTE
chocolate

This rich dark chocolate torte was invented in 19th century Vienna. The simple apricot jam filling and rich ganache topping make it a truly special dessert. Try serving it with a little whipped cream.

INGREDIENTS
18 tbsp butter, softened
1¼ cups granulated sugar
9oz (250g) good-quality
    dark chocolate, melted
½ tsp pure vanilla extract
5 eggs, separated
2 cups all-purpose flour
6–8 tbsp apricot glaze,
    or strained apricot jam
whipped cream, to serve

For the ganache
¾ cup heavy cream

5½ oz (150g) good-quality
    dark chocolate, finely
    chopped

SPECIAL EQUIPMENT
9in (23cm) round cake pan
piping bag fitted with a fine
    plain round nozzle

PLAN AHEAD
You can store the unglazed
cake in an airtight container
in the freezer up to 3
months ahead.

Beat the batter well after each ingredient is added to ensure that it is evenly incorporated.

Preheat the oven to 350°F (180°C). Line the pan with parchment paper. Beat the butter and sugar in a large bowl until light and fluffy. Then beat in the chocolate and vanilla extract. Add the egg yolks, one at a time, and beat well to combine. Fold in the flour until incorporated.

In a separate bowl, whisk the egg whites to form stiff peaks. Spoon a little of the egg white into the chocolate mixture and combine well. Gently fold in the remaining egg whites until evenly incorporated. Pour the batter into the pan and spread it out evenly.

Bake the cake in the oven for 45–50 minutes, until it feels just firm to the touch and an inserted skewer comes out clean. Remove from the heat and place the pan on a wire rack. Let the cake cool completely, then remove it from the pan and slice in half horizontally.

Heat the apricot glaze in a small saucepan until runny. Place one of the cakes on a wire rack, over a baking sheet. Brush with the glaze and top with the other cake, making sure the flat side of the cake faces the top. Brush the glaze over the top and sides of the cake and let set.

5 For the ganache, gently melt the cream and chocolate in a heatproof bowl over a saucepan of simmering water, making sure it does not touch the water. Stir the ganache occasionally, until thick and glossy. Remove from the heat.

6 Let the ganache cool slightly, stirring occasionally, until it reaches a smooth, coating consistency. If it becomes cold and thick, rewarm it over a pan of gently simmering water. Set aside 3 tablespoons of the ganache in a separate bowl.

7 Pour the ganache over the cake, a little at a time, and use a palette knife to spread it evenly over the top and sides of the cake. Let the cake set in a cool place, then use the palette knife to transfer it carefully to a large serving dish.

8 Gently heat the reserved ganache if it has become too thick. Spoon it into the piping bag and carefully pipe the word "Sacher" across the top of the cake. Let set briefly before serving with whipped cream. You can store the cake in an airtight container for up to 3 days.

🕐 **1 hr 10 mins**
plus cooling and chilling 🍴 **SERVES 8**

TORTE chocolate and salted caramel

This luxurious dessert is as eye-catching as it is delicious. For a mouth-watering contrast in flavor, dark chocolate ganache is studded with sea salt flakes. Apply the ganache when it is cool but still spreadable to achieve a smooth finish.

INGREDIENTS

3 eggs
½ cup granulated sugar
½ cup all-purpose flour
¼ cup cocoa powder

For the mousse
¾ cup granulated sugar
6 tbsp unsalted butter, diced
1 cup heavy cream
1 tbsp powdered gelatin

For the ganache
⅓ cup heavy cream
4oz (115g) good-quality dark chocolate, finely chopped
sea salt flakes, to decorate

SPECIAL EQUIPMENT

8in (20cm) springform cake pan

1 Preheat the oven to 375°F (190°C). Line the pan with parchment paper. Whisk the eggs and sugar in a large bowl for 5 minutes, until the mixture is pale, thick, and has tripled in volume.

2 Sift the flour and cocoa powder into the egg mixture and gently fold them in. Pour the batter evenly into the pan. Bake for 20–25 minutes, until the cake is well-risen and an inserted toothpick comes out clean. Cool in the pan for 10 minutes, then transfer the cake to a wire rack to cool completely.

3 For the mousse, melt the sugar in a large, heavy-bottomed saucepan over medium heat until the edges start to melt. Gently swirl the pan to distribute the heat, until it forms a thick, dark caramel. Then reduce the heat and gradually stir in the butter.

4 Increase the heat to medium. Add ½ cup of the cream in a thin stream, stirring constantly until combined. Then increase the heat and bring to a boil for 1 minute, whisking constantly. Transfer the mousse to a heatproof bowl. Let cool, then whisk in the remaining cream until combined.

5 Mix the gelatin with 2 tablespoons of cold water in a cup and let rest for 1 minute. Then whisk in 1 tablespoon of boiling water until the gelatin dissolves. Whisk the mixture into the mousse until well combined.

6 Slice the cake in half lengthwise. Place the bottom half in the pan and spread the mousse evenly. Top with the remaining half of the cake, cut-side up, pressing down slightly. Chill until needed.

7 For the ganache, heat the cream in a small, heavy-bottomed saucepan until hot, but not boiling. Remove from the heat, add the chocolate, and let melt. Then stir the ganache well to combine and chill until cool and thick enough to pour.

8 Pour the ganache over the cake and spread it out evenly. Sprinkle with sea salt and chill for at least 4 hours before serving. You can store it in an airtight container in the fridge for up to 2 days.

TORTE lemon and raspberry

🕐 **1 hr–1 hr 10 mins**
plus cooling and chilling   🍴 **SERVES 8**

This pretty torte is a perfect dish to serve at a summer celebration. The sponge cake is as light as a feather, and the filling is creamy and tangy at the same time.

INGREDIENTS

3 eggs
½ cup granulated sugar
⅔ cup all-purpose flour
grated zest of ½ small lemon

For the filling

1 tbsp powdered gelatin
5 tbsp lemon juice
¾ cup good-quality lemon curd
8oz (225g) mascarpone cheese
4½oz (125g) raspberries, plus extra to decorate
2 tbsp granulated sugar
confectioners' sugar, to decorate

SPECIAL EQUIPMENT

8in (20cm) springform cake pan

PLAN AHEAD

You can store the unfilled sponge cake in an airtight container in the freezer up to 3 months ahead.

1 Preheat the oven to 375°F (190°C). Line the pan with parchment paper. Whisk the eggs and granulated sugar in a bowl for at least 5 minutes (see Chocolate and salted caramel torte, step 1). Sift the flour into the egg mixture and fold it in gently. Then fold in the lemon zest.

2 Pour the mixture evenly into the pan and bake for 20–25 minutes, until done (see Chocolate and salted caramel torte, step 2). Cool in the pan for 10 minutes, then transfer to a wire rack to cool completely.

3 For the filling, whisk the gelatin with 3 tablespoons of lemon juice in a bowl and let stand for 1 minute. Add 2 tablespoons of hot water to the gelatin, whisking until the gelatin dissolves. Beat the lemon curd and mascarpone in a bowl with a handheld mixer.

4 Add the gelatin to the mascarpone mixture and continue to beat until it is thick. Slice the sponge cake in half lengthwise. Place the bottom half in the pan and spread the filling evenly. Place the raspberries evenly over the filling. Top with the remaining half of the cake and press down firmly.

5 Melt the granulated sugar and remaining lemon juice in a saucepan over low heat until just dissolved. Spoon the drizzle evenly over the cake. Cover the cake with plastic wrap and chill for 4 hours, or overnight. Dust with confectioners' sugar, top with raspberries, and serve. You can store it in an airtight container in the fridge for up to 2 days.

Dusts and powders

With a smooth surface and even color, a torte is the perfect canvas for dusting. Make sure you dust no more than an hour before serving.

Citrus powder This powder has a sharp flavor, rather like sherbet. To make it, bake candied citrus slices (see Blood orange posset, p192). Grind 2–3 slices to a fine powder in a clean spice or coffee grinder. Use it to dust citrus-flavored tortes, such as the Lemon and raspberry torte (see left).

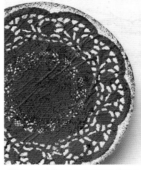

Doily design Place a paper doily or homemade stencil on top of your torte. Sift confectioners' sugar over the surface, then remove the doily carefully—it will leave a delicate and pretty finish. This works well on any unglazed torte.

Matcha powder With a beautiful pale-green color, matcha powder has a very strong green tea flavor, so use a ratio of 1 tsp confectioners' sugar for every ¼ tsp matcha powder. Lay strips of ribbon, spaced apart, on the surface of your unglazed torte. Dust with the powder, remove the ribbons carefully, and serve.

Sugar sprinkles To make sprinkles, preheat the oven to 350°F (180°C). Mix ¼ cup granulated sugar with your choice of food coloring, a drop at a time, until you get the right color. Spread it out on a foil-lined baking sheet and bake for 10 minutes. Let cool, then sprinkle over your torte.

30 mins
plus chilling   **SERVES 8**

CHILLED CHEESECAKE
lime and blueberry

This fruity cheesecake is chilled rather than baked. The filling has a lighter consistency than a baked one, and it is less susceptible to cracking. Make sure you measure the gelatin carefully, because it can affect how the filling sets.

INGREDIENTS

9oz (250g) graham crackers, finely crushed

7 tbsp unsalted butter, melted

For the topping

3½oz (100g) blueberries

1 tbsp granulated sugar

grated zest of ½ lime

For the filling

juice of 2 limes

1 tbsp + 1 tsp powdered gelatin

1¼ cups sour cream

½ cup granulated sugar

1lb 2oz (500g) full-fat cream cheese

grated zest of 1 lime, plus extra to serve

1 tsp vanilla extract

SPECIAL EQUIPMENT

9in (23cm) springform cake pan

1 Line the pan with parchment paper. Mix the cracker crumbs and butter in a bowl until well combined. Spread the mixture in the pan, pressing it down firmly to form a smooth and even crust. Chill until needed.

2 For the topping, gently heat the blueberries, sugar, lime zest, and 1 tablespoon water in a heavy-bottomed saucepan. Stir until the blueberries start to release their juices. Remove from the heat and let cool.

3 For the filling, whisk the lime juice and gelatin in a heavy-bottomed saucepan and leave for 5 minutes. Then heat gently, whisking, until the gelatin dissolves and let cool. Whisk the remaining ingredients in a bowl until combined, then whisk in the gelatin mixture and spread the filling evenly over the graham cracker crust.

4 Spoon over the topping and decorate with the strained juices. Chill for 4–6 hours, or overnight. Remove from the pan and sprinkle with lemon zest to serve. You can store it, covered in the fridge, for up to 2 days.

30 mins
plus chilling

 **SERVES 8–10**

CHILLED CHEESECAKE
triple chocolate

A chocoholic's dream, this cheesecake features a rich white chocolate filling. Top it with milk and dark chocolate swirls that provide added crunch.

INGREDIENTS

9oz (250g) Oreo cookies, filling removed and finely crushed

7 tbsp unsalted butter, melted

10oz (300g) good-quality white chocolate, broken into pieces

1oz (30g) each good-quality dark chocolate and milk chocolate, broken into pieces

8oz (225g) full-fat cream cheese

7oz (200g) mascarpone

¼ cup granulated sugar

1 tsp vanilla extract

½ cup heavy cream, whipped

SPECIAL EQUIPMENT

8½in (22cm) springform cake pan

1 Line the pan with parchment paper. Combine the cookies and butter in a large bowl. Pour the crumbs out into the prepared pan and press them down firmly, using the back of a spoon, to form a thin, even layer. Chill until needed.

2 Melt the white chocolate in a heatproof bowl over a saucepan of simmering water, making sure it does not touch the water. Stir until smooth, remove from the heat, and let cool. Repeat the process for the dark and milk chocolate, using two separate heatproof bowls.

3 Whisk the cream cheese, mascarpone, sugar, and vanilla extract in a large bowl, until well combined and smooth. Whisk in the cooled white chocolate, then fold in the whipped cream. Pour the filling over the cookie crust and spread it out into a smooth layer.

4 Drizzle the melted dark and milk chocolate over the cheesecake and use a skewer to swirl it. Chill the cheesecake for at least 6 hours, or overnight, before serving. You can store the cheesecake, covered, in the fridge for up to 2 days.

 25 mins
plus resting, cooling, and chilling

MAKES 4

MINI CHILLED CHEESECAKES lemon

With a lemon curd topping that produces a dark golden-yellow layer, these mini cheesecakes look very professional.

INGREDIENTS

3 tbsp unsalted butter, melted, plus extra for greasing

4½oz (125g) graham crackers, finely crushed

For the filling

1 heaping tsp (7g) powdered gelatin

¼ cup lemon juice

3½oz (100g) full-fat cream cheese

5½oz (150g) ricotta cheese

¼ cup granulated sugar

grated zest of 1 lemon

For the topping

5½oz (150g) thick-set lemon curd

1 heaping tsp (7g) powdered gelatin

SPECIAL EQUIPMENT

4 x 3in (7.5cm) baking rings

1 Grease the baking rings and set aside. Combine the graham crackers and butter in a large bowl. Pour the crumbs out into the prepared rings and press them down firmly, using the back of a spoon, to form a thin, even layer. Chill until needed.

2 For the filling, sprinkle the gelatin over the lemon juice in a small, heavy-bottomed saucepan. Whisk well and let rest for 5 minutes, then gently heat the mixture, whisking constantly, until the gelatin has just dissolved. Remove from the heat and let cool.

3 Whisk the remaining filling ingredients in a large bowl until well combined and smooth. Whisk in the cooled gelatin mixture until combined. Divide the filling between the graham cracker crusts and smooth out to an even layer. Chill the cakes for 30 minutes.

4 For the topping, whisk 1 tablespoon of water with the lemon curd in a small, heavy-bottomed saucepan. Sprinkle in the gelatin and let rest for 5 minutes. Gently heat the mixture, whisking constantly, until smooth. Remove from the heat and let cool.

5 Pour the topping over the cheesecakes, spreading it out into an even layer. Chill the cheesecakes for at least 4–6 hours, or overnight. To serve, run a knife around the edges of the rings and release the cheesecakes. You can store them, covered, in the fridge for up to 2 days.

CHILLED CHEESECAKES
Alternative curds and coulis

To adapt the classic Lime and blueberry chilled cheesecake (see pp212–13) or the variation recipes (opposite), pair them with these vibrant and full-flavored curds and coulis.

◄ Tangerine curd
Transform the Mini lemon cheesecakes (see opposite) into Mini tangerine cheesecakes. For the topping, use the same quantity of thick-set orange curd instead of the lemon curd, and prepare it as described. You can also replace the lemon juice in the filling with the same quantity of tangerine juice.

▲ Blueberry coulis
Instead of the classic blueberry cheesecake (see pp212–13), you can blend 3½oz (100g) blueberries, 1 tbsp confectioners' sugar, and a little water. Strain, then use to top the cake. Chill. You can also omit the lime juice and zest from the filling and add 2 tsp vanilla extract and 2 tbsp water.

◄ Strawberry coulis
Serve the Triple chocolate cheesecake (see opposite) with a strawberry coulis instead of the melted chocolate. Puree 5½oz (150g) strawberries with 1 tbsp each lemon juice and confectioners' sugar. Strain to remove the seeds and serve with the chilled cheesecake.

◄ Kiwi and lime coulis
Replace the blueberries in the coulis for the Lime and blueberry cheesecake (see pp212–13) with 1 kiwi, diced into ¼in (5mm) cubes. Briefly simmer the juice of 1 lime, 1 tbsp granulated sugar, and 1 tbsp water in a pan until the sugar dissolves. Add the kiwi, use to top the cheesecake, and chill as directed.

Peach coulis ►
Replace the blueberries in the coulis for the Lime and blueberry cheesecake (see pp212–13) with 3½oz (100g) pitted and diced ripe peaches. You can also omit the lime zest from the coulis, and add 1 tsp almond extract to the filling instead of the lime zest and juice.

Mango coulis ▲
Use a mango coulis instead of the Lime and blueberry version (see pp212–13). Puree the flesh of 2 ripe mangoes with juice of 1 lemon and 1 tbsp confectioners' sugar until it is completely smooth. Use to top the cheesecake and chill as directed.

 **1 hr 30 mins**
plus cooling and chilling

SERVES 8

BAKED CHEESECAKE with strawberry sauce

Less delicate than chilled varieties, baked cheesecakes keep for longer in the fridge. The lemon juice and zest gives this velvet-like filling a brightness of flavor. Once you master this classic, you could change the flavorings or sauce, if you prefer.

INGREDIENTS

5 tbsp unsalted butter, at room temperature, plus extra for greasing

9 sheets graham crackers, crushed into fine crumbs (about 1¼ cups crushed)

For the filling

1½lb (675g) cream cheese, at room temperature

⅔ cup sour cream, at room temperature

⅔ cup granulated sugar

1 tsp vanilla extract

pinch of fine sea salt

grated zest of ½ lemon

1 tbsp lemon juice

2 eggs

For the sauce

14oz (400g) strawberries, hulled and thinly sliced lengthwise

1 tbsp lemon juice

1 tbsp granulated sugar

¼ cup strawberry jam, strained to remove seeds

SPECIAL EQUIPMENT

8in (20cm) springform cake pan

1

Preheat the oven to 350ºF (180ºC). Grease and line the cake pan with parchmenet paper. Melt the butter in a small saucepan over low heat, then combine it with the graham cracker crumbs in a large bowl.

2

Transfer the mixture to the prepared pan. Using the back of a spoon, gently press it into the bottom of the pan to form a thin, even layer. Bake for about 10 minutes, then remove and set aside to cool.

3

For the filling, whisk the cream cheese, sour cream, sugar, vanilla extract, salt, and lemon zest and juice until combined. Add the eggs, one at a time, and mix well to combine.

4

Cover the sides and bottom of the cake pan with thick foil and place it in a large roasting pan. Pour the filling evenly over the graham cracker crust. Pour enough boiling water into the roasting pan to come halfway up the sides of the cake pan.

5

Bake for 1 hour, until the cheesecake is set and shrinking away from the sides. Turn off the heat and let the cheesecake cool in the oven for 30 minutes, so that it is less likely to crack as it cools. Let it cool completely on a wire rack before chilling for at least 4 hours.

6

For the sauce, combine the strawberries, lemon juice, and sugar in a bowl and let macerate for about 30 minutes. Gently heat the jam in a small heavy-bottomed saucepan. Combine it with the strawberry mixture and let cool. Remove the cheesecake from the pan and serve it with the sauce. You can keep the cheesecake, well wrapped, in the fridge for up to 3 days.

🕐 **1 hr 50 mins**
  plus cooling and chilling   🍴 **SERVES 8**

BAKED CHEESECAKE *chocolate orange*

Dark chocolate cookies, such as chocolate wafers or Oreos, can replace graham crackers to create a rich cheesecake crust. The cream cheese and mascarpone filling is perfectly smooth with a distinct orange flavor.

INGREDIENTS

7 tbsp unsalted butter, melted and cooled, plus extra for greasing

1 x 14.3oz package oreos (about 32 cookies), cream removed and crushed

For the filling

1lb (450g) cream cheese, at room temperature

8oz (225g) mascarpone cheese, at room temperature

½ cup granulated sugar

½ tsp orange extract

¼ cup freshly squeezed orange juice

grated zest of ½ large orange

2 eggs

For the orange curd

½ cup granulated sugar

1 tbsp cornstarch

3 egg yolks

¼ cup freshly squeezed orange juice

grated zest of ½ large orange, plus extra for decorating

2 tbsp unsalted butter, at room temperature, diced

SPECIAL EQUIPMENT

8in (20cm) spring-form cake pan

1 Preheat the oven to 350°F (180°C). Grease and line the cake pan with parchment paper. Combine the cookie crumbs and butter in a bowl. Spread the mixture in the pan in an even layer. Place on a baking sheet and bake for 10 minutes. Remove and set aside to cool.

2 For the filling, pulse all the ingredients, except the eggs, in a food processor until smooth. Transfer to a bowl and add the eggs, one at a time, whisking well after each addition. Cover the sides and bottom of the cake pan with foil.

3 Place the cake pan in a large roasting pan. Pour the filling over the cookie crust in an even layer. Pour just enough boiling water into the roasting pan, so it comes halfway up the sides of the cake pan.

4 Bake the cheesecake for 1 hour, until the filling is just set and shrinking away from the sides. Turn off the heat and let it cool in the oven for 30 minutes. Remove the cheesecake from the oven and let it cool completely.

5 For the orange curd, combine the sugar and cornstarch in a heavy-bottomed saucepan. Beat in the egg yolks until combined, then add the orange juice and zest and mix well.

6 Heat the mixture for 10–15 minutes, stirring until thickened. Do not allow it to boil. Remove from the heat and gradually beat in the butter, until the orange curd is thick and glossy. Let cool completely.

7 Spread the orange curd over the top of the cheesecake, avoiding the sides. Cover the cake with plastic wrap and chill for 4 hours, before removing from the pan to serve. You can keep it, wrapped, in the fridge for up to 3 days.

CROSTATA di ricotta

⏱ **1 hr** plus chilling and cooling   🍴 **SERVES 8**

This well-loved Italian dessert combines ricotta and candied peel with a sweet and lemony pie crust.

INGREDIENTS

12 tbsp unsalted butter, softened, plus extra for greasing
1½ cups all-purpose flour, sifted, plus extra for dusting
grated zest of 1 lemon
¼ cup granulated sugar
4 egg yolks
pinch of salt
1 egg, beaten, to glaze

For the filling
2¾lb (1.25kg) ricotta cheese
½ cup granulated sugar

1 tbsp all-purpose flour
pinch of salt
grated zest of 1 orange
2 tbsp chopped candied orange peel
1 tsp vanilla extract
¼ cup raisins
⅓ cup sliced almonds
4 egg yolks

SPECIAL EQUIPMENT
9–10in (23–25cm) round springform cake pan

1 Grease the pan and set aside. Place the flour in a bowl. Make a well in the center and add the butter, lemon zest, sugar, egg yolks, and salt. Mix well. Gradually work in the flour to form a dough. Knead it on a floured surface for 2 minutes until smooth. Shape it into a ball, wrap in plastic wrap, and chill for 30 minutes.

2 On a floured surface, roll out three-quarters of the pastry to a 14–15in (35–37cm) round. Use it to line the pan, pressing it down well. Trim the excess. Chill the pie crust and remaining pastry for 15 minutes.

3 For the filling, beat the ricotta, sugar, flour, and salt in a bowl. Then beat in the remaining ingredients, until combined. Spoon the filling into the pie crust evenly and tap the pan lightly to remove air pockets. Brush the edges of the pie with the egg.

4 Preheat the oven to 350°F (180°C). On a floured surface, roll out the remaining pastry to a 10in (25cm) round. Cut it into ½in (1cm) wide strips and use to create a lattice top for the pie. Brush with the remaining egg and chill for 15–30 minutes until firm.

5 Place the cheesecake on a baking sheet and bake on the bottom rack of the oven for 1 hour, until golden. Let cool slightly, then remove from the pan. Serve cooled to room temperature. Serve on the same day.

⏱ **50–55 mins** plus cooling   🍴 **MAKES 4**

BAKED CHEESECAKES tiramisu

Tiramisu flavors work perfectly with a creamy cheesecake filling. Serve these little treats alongside a glass of Amaretto or strong coffee.

INGREDIENTS
5 sheets graham crackers (½ cup crushed)
1¾oz (50g) Amaretti cookies, finely crushed
4 tbsp unsalted butter, melted and cooled
10oz (300g) ricotta cheese
7oz (200g) full-fat cream cheese
½ cup granulated sugar
2 eggs
1 tsp vanilla extract
1 tbsp Amaretto liqueur
1 tsp instant espresso powder
1 tbsp coffee liqueur
cocoa powder, for dusting

SPECIAL EQUIPMENT
4 x 4in (10cm) round loose-bottomed cake pans

1 Preheat the oven to 350°F (180°C). Line the cake pans with parchment paper. Combine the graham crackers, cookies, and butter in a bowl. Distribute the mixture equally between the pans, pressing it into thin layers. Bake in the oven for 5 minutes. Remove and set aside to cool.

2 Pulse the ricotta, cream cheese, sugar, eggs, vanilla extract, and Amaretto in a food processor until smooth. Dissolve the espresso powder in 1 tablespoon of boiling water. Stir in the coffee liqueur, cool slightly, then combine with 3 tablespoons of the cheese mixture.

3 Place the pans on a baking sheet. Divide the filling between them and drizzle with the coffee mixture. Bake in the oven for 25–30 minutes, until the filling is just set and shrinking away from the sides.

4 Turn off the heat and leave them in the oven to cool for 30 minutes. Then remove and cool completely, before chilling for 4 hours or overnight. Remove the cakes from the pans and serve dusted with cocoa powder. You can keep them, wrapped, in the fridge for up to 3 days.

🕐 **1 hr 10 mins**
plus cooling

🍴 **SERVES 8–10**

CAKE vanilla and strawberry

In this recipe, the egg yolks and whites are whisked separately to give you the perfect sponge cake: light, airy, and well-risen. The combination of whipped cream and strawberries makes this a classic summer dessert.

INGREDIENTS

3 tbsp unsalted butter, melted, plus extra, for greasing
1 cup all-purpose flour
¾ tsp baking powder
¼ tsp salt
2 tbsp cornstarch
6 large eggs, separated
1 tsp cream of tartar
¾ cup granulated sugar
1½ tsp vanilla extract
3 tbsp whole milk, at room temperature

For the filling
⅔ cup heavy cream

1 tsp confectioners' sugar
7oz (200g) strawberries, hulled and halved

For the frosting
1½ cups whipping cream
3 tbsp confectioners' sugar
½ tsp vanilla extract

SPECIAL EQUIPMENT
2 x 8in (20cm) cake pans

PLAN AHEAD
You can bake and store the unfilled sponge cakes in an airtight container for up to 2–3 days ahead.

1

Preheat the oven to 350°F (180°C). Lightly grease and line the cake pans with parchment paper. Sift the flour, baking powder, salt, and cornstarch into a small bowl and set aside.

2

Whisk the egg whites in a large bowl until light and foamy. Whisk in the cream of tartar until soft peaks form, then add half of the sugar. Beat the mixture well to form stiff peaks.

Gradually fold in the flour mixture until incorporated.

3

In a separate bowl, beat the egg yolks and remaining sugar for 4–5 minutes until thick and pale yellow. Add the vanilla extract, butter, and milk, and mix well. Fold in the flour mixture, until combined.

Add the egg white mixture a little at a time.

4

Fold in the egg white mixture until combined. Divide the batter evenly between the pans. Bake for 20–25 minutes, until the cakes are golden and an inserted toothpick comes out clean. Cool in the pan for 10 minutes, then let cool completely on a wire rack.

For the filling, beat the heavy cream and confectioners' sugar in a bowl to form stiff peaks. Coarsely chop half the strawberries and fold them into the cream and sugar mixture.

5

6

Spread the filling on one of the cakes and top with the other. For the frosting, whisk the whipping cream, confectioners' sugar, and vanilla extract to form stiff peaks and spread over the cake. Top with the remaining strawberries and serve. You can store the cake in the fridge for 1–2 days.

⏱ **1 hr 30 mins** plus chilling 🍴 **SERVES 12**

TRES LECHES with cherries

The name for this cake translates from Spanish into "three-milk cake." It is popular throughout South America. To achieve the delicately moist texture and sweet flavor, soak the cake in a sauce made from cream, condensed milk, and evaporated milk.

INGREDIENTS

unsalted butter, for greasing
1¼ cups all-purpose flour, plus extra for dusting
6 large eggs, separated
¼ tsp cream of tartar
1¼ cups granulated sugar
¼ cup whole milk
1½ tsp vanilla extract
1¾ tsp baking powder
¼ tsp salt
12 Maraschino cherries

For the tres leches

1 cup heavy cream
¾ cup condensed milk
½ cup evaporated milk
1 tsp vanilla extract

For the frosting

1½ cups heavy cream
3 tbsp confectioners' sugar
½ tsp pure vanilla extract

SPECIAL EQUIPMENT

9 x 13in (23 x 33cm) cake pan

1 Preheat the oven to 350°F (180°C). Grease and flour the cake pan. Beat the egg whites in a large bowl until fluffy. Add the cream of tartar and beat to form soft peaks. Gradually add ¼ cup of the granulated sugar and beat to form stiff peaks. Set aside.

2 Beat the egg yolks and remaining sugar in a large bowl until thick and pale yellow in color. Add the milk and vanilla extract and beat until smooth. Place the flour, baking powder, and salt in a separate bowl and mix well to combine.

3 Gradually add the dry ingredients to the egg yolk mixture and beat until smooth, then fold in the egg white mixture, a little at a time, until combined. Pour the batter into the pan and smooth over the top.

4 Bake for 30–35 minutes. Remove and cool the cake in the pan for 5 minutes before letting cool completely on a wire rack. For the tres leches, combine all the ingredients in a bowl.

5 Place the cooled cake on a serving dish and pierce it in several places with a skewer, making sure it goes all the way through. Pour the tres leches over the top and sides of the cake. Cover with plastic wrap and chill for 3 hours, until the liquid has been absorbed.

6 For the frosting, beat all the ingredients to form stiff peaks and spread over the cake. Slice the cake into 12 even-sized pieces, top each with a Maraschino cherry, and serve chilled. You can store the cake in an airtight container in the fridge for 4 days.

⏱ **55 mins** plus cooling   🍴 **SERVES 8–10**

CAKE Victoria

Give the traditional British cake a fresh spin with this cream-raspberry filling—lovely to serve in the summer months.

INGREDIENTS

16 tbsp unsalted butter, plus extra for greasing

1 cup granulated sugar

4 large eggs, at room temperature

1½ tsp pure vanilla extract

¼ cup whole milk

1½ cups self-rising flour

½ tsp salt

6oz (175g) raspberries, halved

For the filling

8oz (225g) mascarpone cheese, at room temperature

¾ cup heavy cream

¼ cup confectioners' sugar, plus extra for dusting

½ tsp vanilla extract

SPECIAL EQUIPMENT

2 x 9in (23cm) round cake pans

PLAN AHEAD

You can prepare and store the unfilled sponge cakes in an airtight container for 2–3 days ahead.

1 Preheat the oven to 350°F (180°C). Grease and line the cake pans with parchment paper. Place the butter and granulated sugar in a large bowl and beat well with a handheld mixer until light and fluffy. Add the eggs, one at a time, beating well after each addition.

2 Add the vanilla extract and milk and beat until evenly combined. Sift the flour and salt into a bowl and add to the wet mixture, a little at a time, mixing until just combined. Do not overmix.

3 Divide the batter evenly between the cake pans and smooth over the tops with a spatula. Bake for 20–25 minutes, until a skewer inserted into the center of the cakes comes out clean. Let the cakes cool in the pans for 10 minutes, then remove and place on a wire rack to cool completely.

4 For the filling, place all the ingredients in a large bowl and beat well to form stiff peaks. Spread the filling on one of the cakes and top with a layer of the raspberries. Cover it with the second cake, dust with confectioners' sugar, and serve. You can store the cake in the fridge for 1–2 days.

⏱ **1 hr** plus cooling   🍴 **SERVES 8**

CAKE angel food

The name "angel food cake" comes from the airy texture of the cake—so light, it is suitable for angels. There is no fat in the recipe, so it does not keep. Serve on the same day.

INGREDIENTS

¾ cup all-purpose flour

2 tbsp cornstarch

¼ tsp salt

1½ cups granulated sugar

11 egg whites, at room temperature

1½ tsp cream of tartar

1½ tsp vanilla extract

1 tsp lemon juice

6oz (175g) blueberries, to serve

confectioners' sugar, for dusting

SPECIAL EQUIPMENT

10in (25cm) tube cake pan

1 Preheat the oven to 350°F (180°C). Sift the flour, cornstarch, salt, and half the granulated sugar into a bowl. Set aside. Place the egg whites in a separate bowl and beat with a handheld mixer until foamy. Add the cream of tartar and beat again to form soft peaks.

2 Gradually add the remaining sugar and beat until the mixture is combined and forms soft peaks. Fold in the vanilla extract and lemon juice with a spatula until just combined. Gradually sift the flour mixture over and fold it in gently until just combined. Do not overmix.

3 Pour the batter into the cake pan and smooth over the top. Tap the pan on a work surface a few times to release any air bubbles. Bake the cake for 30–35 minutes, until golden and firm to the touch. Invert the pan over a serving plate and let cool for 2–3 hours.

4 Run a knife around the cake edge to help to remove it from the pan. Place the cake, bottom-side up, on a large plate. Scatter with the blueberries and dust with confectioners' sugar. Serve on the same day.

🕐 **45 mins**
plus cooling and macerating

🍴 **MAKES 4**

SHORTCAKES strawberry

This recipe is a classic, and is beloved throughout the country. The texture resembles an English scone. These shortcakes are large—in true American style—but they are so delicious that they will quickly disappear.

INGREDIENTS
5 tbsp unsalted butter, chilled and diced, plus extra for greasing
2 cups all-purpose flour, plus extra for dusting
2 tsp baking powder
¼ cup granulated sugar
pinch of salt
1 egg, beaten
⅔ cup buttermilk
confectioners' sugar, to dust

For the filling
5½oz (150g) strawberries, hulled and thinly sliced
1 tbsp granulated sugar
⅔ cup heavy cream
1 tsp vanilla extract

SPECIAL EQUIPMENT
3in (7.5cm) round pastry cutter

1 Preheat the oven to 400°F (200°C). Grease and line a baking sheet with parchment paper. Combine the flour, baking powder, granulated sugar, and salt in a large bowl. Rub in the butter until the mixture resembles coarse bread crumbs.

2 Whisk the beaten egg and buttermilk in a separate bowl and pour into the dry mixture. Using your fingertips, bring the mixture together to form a soft, loose dough.

3 On a floured surface, roll out the dough to a large circle, ¾in (2cm) thick. Cut out 4 rounds with the pastry cutter and place on the baking sheet. Bake on the top rack of the oven for 15 minutes, until risen. Remove and place on a wire rack to cool completely.

4 For the filling, combine the strawberries and granulated sugar in a bowl and let macerate for 1 hour. Whisk the cream and vanilla extract in a bowl to form stiff peaks. Split the shortcakes and sandwich with the cream and the strawberries. Dust with confectioners' sugar and serve.

⏱ **1 hr** plus cooling   🍴 **SERVES 4–6**

SHORTCAKE roasted peach

Play around with proportions and serve an oversized peach shortcake. Shortcakes—like scones—are incredibly easy to make, but should be served right away, or within a few hours of cooling.

INGREDIENTS

2 peaches, pitted and cut into thin wedges

2 tbsp unsalted butter, chilled and diced

¼ cup light brown sugar

For the shortcake

2 cups all-purpose flour, plus extra for dusting

2 tsp baking powder

¼ cup granulated sugar

pinch of salt

5 tbsp unsalted butter, chilled and diced

1 egg, beaten

⅔ cup buttermilk

For the filling

⅔ cup heavy cream

1 tsp vanilla extract

confectioners' sugar, to serve

PLAN AHEAD

You can store the roasted peaches in an airtight container in the fridge up to 3 days ahead. Bring to room temperature before serving.

1 Preheat the oven to 400°F (200°C). Arrange the peaches in an ovenproof dish large enough to hold them in a single layer. Dot with the butter and sprinkle with the brown sugar.

2 Bake the peaches on the top rack of the oven for 10–15 minutes, until just soft when pierced with a knife. Remove from the oven and let cool.

3 For the shortcake, combine the flour, baking powder, granulated sugar, and salt in a large bowl. Rub in the butter until the mixture resembles bread crumbs.

4 Whisk the egg and buttermilk in a separate bowl and add to the dry mixture. Use your fingertips to bring them together to form a soft, loose dough.

5 Gently roll out the dough on a lightly floured work surface to a 6in (15cm) circle, about ¾in (2cm) thick. Place on a baking sheet.

6 Bake on the top rack of the oven for 20–25 minutes, until well-risen and lightly colored. Remove from the heat. Cool completely on a wire rack, then use a knife to split the shortcake in half.

7 For the filling, whisk the cream and vanilla extract in a bowl to form soft peaks. Sandwich the shortcake with the filling and peaches and pour over a little cooking liquid. Serve dusted with confectioners' sugar.

⏱ **45 mins**
plus cooling and chilling   🍴 **MAKES 6**

SHORTCAKE SANDWICHES
ice cream

For a playful take on the classic, speckle your shortcakes with fresh strawberries and sandwich them with ice cream.

INGREDIENTS
8 tbsp unsalted
  butter, softened

⅔ cup granulated sugar,
  plus extra for dusting

½ tsp vanilla extract

1 egg yolk

1⅔ cups all-purpose flour

½ tsp baking powder

3½oz (100g) strawberries,
  hulled and diced

6oz (175g) good-quality
  vanilla ice cream

PLAN AHEAD
You can store the unfilled shortcakes in an airtight container up to 1 day ahead.

1 Preheat oven to 350°F (180°C). Line two baking sheets with parchment paper and set aside. Use a handheld mixer to beat the butter and sugar in a large bowl until light and fluffy.

2 Beat in the vanilla extract and egg yolk. Sift the flour and baking powder into the mixture and mix to combine. Add the strawberries and mix well. Shape the dough into 12 equal-sized balls, rolling them briefly between your hands.

3 Flatten the balls slightly and place on the baking sheets. Sprinkle with the sugar. Bake for 15–18 minutes, until the shortcakes are risen and lightly golden at the edges. Remove and let cool on the sheet for 10 minutes, then place on a wire rack to cool completely.

4 To assemble the sandwiches, let the ice cream soften at room temperature for a few minutes, then sandwich two of the shortcakes with a spoonful of the softened ice cream. Place in the freezer for 5–10 minutes before serving.

⏱ **20 mins**
plus chilling and cooling   🍴 **MAKES 4**

SHORTCAKES stacked
strawberry

This elegant dessert looks wonderful served with a little fruit coulis (see p215). Resting the stacks in the fridge helps to soften the layers of buttery treats.

INGREDIENTS
6 tbsp unsalted butter,
  softened

⅔ cup granulated sugar

1 egg yolk

½ tsp vanilla extract

1¼ cups all-purpose flour,
  plus extra for dusting

For the filling
1 cup heavy cream

1 tbsp confectioners' sugar,
  plus extra for dusting

9oz (250g) strawberries,
  hulled and thinly sliced

SPECIAL EQUIPMENT
3¼in (8cm) cookie cutter
4 x 3¼in (8cm) pastry rings

PLAN AHEAD
You can store the unfilled shortcakes in an airtight container up to 3 days ahead.

1 Beat the butter and granulated sugar in a bowl until light and fluffy. Mix in the egg yolk and vanilla extract. Add the flour, and add 2 tablespoons cold water, and bring together to form a soft, loose dough. Cover in plastic wrap and chill for 30 minutes.

2 Preheat the oven to 350°F (180°C) and line three baking sheets with parchment paper. On a floured surface, roll out the dough thinly. Use the cookie cutter to cut out 16 circles and place them on a baking sheet. Bake for 10 minutes, until the edges begin to color.

3 Remove from the heat and cool completely on a wire rack, then place one shortcake in each pastry ring on a lined baking sheet. For the filling, whisk the cream and confectioners' sugar in a bowl to form stiff peaks.

4 Spread a spoonful of the cream over each shortcake to make a ¼in (5mm) thick layer. Cover with a layer of the strawberries. Repeat to add two more layers each of the shortcakes, cream, and strawberries. Add another layer of cream and top with a shortcake.

5 Cover with plastic wrap and chill for at least 6 hours, or overnight. Carefully remove the pastry rings and dust the shortcake stacks with confectioners' sugar to serve. You can store the dessert, covered in plastic wrap, in the fridge for up to 1 day.

1 hr
plus cooling and chilling

SERVES 8–10

CAKE devil's food

This rich cake is dark and moist, with the espresso powder adding an extra layer of flavor to the chocolate cake. You can serve devil's food cake with a bowl of whipped cream, sweetened with a little confectioners' sugar and a drop of vanilla extract.

INGREDIENTS

1 cup vegetable or grapeseed oil, plus extra for greasing

1 tsp instant espresso powder

¾ cup natural cocoa powder

2 large eggs, plus 1 yolk, lightly beaten

½ cup granulated sugar

1 cup dark brown sugar

1 tsp vanilla extract

2 cups all-purpose flour

1 tsp salt

1½ tsp baking soda

½ tsp baking powder

1 cup sour cream, at room temperature

For the frosting

1¾ cups heavy cream

¼ tsp salt

12oz (350g) good-quality dark chocolate, finely chopped

3 tbsp unsalted butter, softened

1 tsp vanilla extract

SPECIAL EQUIPMENT

2 x 8in (20cm) round cake pans

PLAN AHEAD

You can wrap the unfrosted cake in plastic wrap and store it for up to 2 days ahead.

1

Preheat the oven to 350°F (180°C). Lightly grease and line the cake pans with parchment paper. Place the espresso powder and cocoa powder in a small bowl. Pour in 1 cup hot water, mix well, and let cool.

2

In a large bowl, whisk the oil, eggs, egg yolk, and both types of sugar until smooth. Add the vanilla extract and whisk well to combine. In a separate bowl, sift together the flour, salt, baking soda, and baking powder. Mix well.

3

Gradually add the dry ingredients and sour cream to the wet mixture, alternately, and combine well. Add the espresso mixture and stir lightly until incorporated.

Keep stirring until the mixture is smooth and without streaks.

4

Divide the batter between the cake pans. Bake the cakes for 35–40 minutes, until an inserted skewer comes out clean. Remove and cool the cakes in the pans for 15 minutes, then transfer to a wire rack to cool completely.

5

Whisk the frosting until smooth before chilling.

For the frosting, bring the heavy cream to a simmer over medium-low heat. Place it in a large bowl. Whisk in the salt and chocolate, then stir in the butter and vanilla extract. Cover and chill for 2 hours, stirring occasionally, until thick.

6

Beat the chilled frosting for 1 minute, until light and fluffy. Sandwich the cakes with a generous amount of the frosting, then cover the top and sides with the remaining frosting and serve. You can keep the cake in an airtight container in the fridge for 2–3 days.

🕐 **55 mins** plus cooling   🍴 **SERVES 8–10**

CAKE German chocolate

Everything about this American classic is rich and decadent. With its triple-layered cake and fantastic frosting, this cake makes a perfect centerpiece to a dessert table.

INGREDIENTS

12 tbsp unsalted butter, softened and diced, plus extra for greasing

4oz (115g) unsweetened chocolate

1 cup granulated sugar

1 cup dark brown sugar

4 large eggs, lightly beaten

1½ tsp vanilla extract

1¼ cups buttermilk

2 cups all-purpose flour

1¼ tsp baking powder

¾ tsp baking soda

1 tsp salt

For the frosting

¾ cup whole milk

1 cup light brown sugar

⅛ tsp salt

2 large egg yolks, lightly beaten

1 tsp vanilla extract

6 tbsp unsalted butter, diced

2 cups unsweetened, dried coconut flakes

¾ cup walnuts, chopped

SPECIAL EQUIPMENT

3 x 8in (20cm) cake pans

PLAN AHEAD

You can store the unglazed cakes, wrapped in plastic wrap, 1–2 days ahead.

1 Preheat the oven to 350°F (180°C). Grease and line the pans with parchment paper. Melt the chocolate in a heatproof bowl over a saucepan of simmering water, making sure it does not touch the water. Remove and cool to room temperature.

2 Beat the butter and both types of sugar in a large bowl until light and fluffy. Gradually beat in the eggs until combined. Then beat in the vanilla extract until smooth. Add the chocolate and combine well, scraping down the sides of the bowl.

3 Mix the buttermilk with ¼ cup lukewarm water. Sift the flour, baking powder, baking soda, and salt into a bowl. Gradually add the dry mixture and buttermilk mixture alternately to the chocolate batter. Mix until combined and smooth.

4 Divide the batter evenly between the cake pans and bake for 30–35 minutes, until an inserted toothpick comes out clean. Cool the cakes in the pans for 10–15 minutes, then transfer to a wire rack to cool completely.

5 For the frosting, place the milk, brown sugar, salt, egg yolks, vanilla extract, and butter in a large saucepan over medium heat. Whisk until smooth and bring to a boil. Reduce the heat to a simmer, cooking for another 5–6 minutes, until thickened.

6 Remove from the heat, add the coconut and walnuts, and mix well. Cool to room temperature and sandwich the cakes with two-thirds of the frosting. Top the cake with the remaining frosting and serve. You can store the cake in an airtight container for 3–4 days.

🕐 **1 hr 15 mins** plus cooling   🍴 SERVES 6–8

GÂTEAU black forest

This dessert derives its name from Kirsch, a cherry liqueur that originated in the Black Forest region of Germany.

INGREDIENTS
3 tbsp unsalted butter, melted, plus extra for greasing
6 large eggs, separated
1 cup granulated sugar
1½ tsp vanilla extract
3 tbsp whole milk, at room temperature
¾ cup all-purpose flour
¾ tsp baking powder
2 tbsp cornstarch
¼ tsp salt
6 tbsp natural cocoa powder
1 tsp cream of tartar

For the filling
5 tbsp cherry juice
2½ tbsp Kirsch
pinch of salt
3½ tbsp granulated sugar
14½oz (400g) tart cherries, pitted
8oz (225g) mascarpone cheese, at room temperature
1½ cups heavy cream
¼ tsp vanilla extract
1½oz (45g) grated chocolate, to decorate

SPECIAL EQUIPMENT
9in (23cm) springform cake pan

PLAN AHEAD
You can store the unglazed cake, wrapped in plastic wrap, up to 1 day ahead.

1 Preheat the oven to 350°F (180°C). Grease and line the pan with parchment paper. Set aside. Beat the egg yolks and half the sugar in a bowl until thick and pale, then beat in the vanilla extract, butter, and milk until combined.

2 Sift the flour, baking powder, cornstarch, salt, and cocoa powder into a bowl. Gradually fold in the egg yolk mixture and set aside. In a separate bowl, beat the egg whites until foamy. Beat in the cream of tartar to form soft peaks, then gradually beat in the remaining sugar to form stiff peaks.

3 Gradually fold the egg white mixture into the batter until just combined, then pour it into the pan, bake for 40–45 minutes, and let cool (see German chocolate cake, step 4). Use a long, serrated knife to slice the cake into two.

4 For the filling, heat the cherry juice, Kirsch, salt, and 1½ tbsp of the sugar in a saucepan over medium-low heat. Stir until the sugar has dissolved. Add the cherries and stir to coat. Remove the cherries from the pan, reserving the syrup, and place them in a bowl. Let cool.

5 Beat the mascarpone in a bowl until smooth. Gradually add the cream and beat well to combine. Gradually add the vanilla extract and remaining sugar and beat to form soft peaks.

6 Place one of the cakes on a serving dish and brush generously with the cherry syrup. Spread over half of the cream mixture and top with two-thirds of the cherries. Sprinkle with half of the chocolate shavings.

7 Top with the second cake and brush with the syrup. Top with the remaining cream, grated chocolate, and cherries, and serve. You can store the cake, covered in the fridge, for 2–3 days.

🕐 **50 mins** plus cooling   🍴 SERVES 8–10

CAKE red velvet

This vividly colored cake is light and fluffy, thanks to the buttermilk in the cake layers.

INGREDIENTS
1 cup vegetable oil, plus extra for greasing
2 cups all-purpose flour
2 tbsp natural cocoa powder
1 tsp salt
1 tsp baking soda
2 large eggs, plus one yolk, lightly beaten
1½ cups granulated sugar
1¼ cups buttermilk
1½ tsp vanilla extract
1 tsp apple cider vinegar
2–3 tsp red food coloring paste

For the frosting
12oz (350g) cream cheese
6 tbsp unsalted butter, at room temperature
¾ tsp vanilla extract
pinch of salt
3 cups confectioners' sugar

SPECIAL EQUIPMENT
2 x 8in (20cm) cake pans

PLAN AHEAD
You can store the unglazed cake, wrapped in plastic wrap, for 1–2 days ahead.

1 Preheat the oven to 350°F (180°C). Grease and line the cake pans with parchment paper. Combine the flour, cocoa powder, salt, and baking soda in a bowl. In a separate bowl, whisk the oil, eggs and yolk, sugar, buttermilk, vanilla extract, cider vinegar, and food coloring paste until well combined.

2 Gradually fold the dry mixture into the wet mixture, until smooth and combined. Divide the batter between the pans. Bake the cake and let cool (see German chocolate cake, step 4). For the frosting, beat together all the ingredients in a bowl until well combined.

3 Spread the frosting generously over one cake, then cover with the second cake, rounded side up. Use the remaining frosting to cover the top and sides, and serve. You can store the cake in an airtight container for 3–4 days.

 **1 hr 30 mins** plus cooling   **SERVES 8-10**

CARROT CAKE with cream cheese frosting

Adding grated carrots to a cake batter makes it moist and sweet. The carrots are not discernible once the cake is cooked, but impart the moist texture. Walnuts add extra crunch, while the frosting gives it a rich, creamy finish.

INGREDIENTS

1¼ cups sunflower oil, plus extra for greasing

2 cups self-rising flour, sifted

1 tsp ground cinnamon

½ tsp ground ginger

¼ tsp grated nutmeg

1⅓ cups granulated sugar

4 eggs

2 cups grated carrots, squeezed to remove excess moisture

¾ cup walnuts, coarsely chopped

For the frosting

7 tbsp unsalted butter, softened

3½oz (100g) cream cheese, at room temperature

3½ cups confectioners' sugar

grated zest of 1 large orange, plus extra to decorate

SPECIAL EQUIPMENT

2 x 9in (23cm) cake pans

PLAN AHEAD

You can store the unglazed cakes in an airtight container up to 5 days ahead.

Preheat the oven to 350°F (180°C). Grease and line the pans with parchment paper. Combine the flour, spices, and granulated sugar in a bowl. Beat the eggs and oil in a pitcher and add to the dry ingredients. Add the carrots and walnuts and stir to form a stiff batter.

1

Divide the batter equally between the pans. Bake for 45–50 minutes, until the cakes are golden brown and an inserted toothpick comes out clean. Cool in the pans on a wire rack for 10 minutes, then remove the cakes from the pans and place directly on the rack to cool completely.

2

The frosting should be smooth and fluffy.

For the frosting, beat the butter and cream cheese in a bowl until smooth. Gradually beat in the confectioners' sugar until combined. Add the orange zest and mix well.

3

Sandwich the cakes with one-third of the frosting. Use the remaining frosting to cover the top and sides of the cake. Sprinkle with a little orange zest and serve. You can store the cake in an airtight container for up to 5 days.

4

🕐 **1 hr 5 mins** plus cooling   🍴 **SERVES 8**   🌡 Also great **HOT**

CAKE zucchini and hazelnut

Healthier than carrot cake, this recipe is perfect for when zucchini is in season. The cake is also delicious warm.

INGREDIENTS

1 cup sunflower oil, plus extra for greasing

1 cup hazelnuts

3 large eggs

1 tsp vanilla extract

1 cup granulated sugar

1½ cups grated zucchini, squeezed to remove excess moisture

1½ cups self-rising flour

⅓ cup whole wheat flour

pinch of salt

1 tsp ground cinnamon

finely grated zest of 1 lemon

confectioners' sugar, to dust

SPECIAL EQUIPMENT

9in (23cm) springform cake pan

1 Preheat the oven to 350°F (180°C). Grease the pan, line with parchment paper, and set aside. Spread the hazelnuts on a baking sheet and bake for 5 minutes, until lightly browned. Remove from the heat and rub them with clean paper towels to remove any excess skin. Coarsely chop them and set aside.

2 Whisk the oil, eggs, vanilla extract, and granulated sugar in a large bowl until light and smooth. Fold in the zucchini and hazelnuts until combined, then sift in the flour, pouring in any bran left in the sieve. Add the remaining ingredients and fold well to combine.

3 Pour the batter into the pan and bake for 45 minutes, until well-risen and springy to the touch. Remove from the heat and cool in the pan for 10 minutes, then transfer the cake to a wire rack to cool completely. Serve dusted with confectioners' sugar. You can keep the cake in an airtight container for up to 3 days.

🕐 **45 mins** plus cooling and setting   🍴 **SERVES 8**

CAKE beet and chocolate

Adding pureed beets to chocolate cake gives it a deep and earthy flavor and extra moist crumb.

INGREDIENTS

⅔ cup sunflower oil, plus extra for greasing

7oz (200g) cooked and peeled beets

2 eggs

¾ cup granulated sugar

1¼ cups all-purpose flour

1 tsp baking powder

2 tbsp cocoa powder

1 tbsp freeze-dried raspberry pieces

For the ganache

⅓ cup heavy cream

4oz (115g) dark chocolate, finely chopped

SPECIAL EQUIPMENT

9in (23cm) springform cake pan

PLAN AHEAD

You can store the unglazed cake in an airtight container up to 3 days ahead.

1 Preheat the oven to 350°F (180°C). Grease the pan, line with parchment paper, and set aside. Pulse the beets in a food processor to form a smooth puree, scraping down the sides if needed. In a large bowl, whisk the eggs, oil, and sugar until combined.

2 Sift the flour, baking powder, and cocoa powder into the egg mixture until combined. Fold in the beet puree and combine well. Pour the batter into the pan and bake for 30–35 minutes, until it is well risen and an inserted toothpick comes out clean.

3 Remove from the heat and cool in the pan for 10 minutes, then transfer the cake to a wire rack to cool completely. For the ganache, heat the cream in a small, heavy-bottomed saucepan until steaming.

4 Remove from the heat, add the chocolate, and stir well to melt and combine. Let cool and thicken. Pour it over the cake and smooth it out with a palette knife. Sprinkle with the raspberries and let set at room temperature before serving.

🕐 **55 mins** plus cooling   🍴 **MAKES 6**   🌡 Also great **HOT**

CAKES honey spice

These spiced cakes are served with a delicately flavored orange and cardamom cream. They are wonderful served fresh from the oven.

INGREDIENTS

5 tbsp unsalted butter, plus extra for greasing

¼ cup honey

3 tbsp dark brown sugar

¾ cup all-purpose flour

1 tsp baking powder

½ tsp ground cinnamon

½ tsp ground ginger

⅛ tsp grated nutmeg

⅛ tsp ground cloves

grated zest of 1 orange

1 egg

For the cream

½ cup whipping cream or heavy cream

1 tbsp confectioners' sugar, plus extra to dust

grated zest of 1 orange

pinch of ground cardamom

SPECIAL EQUIPMENT

6 x 4fl oz (120ml) muffin pans

PLAN AHEAD

You can prepare and store the orange cream, covered in the fridge, up to 1 day ahead.

1 Preheat the oven to 350°F (180°C). Grease the muffin pans and set aside. Melt the honey, butter, and brown sugar in a large saucepan over medium heat, stirring frequently, until the sugar dissolves. Transfer to a heatproof pitcher and let cool.

2 Sift the flour, baking powder, and spices into a large bowl. Stir in the orange zest and make a well in the center. Beat the egg into the cooled honey mixture. Add the liquid mixture to the dry mixture, gently folding them together to make a smooth batter.

3 Pour the batter into the prepared muffin pans, making sure they are only three-quarters full. Bake the cakes for 30 minutes, until well-risen and golden brown. Remove from the heat and let cool slightly before transferring to a wire rack to cool.

4 For the cream, whisk the cream, confectioners' sugar, and zest in a bowl to form soft peaks. Then add the cardamom, a little at a time, to taste. Dust the cakes with confectioners' sugar and serve immediately with the cream. Best served on the same day.

 **50 mins–1 hr**
plus cooling

SERVES 10

BUNDT CAKE vanilla

This ring-shaped cake originated in northern Germany and is now popular all over the world. It is traditionally a simply flavored cake that is dusted with confectioners' sugar or drizzled with glaze before serving.

INGREDIENTS
16 tbsp butter, plus extra for greasing
2¾ cups all-purpose flour, plus extra for dusting
2 tsp baking powder
1 tsp salt
1 cup granulated sugar
¾ cup light brown sugar
3 large eggs, plus one yolk, lightly beaten
1 tbsp vanilla extract
¾ cup whole milk
raspberries, to serve (optional)

For the glaze
3–4 tbsp heavy cream
2 cups confectioners' sugar
¼ tsp vanilla extract

SPECIAL EQUIPMENT
10in (25cm) bundt pan

PLAN AHEAD
You can bake, wrap in plastic wrap, and store the unglazed cake up to 1 day ahead.

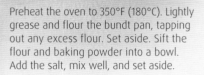

1

Preheat the oven to 350°F (180°C). Lightly grease and flour the bundt pan, tapping out any excess flour. Set aside. Sift the flour and baking powder into a bowl. Add the salt, mix well, and set aside.

2

Beat the butter and both of the sugars in a large bowl with a handheld mixer for 3–4 minutes until light and fluffy. Add half of the beaten eggs and mix until well combined.

3

Mix in the remaining beaten eggs until well combined. Beat in the vanilla extract until smooth. Scrape down the sides of the bowl as needed.

4

Add the flour and milk, a little at a time, and beat the mixture until well combined and smooth. Scrape down the sides of the bowl and pour the batter into the pan.

Bake for 40–50 minutes, rotating the pan halfway through, until golden. Transfer to a wire rack and cool for 1 hour before removing the cake from the pan.

5

Insert a skewer into the baked cake—it should come out clean.

Place the heavy cream in a bowl. Mix in the confectioners' sugar and extract, gradually, until thick. Pour it over the cake. Serve with raspberries, if desired.

6

Drizzle spoonfuls of the glaze over the cake, allowing it to run down the sides.

🕐 **1 hr 30 mins**
plus cooling

🍴 **SERVES 10**

BUNDT CAKE lemon and blueberry

Lemon and blueberry are a classic flavor pairing—sweet and sharp at the same time. Toss the berries in all-purpose flour before you fold them into the batter—this keeps them from sinking to the bottom of the cake.

INGREDIENTS

16 tbsp unsalted butter, plus extra, for greasing

3 cups all-purpose flour, plus 2–3 tbsp extra for dusting

1¾ cups granulated sugar

3 large eggs, lightly beaten

1½ tsp vanilla extract

1 tbsp grated lemon zest, plus extra to serve

2¾ tsp baking powder

1 tsp salt

¾ cup buttermilk, at room temperature

9oz (250g) blueberries, plus extra to serve

For the glaze

2 cups confectioners' sugar

1 tbsp lemon juice

pinch of salt

2 tbsp milk

SPECIAL EQUIPMENT

10in (25cm) bundt pan

PLAN AHEAD

You can bake, wrap in plastic wrap, and store the cooled, unglazed cake up to 1 day ahead.

1 Preheat the oven to 350°F (180°C). Lightly grease and flour the bundt pan, tapping out excess flour. Beat the butter and granulated sugar in a bowl until light and fluffy. Gradually beat in the eggs until combined.

2 Beat the vanilla extract and lemon zest into the butter mixture until smooth. Combine the flour, baking powder, and salt in a separate bowl. Gradually add the flour mixture and buttermilk to the butter mixture alternately, stirring to combine.

3 Toss the blueberries in 2–3 tablespoons of flour and gently fold into the batter. Scrape down the sides of the bowl and mix well.

4 Pour the batter into the prepared pan and bake for 50–60 minutes, rotating the pan halfway through, until golden. Insert a skewer into the baked cake—it should come out clean. Cool on a wire rack for 1 hour before removing the cake from the pan.

5 For the glaze, mix the confectioners' sugar, lemon juice, and salt in a bowl until combined. Gradually add the milk, whisking until smooth, and pour over the cake. Sprinkle the cake with lemon zest and serve immediately, with a handful of blueberries. You can store the cake in an airtight container for up to 3 days.

🕐 **1 hr 20 mins**
plus cooling   🍴 **SERVES 10**

BUNDT CAKE lemon and poppy seed

Poppy seeds add a lovely crunch to this tangy cake. Grease and flour the pan well to help turn the cake out.

INGREDIENTS
16 tbsp unsalted butter, plus extra, for greasing

3 cups all-purpose flour, plus extra, for dusting

2¼ cups granulated sugar

5 large eggs, lightly beaten

1 tsp vanilla extract

1 heaping tbsp grated lemon zest

1¾ tsp baking powder

½ tsp baking soda

1 tsp salt

¼ cup lemon juice

1 cup plain yogurt

1 tbsp poppy seeds

For the glaze
2 cups confectioners' sugar

pinch of salt

2oz (60g) softened cream cheese

1 tbsp butter

3 tbsp milk

SPECIAL EQUIPMENT
10in (25cm) bundt pan

PLAN AHEAD
You can bake, wrap in plastic wrap, and store the cooled, unglazed cake up to 1 day ahead.

1 Preheat the oven and prepare the bundt pan (see Lemon and blueberry bundt cake, step 1). Beat the butter and granulated sugar in a bowl until light and fluffy. Gradually beat in the eggs until combined. Add the vanilla extract and lemon zest, beating until smooth.

2 Place the flour, baking powder, baking soda, and salt in a bowl. In a separate bowl, combine the lemon juice and yogurt. Gradually stir both mixtures into the butter mixture, alternately, until well combined.

3 Fold in the poppy seeds, mix well, then pour into the prepared pan. Bake for 50–55 minutes, rotating the pan halfway through, until golden. Test for doneness (see Lemon and blueberry bundt cake, step 4). Transfer to a wire rack to cool for 1 hour, then remove the cake from the pan.

4 For the glaze, place the confectioners' sugar, salt, cream cheese, and butter in a large bowl and mix to combine. Gradually add the milk, stirring until smooth and glossy. Pour it over the cake. Serve the cake immediately after glazing. You can store it in an airtight container for up to 3 days.

🕐 **1 hr**
plus cooling   🍴 **MAKES 12**

MINI BUNDTS marbled

Mini bundt pans are available in specialty baking shops and produce appealing individual cakes. These delights are great when paired with coffee at the end of a meal.

INGREDIENTS
8 tbsp unsalted butter, plus extra, for greasing

1½ cups all-purpose flour, plus extra for dusting

2 tbsp cornstarch

½ tsp salt

½ tsp baking powder

½ tsp instant espresso powder

3 tsp natural cocoa powder, plus extra to decorate

1 cup granulated sugar

2 large eggs, lightly beaten

1 tsp pure vanilla extract

⅓ cup sour cream

confectioners' sugar, to decorate

SPECIAL EQUIPMENT
Mini bundt pans, each mold measuring 3½fl oz (100ml)

1 Preheat the oven and prepare the mini bundt pans (see Lemon and blueberry bundt cake, step 1). Boil a pan half-full of water and let cool for 5 minutes. Sift the flour, cornstarch, salt, and baking powder into a bowl. In a separate bowl, place the espresso and cocoa powders, pour in 1 tablespoon of the water, and set aside.

2 Beat the butter and granulated sugar in a bowl until fluffy. Gradually add the eggs and beat to combine. Add the vanilla extract and beat until smooth.

3 Gradually fold in the flour mixture and cream into the butter mixture alternately until well incorporated and smooth. Place half the batter in a separate bowl, add the espresso mixture, and stir well to combine.

4 Fill each bundt mold with equal quantities of both batters. Swirl the batters with a toothpick to create a marbled effect. Bake for 15–20 minutes, rotating the pans halfway through, until golden. Insert a toothpick into the baked cakes—it should come out clean.

5 Transfer the pan to a wire rack to cool for 45 minutes, then remove the cakes from the pan. Dust with confectioners' sugar and cocoa powder to serve. You can store them in an airtight container for 3 days.

30 mins
plus chilling and cooling

SERVES 10–12

ROULADE chocolate and summer fruit

A roulade is a fabulous dessert choice for entertaining—it is one of the best recipes to feed a crowd. Rolling up a roulade is not as difficult as it seems. As shown here, wrap it in parchment paper and then a kitchen towel for guaranteed success.

INGREDIENTS
1 tbsp unsalted butter, melted, for brushing
½ cup cocoa powder, plus extra for dusting
5 eggs, separated
⅔ cup granulated sugar
1 tbsp all-purpose flour

For the filling
1 cup heavy cream
1 tsp vanilla extract
1 tbsp confectioners' sugar

4½oz (125g) strawberries, hulled and quartered
4½oz (125g) raspberries

SPECIAL EQUIPMENT
12 x 15in (30 x 37cm) jelly roll pan

PLAN AHEAD
You can make the sponge cake 1 day ahead. Roll it in the kitchen towel, then cover with a layer of foil.

1

Preheat the oven to 425°F (220°C). Line the pan with parchment paper, brush it lightly with butter, and chill for 5 minutes. Dust the parchment evenly with cocoa powder, pouring off any excess.

Dust very lightly using a small strainer.

2

In a large bowl, beat the egg yolks and ½ cup granulated sugar with a handheld mixer until light and fluffy. In a separate bowl, whisk the egg whites to form stiff peaks. Then whisk in the remaining granulated sugar until glossy. Sift the cocoa powder and flour into a small bowl.

3

In three batches, gradually fold the cocoa and the egg white mixtures into the egg yolk mixture. Fold carefully so that you lose as little air as possible, until combined. Pour the batter into the pan. Tip the pan lightly to ensure the batter spreads evenly.

4

Bake for 7–10 minutes, until an inserted toothpick comes out clean. Remove from the oven and cool the cake in the pan for 2 minutes, then transfer to a sheet of parchment paper dusted with cocoa powder. Roll up the cake in the parchment, wrap in a clean kitchen towel, and let cool completely.

Carefully roll up the cake in the kitchen towel.

5

For the filling, whisk the cream, vanilla extract, and confectioners' sugar in a bowl to form stiff peaks. Unroll the cake and spread with the cream, leaving a ½in (1cm) border. Scatter with the berries, gently pressing them into the cream.

6

Re-roll the cake as before, using the parchment to support it, and trim the edges. Carefully transfer the roulade to a serving plate, dust with cocoa powder, and serve immediately.

🕐 **35 mins**
plus cooling

🍴 **SERVES 10–12**

ROULADE peach melba

With a meringue base, this roulade is incredibly light. Softening the base with vinegar and cornstarch helps it to remain flexible and easy to roll around the filling. A bonus of this recipe is that you can make it entirely from pantry ingredients.

INGREDIENTS

5 egg whites, at room temperature

1 cup granulated sugar

½ tsp white wine vinegar, or rice wine vinegar

1 tsp cornstarch

½ tsp vanilla extract

confectioners' sugar, to dust

For the coulis

4½oz (125g) frozen raspberries

2 tbsp granulated sugar

For the filling

1 cup heavy cream

1 x 14oz (400g) can peaches, drained and diced

SPECIAL EQUIPMENT

12 x 15in (30 x 37cm) jelly roll pan

1 Preheat the oven to 350°F (180°C). Line the pan with parchment paper and set aside. Whisk the egg whites in a bowl to form stiff peaks. Gradually add the granulated sugar, whisking constantly until the mixture is well combined, thick, and glossy.

2 Fold the vinegar, cornstarch, and vanilla extract into the meringue mixture. Mix gently, trying to lose as little air as possible, and pour into the prepared pan. Bake the meringue for 15 minutes. Remove from the heat and let cool in the pan.

3 For the coulis, place the raspberries and granulated sugar in a small, heavy-bottomed saucepan over gentle heat. Cook for 5–7 minutes, stirring occasionally, until the raspberries soften and the sugar dissolves. Strain the mixture into a bowl and chill until needed.

4 For the filling, whisk the cream in a bowl to form stiff peaks. Spread a sheet of parchment paper over a clean work surface and sprinkle it with a little confectioners' sugar. Place a large serving platter next to the parchment so that the roulade can be easily moved onto it after it is rolled.

5 Carefully transfer the meringue to the parchment. Spread the cream over the meringue evenly, leaving a ½in (1cm) border. Spread the raspberry coulis over the cream. Gently pat the peaches dry with paper towels to remove any excess liquid.

6 Scatter the peaches over the coulis and gently press them into place. Carefully roll the meringue using the parchment to support it, then roll it onto the serving platter, dust with confectioners' sugar, and serve immediately.

ROULADE
black forest

Canned cherries and fruity Kirsch pair well with thick cream in this decadent version of the classic roulade.

INGREDIENTS

12 x 15in (30 x 37cm) chocolate sponge cake (see Chocolate and summer fruit roulade pp240–41)

cocoa powder, for dusting

For the filling
1 cup heavy cream
1 tsp vanilla extract

1 tbsp confectioners' sugar
3 tbsp Kirsch
1 x 14oz (400g) can pitted black cherries, drained and halved

PLAN AHEAD
You can make the sponge cake 1 day ahead. Roll it in the kitchen towel, then cover with a layer of foil.

1 For the filling, place the cream, vanilla extract, and sugar in a large bowl and whisk well to form stiff peaks. Roll out the prepared sponge cake over a clean work surface covered with a clean kitchen towel.

2 Sprinkle the Kirsch evenly over the cake. Spread the cream over the sponge cake evenly, leaving a ½in (1cm) border. Scatter with the cherries and gently press them into place.

3 Using the kitchen towel for support, gently roll up the cake and trim the edges. Carefully transfer the roulade to a large serving plate and dust with cocoa powder. Serve immediately.

30–35 mins plus cooling **SERVES 8–10**

JELLY ROLL raspberry

Homemade jelly rolls are a world away from crusty store-bought varieties. Traditional raspberry jam is used here, but you can replace it with peach, apricot, or even fig jam.

INGREDIENTS

3 large eggs
½ cup granulated sugar, plus extra for sprinkling
pinch of salt
⅓ cup self-rising flour, sifted
1 tsp vanilla extract
6 tbsp raspberry jam

SPECIAL EQUIPMENT
9 x 13in (23 x 33cm) jelly roll pan

PLAN AHEAD
You can make the sponge cake 1 day ahead. Roll it in the kitchen towel, then cover with a layer of foil.

1 Preheat the oven to 400°F (200°C). Line the pan with parchment paper and set aside. Whisk the eggs, sugar, and salt in a heatproof bowl set over a saucepan of simmering water, making sure it does not touch the water, until thick. The mixture should leave trails on the surface when the whisk is lifted.

2 Remove from the heat and whisk the mixture for 1–2 minutes, until cool. Gently fold in the flour and vanilla extract, so that you lose as little air as possible. Pour the mixture evenly into the pan. Bake for 12–15 minutes, until the cake is springy and shrinking away from the sides.

3 Place a sheet of parchment paper on a clean work surface. Sprinkle evenly with a little sugar transfer the cake to it. Cool for 5 minutes, then gently peel off the parchment paper.

4 Warm the jam in a saucepan over gentle heat and spread over the cake. Make a ¾in (2cm) indent along one short side, ¾in (2cm) from the edge. Roll the cake from this edge, using the parchment to support it.

5 Let the cake cool completely, then remove the parchment and place the roulade, seam downward, on a serving plate. Sprinkle with sugar and serve. You can keep it in an airtight container for 2 days, or freeze it for up to 8 weeks.

🕐 **25 mins**
plus cooling

🍴 **MAKES 24**

MACAROONS almond

Perfect to serve as an after-dinner treat for those with a gluten intolerance, these macaroons are made with a mixture of ground almonds and rice flour, which gives them a light, delicate texture.

INGREDIENTS
2 egg whites
1 cup granulated sugar
1¼ cups ground almonds
3 tbsp rice flour
2–3 drops of almond extract
24 blanched almonds

SPECIAL EQUIPMENT
2 sheets of edible wafer paper

1 Preheat the oven to 350°F (180°C). Line two baking sheets with edible wafer paper and set aside. Whisk the egg whites in a large bowl with a handheld mixer until they are stiff and form soft peaks.

2 Add the sugar, a tablespoon at a time, and blend until the mixture is thick and glossy. Gently fold in the ground almonds, rice flour, and almond extract. Mix until combined.

4

Bake the macaroons in the oven for 12–15 minutes, until lightly colored. Place on a wire rack to cool completely, then tear the macaroons off the sheets and serve. You can store them in an airtight container for 2–3 days.

3 Use two warmed tablespoons to scoop up and shape the dough into 24 rounds, placing them spaced well apart on the baking sheets. Clean the spoon between scoops. Place a blanched almond in the center of each round.

🕐 **30 mins** plus chilling   🍴 **MAKES 24**

MACAROONS coffee and hazelnut

Ground hazelnuts give these macaroons a darker, nuttier flavor than ground almonds—perfect when matched with strong coffee. You can also crumble them over a coffee granita.

INGREDIENTS
2 egg whites
1 cup granulated sugar
1⅓ cups ground
   hazelnuts
3 tbsp rice flour
1 tsp strong instant coffee
   powder, dissolved in 1 tsp
   boiling water and cooled
24 blanched hazelnuts

SPECIAL EQUIPMENT
2 sheets of edible wafer
   paper

1 Preheat the oven to 350°F (180°C). Line two baking sheets with edible wafer paper. Whisk the egg whites in a bowl to form stiff peaks. Add the sugar, a tablespoon at a time, and whisk until thick and combined.

2 Gently fold the ground hazelnuts and rice flour into the mixture, then fold in the coffee mixture and mix until evenly incorporated. Cover and chill for about 30 minutes.

3 Use two warmed tablespoons to shape the dough into 24 rounds, placing them spaced apart on the baking sheets. Clean the spoons between scoops. Place a blanched hazelnut in the center of each round.

4 Bake the macaroons on the top shelf of the oven for 12–15 minutes, until lightly colored. Let cool on the sheets for 5 minutes, then place on a wire rack to cool completely before tearing them from the sheets and serving. You can store them in an airtight container for 2–3 days.

🕐 **45 mins** plus cooling   🍴 **MAKES 15**

MACAROONS pineapple and coconut

Pineapple provides a good contrast to sweet coconut in these little delicacies, inspired by tropical flavors.

INGREDIENTS
2½ cups sweetened
   shredded coconut
¾ cup condensed
   milk
½ cup diced pineapple
2 large egg whites
pinch of cream of tartar

1 Preheat the oven to 375°F (190°C). Line a baking sheet with baking parchment. Place the coconut, milk, and pineapple in a large bowl and mix well. In a separate bowl, beat the egg whites and cream of tartar to form stiff peaks.

2 Gently fold the egg white mixture into the coconut mixture, a little at a time, until it is well combined. Use two tablespoons to scoop and shape the dough into 15 rounds, placing them spaced well apart on the lined baking sheet. Clean the spoons between scoops.

3 Bake the macaroons for 20–25 minutes, rotating the sheets after 15 minutes, until golden. Let cool completely on the baking sheets, then serve. You can store the macaroons in an airtight container in the fridge for up to 4 days, or freeze them for up to 1 month. Thaw before serving.

45 mins
plus cooling and chilling　　**MAKES 24**

MACAROONS chocolate
and raspberry

Mixing fresh raspberries into the macaroon mixture results in a wonderfully vibrant color, and distributes nuggets of tangy fruit throughout the dessert.

INGREDIENTS

6oz (175g) raspberries

4½ cups shredded coconut

⅔ cup condensed milk

2 large egg whites

⅛ tsp cream of tartar

12oz (350g) good-quality dark chocolate

1 Preheat the oven to 375°F (190°C). Line two baking sheets with baking parchment. In a small bowl, crush the raspberries with the back of a spoon. In a separate bowl, combine the raspberries, coconut, and milk and set aside.

2 Beat the egg whites and cream of tartar to form stiff peaks. Gently fold the egg whites into the coconut mixture, a little at a time, until well combined. Scoop and shape 24 rounds of dough using two tablespoons (see Coffee and hazelnut macaroons, step 3).

3 Bake the macaroons for 20–25 minutes, rotating the sheets after 15 minutes, until lightly golden. Let cool completely on the baking sheets. Melt the chocolate in a heatproof bowl over a saucepan of gently simmering water, making sure it does not touch the water.

4 Remove from the heat and cool for 3–4 minutes, then dip the bottom of the macaroons in the chocolate and place them on a baking sheet, lined with parchment paper. Drizzle chocolate over the macaroons, if desired.

5 Chill the macaroons for 15–20 minutes, until the chocolate has hardened. Serve at room temperature. You can store the macaroons in an airtight container in the fridge for up to 4 days, or freeze them for up to 1 month. Thaw before serving.

🕐 **1 hr 25 mins**
plus cooling and setting

🍴 **MAKES 16**

BARS millionaire's shortbread

The variety of rich ingredients in this recipe is said to be the reason for its indulgent name. You can cut the bars into bite-sized pieces and serve it with coffee. It also works well as a sweet canapé.

INGREDIENTS

12 tbsp unsalted butter, softened, plus extra for greasing

1½ cups all-purpose flour

½ cup granulated sugar

For the caramel filling

4 tbsp unsalted butter

⅓ cup light brown sugar

1 x 14oz (400g) can condensed milk

For the topping

7oz (200g) milk chocolate

2 tbsp unsalted butter

1¾oz (50g) good-quality dark chocolate

SPECIAL EQUIPMENT

8in (20cm) square cake pan

Preheat the oven to 325°F (160°C). Grease and line the pan with parchment paper. Combine the flour and sugar in a bowl. Rub in the butter until the mixture resembles bread crumbs. Spread it in the pan and bake for 35–40 minutes. Remove and let cool in the pan.

1

Press the mixture down for a smooth, even layer.

2

For the filling, melt the butter and sugar in a heavy-bottomed saucepan over medium heat. Add the milk and bring to a boil, stirring. Reduce the heat to a simmer and cook for 5 minutes, stirring, until it is thick and lightly colored. Pour it over the base and let cool.

For the topping, melt the milk chocolate and butter in a heatproof bowl over a pan of simmering water, making sure it does not touch the water. Stir until smooth, then melt the dark chocolate in a separate bowl until smooth.

3

Pour the milk chocolate mixture over the caramel and smooth over the top. Top with the dark chocolate in a zigzag pattern, and drag a skewer through both layers of chocolate. Let cool and harden. Cut it into 16 even-sized squares to serve. You can store the shortbread in an airtight container for up to 5 days.

4

Use the skewer to create a marbled effect.

🕐 **30 mins** plus chilling   🍴 **MAKES 16**

BAR Nanaimo

These rich and moist no-bake bars are said to originate from Nanaimo, which is a town in British Columbia.

1 Grease and line an **8in (20cm) square baking pan**. Melt **8 tbsp unsalted butter** in a heavy-bottomed saucepan over low heat. Add **5 tbsp cocoa powder** and **¼ cup granulated sugar**, and cook for 2 minutes, whisking, until the sugar has dissolved.

2 Remove the cocoa mixture from the heat. Whisk in **1 large beaten egg**, until well combined. Return the mixture to low heat and cook it for 1–2 minutes, whisking frequently, until it has thickened. Remove from the heat.

3 Place **2 cups crushed graham crackers**, **¾ cup sliced almonds**, and **⅔ cup unsweetened, dried coconut flakes** in a large bowl. Pour in the cocoa and egg mixture and combine well. Transfer the mixture to the pan, pressing down to form an even, firm layer. Chill for 30 minutes.

4 Whisk **4 tbsp softened unsalted butter** in a large bowl until light and fluffy. Add **2 cups confectioners' sugar**, **2 tbsp vanilla pudding mix**, **½ tsp vanilla extract**, and **2–3 tbsp milk**, and beat until it is a smooth, spreadable frosting. Smooth it over the base and chill for 30 minutes.

5 Melt **5½oz (150g) good-quality dark chocolate** and **2 tbsp unsalted butter** in a heatproof bowl over a pan of simmering water. Cool it to room temperature and pour the vanilla layer in the pan. Spread it out evenly and chill for 1 hour, then remove from the pan and slice into 16 even-sized pieces. You can store the bars in an airtight container for up to 5 days.

Tiffin

🕐 **20 mins** plus chilling   🍴 **MAKES 25**

BAR tiffin

Crunchy and chewy at the same time, these delicious bars were invented in Scotland at the beginning of the 20th century.

1 Grease and line an **8in (20cm) square baking pan**. Melt **11 tbsp unsalted butter**, **½ cup golden or corn syrup**, and **½ cup cocoa powder** in a saucepan over low heat, whisking until smooth.

2 Combine **2½ cups crushed graham crackers** and **5½oz (150g) dried fruit** in a large bowl. Pour in the butter mixture and mix until combined. Transfer the mixture to the prepared pan and spread it out to a firm, even layer. Chill for at least 30 minutes.

3 Meanwhile, melt **9oz (250g) milk chocolate** in a heatproof bowl over a saucepan of simmering water. Do not allow the bowl to touch the water. Cool to room temperature before spreading it over the graham cracker and fruit base. Chill for 30 minutes, then remove from the pan and slice into 25 even-sized pieces. You can store the bars in an airtight container for up to 5 days.

Nanaimo

20 mins plus chilling   **MAKES 16**

BAR rocky road

This American classic derives its name from its chunky texture and is stuffed with dried fruits, nuts, and sweet treats.

1 Grease and line an **8in (20cm) square baking pan**. Melt **9oz (250g) good-quality dark chocolate, 7 tbsp unsalted butter**, and **2 tbsp corn syrup** in a large heatproof bowl over a pan of simmering water. Cool to room temperature.

2 Add **1½ cups coarsely chopped pretzel sticks, 1½ cups mini marshmallows, ⅓ cup coarsely chopped almonds**, and **⅓ cup coarsely chopped dried cherries** to the chocolate mixture. Stir well until combined.

3 Transfer the mixture to the prepared pan. Spread it out to a firm and even layer and chill for at least 2 hours. Remove from the pan and slice into 16 even-sized pieces. You can store the bars in an airtight container for up to 5 days.

Rocky road

Melts and marbles

It is so easy to mix molten chocolate or sugar to create stunning decorations for bars. Use good-quality chocolate for best results.

Marbling Marble Millionaire's shortbread (see pp248–49) with 2oz (60g) melted white chocolate. Spread the melted milk chocolate over the base, as described in the recipe, then pour the white chocolate over the top, dragging a wooden chopstick through both layers. Allow to set, and chill.

Feathering This gives a professional look to Millionaire's shortbread (see pp248–49). Top the filling with the milk chocolate and smooth it out. Working quickly, use a piping bag to pipe thin lines of the melted dark chocolate across the surface. Drag a toothpick through the lines to feather them, then let set.

Spun sugar Melt 1 cup granulated sugar over low heat until it turns to a dark, liquid caramel. Use a fork to drizzle the caramel quickly in thin zigzag lines over parchment paper. When each little knot of spun sugar sets, use to top small pieces of Millionaire's shortbread (see pp248–49).

Zigzag shapes Divide the base for the Nanaimos (see opposite) between 12 mini muffin pans. Pack them down and chill for 30 minutes. Remove from the pan and pipe mini rosettes of the filling on each one. Chill for 30 minutes. On a lined baking sheet, drizzle melted chocolate into zigzags, and allow to set. Use them to top the Nanaimos and serve.

INGREDIENTS
½ cup packed dark brown sugar

¼ cup granulated sugar

8 tbsp unsalted butter, softened

1 egg, at room temperature

¾ tsp vanilla extract

1¼ cups all-purpose flour

½ tsp salt

½ tsp baking powder

1 cup dark chocolate chips

PLAN AHEAD
You can store the dough in the fridge for up to 3 days ahead, or freeze it for 4–5 weeks.

🕐 **20 mins**
plus chilling and cooling

🍴 **MAKES 12**

COOKIES chocolate chip

Not only an after-school snack, these cookies are also the perfect after-dinner choice, especially when served with coffee or ice cream. You can also crumble them and serve them on top of sundaes or parfaits.

Beat both of the sugars and the butter in a large bowl for 3–4 minutes, until light and fluffy. Beat in the egg, scraping down the sides of the bowl. Beat in the vanilla extract. Combine the flour, salt, and baking powder in a separate bowl.

Gradually fold the dry ingredients into the wet mixture until just combined, then fold in the chocolate chips until they are evenly incorporated. Wrap the dough in plastic wrap. Chill for 2–3 hours, or overnight, until firm.

3

Preheat the oven to 350°F (180°C). Line two baking sheets with parchment paper. Shape the dough into 12 equal-sized balls, each about 2in (5cm) in size. Place them on the baking sheets, spaced at least 2in (5cm) apart.

Bake for 13–14 minutes, rotating the baking sheets halfway through. Remove and cool the cookies on the baking sheets for 5 minutes. Transfer to a wire rack to cool completely, and serve. You can store the cookies in an airtight container in the fridge for 4–5 days, or freeze them for up to 8 months.

4

🕐 **20 mins**
plus chilling and cooling   🍴 **MAKES 10**

COOKIES snickerdoodles

These soft cookies are really a cross between a cake and a cookie. Their light and buttery texture is best enjoyed fresh from the oven.

1 Beat **6 tbsp unsalted butter**, **½ cup dark brown sugar**, and **¼ cup granulated sugar** in a large bowl until light and fluffy. Add **1 egg** and stir to combine. Then stir in **½ tsp vanilla extract** until well combined, scraping down the sides of the bowl if needed.

2 Place **1¼ cups all-purpose flour**, **½ tsp salt**, **⅛ tsp cinnamon**, **½ tsp baking power**, **½ tsp cream of tartar**, and **1 tbsp cornstarch** in a separate bowl and mix well. Gradually add to the sugar and butter mixture, stirring until just incorporated. Cover the dough with plastic wrap and chill for 2–3 hours, or until firm.

3 Preheat the oven to 350°F (180°C). Line two large baking sheets with parchment paper and set aside. Place **¼ cup granulated sugar** and **1½ tbsp ground cinnamon** in a small bowl. Mix well to combine.

4 Divide and shape the dough into 10 equal-sized balls, each about 2in (5cm) in size. Lightly coat each dough ball with the cinnamon mixture. Transfer them to the lined baking sheets, spacing them at least 2in (5cm) apart.

5 Bake the cookies for 14–16 minutes, rotating the baking sheets halfway through, until golden at the edges and shiny. Remove and cool them on the baking sheets for 5 minutes before placing on a wire rack to cool completely. You can store them in an airtight container for up to 4–5 days, or freeze them for up to 8 months.

PLAN AHEAD
You can wrap the dough in plastic wrap and store it in the fridge for up to 3 days ahead, or freeze it for 4–5 weeks. Bring to room temperature before baking.

Snickerdoodles

Snickerdoodles

🕐 **30 mins**
plus cooling   🍴 **MAKES 16**

COOKIES cranberry and oatmeal

Vitamin-rich cranberries and heart-healthy oats make these cookies a healthy dessert option. Serve them with Greek yogurt and honey.

1 Preheat the oven to 350ºF (180ºC). Beat **7 tbsp softened unsalted butter**, **¼ cup dark brown sugar**, and **⅔ cup granulated sugar** in a large bowl until light and fluffy. Add **1 egg** and beat well to combine.

2 Sift **¾ cup all-purpose flour**, **¼ tsp baking powder**, **¼ tsp ground cinnamon**, and **a pinch of salt** into a bowl. Combine the dry ingredients with the wet mixture, then gently fold in **1 cup rolled oats** and **2oz (60g) dried cranberries** until incorporated.

3 Line two baking sheets and place 8 heaping tablespoons of the mixture on each, spaced well apart. Bake the cookies in the oven for 15 minutes, or until they begin to brown at the edges, but are still chewy in the center.

4 Remove and cool them on the baking sheets for 5 minutes before placing on a wire rack to cool completely. You can store the cookies in an airtight container for up to 3 days.

PLAN AHEAD
You can freeze the dough on a baking sheet until frozen, then transfer to a plastic bag and freeze it for 4–5 weeks ahead. Bring to room temperature before baking.

🕐 **30 mins**
plus chilling and cooling

🍴 **MAKES 16**

COOKIES s'mores

Reminiscent of childhood campfires, the flavors of s'mores are comforting, indulgent, and oh so addictive.

1 Beat **¾ cup dark brown sugar**, **½ cup granulated sugar**, and **8 tbsp unsalted butter** in a large bowl until light and fluffy. Add **1 egg** and beat well to combine, then whisk in **1 tsp vanilla extract** until combined, scraping down the sides of the bowl if needed.

2 Place **1½ cups all-purpose flour**, **¾ tsp baking soda**, and **½ tsp salt** in a small bowl and mix until well combined. Add the dry ingredients to the wet mixture, a little at a time, until just combined.

3 Use a spatula to fold **½ cup mini marshmallows**, **½ cup crushed graham crackers**, and **½ cup each of dark and milk chocolate chips** into the mixture until incorporated. Cover the dough with plastic wrap and chill for 2–3 hours, or until firm.

4 Preheat the oven to 350°F (180°C) and line two large baking sheets with parchment paper. Divide and shape the dough into 16 equal-sized balls, each about 2in (5cm) in size. Place eight balls on each baking sheet, at least 2in (5cm) apart.

5 Bake the cookies for 13–14 minutes, rotating the baking sheets halfway through, until browning at the edges. Remove and cool them on the baking sheets for 5 minutes before placing on a wire rack to cool completely. You can store them in an airtight container in the fridge for up to 4–5 days, or freeze them for up to 8 months.

PLAN AHEAD
You can wrap the dough in plastic wrap and store it in the fridge for up to 3 days ahead, or freeze it for 4–5 weeks. Bring to room temperature before baking.

Cranberry and oatmeal

S'mores

1 hr
plus cooling

MAKES 12–15

BISCOTTI almond

These crisp Italian cookies are often served with dessert wine at the end of a meal. Twice baked, they are usually dry and hard, but soften well when dipped into sweet, heady wine. Their lack of moisture means that they store well.

INGREDIENTS

¾ cup whole almonds, shelled and skinned

4 tbsp unsalted butter

1⅓ cups self-rising flour, plus extra for dusting

½ cup granulated sugar

2 eggs

1 tsp vanilla extract

1

Preheat the oven to 350°F (180°C). Spread the almonds on a nonstick baking sheet. Bake in the oven for 5–10 minutes, tossing them halfway through, until slightly colored. Remove and let cool.

2

Melt the butter in small saucepan over low heat. Remove and let cool slightly. Sift the flour into a large bowl. Coarsely chop the almonds and add them to the flour along with the sugar and mix well.

3

Mix together the butter, eggs, and vanilla extract in a bowl until combined. Gradually stir the wet mixture into the dry ingredients. Bring them together to form a dough, adding more flour if it is too wet and difficult to shape.

4

On a lightly floured surface, shape the dough into two logs, each about 8in(20cm) long. Place the logs on a lined baking sheet and bake in the oven for 20 minutes.

Make sure the logs are spaced apart on the baking sheet, as they will increase in size.

5

Remove and let the logs cool slightly on a cutting board. Then use a serrated knife to chop them, on a slant, into 1–2in (3–5cm) thick slices. Place the slices on a baking sheet and bake for 10 minutes.

6

Remove the biscotti from the oven, turn them over, and bake for another 5 minutes. Remove and place on a wire rack to cool and harden before serving. You can store the biscotti in an airtight container for up to 1 week, or freeze them, spaced out on a sheet, for up to 8 weeks.

Chocolate

🕐 **1 hr 15 mins**
plus cooling 🍴 **MAKES 20**

BISCOTTI chocolate

Simple biscotti dough is easy to embellish. Here, cocoa powder is added to the mixture, along with some coarsely chopped pecans.

1 Preheat the oven to 350°F (180°C). Spread ½ **cup pecans** on a baking sheet and bake for 5 minutes, until slightly colored. Let them cool slightly, and then chop into small pieces. Melt **4 tbsp** butter, then cool.

2 Sift ¾ **cup all-purpose flour**, **1 tsp baking powder**, ½ **tsp salt,** and ¼ **cup cocoa powder** into a large bowl. Add ½ **cup granulated sugar**, ¼ **cup dark chocolate chips**, and the pecans and mix well. Whisk together **2 eggs** and the cooled butter in a separate bowl and combine with the dry ingredients.

3 Bring the mixture together to form a dough. On a lightly floured surface, shape the dough into two logs, each about 8in (20cm) long and 2in (5cm) wide. Place the logs on a lined baking sheet and bake for about 25 minutes.

4 Remove and let cool for 20 minutes on a cutting board. Using a serrated knife, cut the logs diagonally into ¾in (2cm) thick slices. Place the slices on baking sheets, making sure they are spaced well apart.

5 Bake the biscotti for 10 minutes, then turn them over and bake for another 10 minutes. Remove and transfer to a wire rack to harden and cool completely before serving. You can store the biscotti in an airtight container for up to 1 week.

Pistachio and cranberry

BISCOTTI pistachio and cranberry

🕐 **1 hr** plus cooling   🍴 **MAKES 12–15**

Flecked with green and red, these pretty biscotti make a fantastic addition to the table during the festive season.

1 Preheat the oven to 350°F (180°C). Spread **1 cup shelled, whole pistachios** on a baking sheet, and bake for 5–10 minutes. Remove, cool to room temperature, and rub between paper towels to remove the skins. Coarsely chop the pistachios and place them in a large bowl.

2 Add **⅓ cup dried cranberries**, **1⅓ cups self-rising flour**, **½ cup granulated sugar**, and **finely grated zest of 1 orange** and mix well. In a separate bowl, whisk **2 eggs**, **1 tsp vanilla extract**, and **4 tbsp melted and cooled unsalted butter**. Combine the wet mixture with the dry ingredients to form a dough.

3 On a lightly floured surface, shape the dough into two logs, each about 8in (20cm) long and 3in (7.5cm) thick. Place them on a baking sheet lined with silicone or parchment paper and bake in the oven for 20 minutes.

4 Remove and let cool slightly on a cutting board. Use a serrated knife to chop the logs on a slant into 1–2in (3–5cm) thick slices. Place on a baking sheet, making sure the slices are spaced well apart.

5 Bake the biscotti for 10 minutes, then turn them over and bake for another 5 minutes. Remove and transfer to a wire rack to harden and cool completely before serving. You can store the biscotti in an airtight container for up to 1 week.

BISCOTTI ginger

🕐 **1 hr 5 mins** plus cooling   🍴 **MAKES 20**

Using both ground and crystallized ginger gives these gently spiced biscotti a complex flavor and texture.

1 Preheat the oven to 350°F (180°C). Sift **1½ cups self-rising flour** into a large bowl. Add **½ cup granulated sugar** and **⅓ cup finely chopped crystallized ginger** and mix well. Then add **1½ tsp ground ginger**, **1½ tsp cinnamon**, and **¼ tsp grated nutmeg**. Mix well to combine.

2 In a separate bowl, beat together **2 eggs**, **1 tsp vanilla extract**, and **4 tbsp melted and cooled unsalted butter** until well mixed. Combine the wet mixture with the dry ingredients to form a loose dough. On a lightly floured surface, shape the dough into two logs, each about 8in (20cm) long and 2in (5cm) wide. Place the logs on a lined baking sheet.

3 Bake for 25 minutes. Remove and leave the logs to cool for 20 minutes on a cutting board. Then use a serrated knife to cut the logs diagonally into ¾in (2cm) thick slices. Place the slices on baking sheets, making sure they are spaced well apart.

4 Bake the biscotti for 10 minutes, then turn them over and bake for another 10 minutes until golden and hard. Remove and let harden and cool completely on a wire rack before serving. You can store the biscotti in an airtight container for up to 1 week.

Ginger

🕐 **30 mins**
plus cooling

🍴 **MAKES 30**

SABLÉS classic

These all-butter shortbread cookies are a French classic. They are a versatile dessert choice—you can use them to sandwich ice cream, as shown here, or roll them as thinly as you dare and use them to decorate a mousse or parfait.

INGREDIENTS

1¼ cups all-purpose flour, plus extra for dusting

½ cup granulated sugar

11 tbsp unsalted butter, softened and diced

1 egg yolk

1 tsp vanilla extract

vanilla ice cream, to serve (optional)

blueberries, to serve (optional)

SPECIAL EQUIPMENT

2¾in (7cm) round pastry cutter

PLAN AHEAD

You can wrap the dough in plastic wrap and chill it for up to 3 days ahead, or freeze it for up to 3 months. Thaw it in the fridge overnight before using.

1

Preheat the oven to 350°F (180°C). Sift the flour and sugar into a large bowl and mix well. Rub in the butter until the mixture resembles coarse bread crumbs. Add the egg yolk and vanilla extract, then bring together to form a soft dough.

2

On a lightly floured surface, briefly knead the dough until smooth and roll it out to a thickness of ¼in (5mm). Use a palette knife to move the dough around to prevent it from sticking, if needed.

If the dough is too sticky to roll, chill it for 15 minutes and try again.

3

Use the pastry cutter to cut out 30 rounds and transfer them to nonstick baking sheets.

Re-roll the offcuts to the same thickness and cut out more rounds.

4

Bake in batches for 10–15 minutes, until the biscuits are golden brown at the edges. Cool them on the baking sheets until firm enough to handle, then transfer to a wire rack to cool completely. Sandwich the sablés with vanilla ice cream and serve with blueberries, if desired. You can store them in an airtight container for up to 5 days.

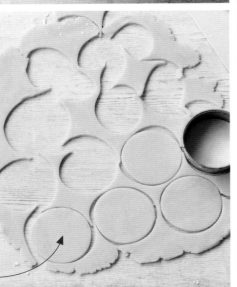

🕐 **30 mins** plus cooling   🍴 **MAKES 30**

SABLÉS ginger

Crystallized ginger gives these elegant sablés extra crunch, sweetness, and a lovely warmth of flavor.

1 Preheat the oven to 350°F (180°C). Place ½ **cup granulated sugar** and 1½ **cups sifted all-purpose flour** in a large bowl and mix well. Rub in **11 tbsp softened unsalted butter** until the mixture resembles bread crumbs.

2 Stir in **1 tsp ground ginger** and ⅓ **cup finely chopped crystallized ginger**. Then add **1 egg yolk** and **1 tsp vanilla extract** and bring together to form a dough. On a floured surface, briefly knead the dough until smooth.

3 On a well-floured surface, roll the dough out to a ¼in (5mm) thickness. Use a **3in (7.5cm) pastry cutter** to cut out 30 rounds, re-rolling the offcuts to the same thickness until you have used all of the dough. Place the cookies, spaced apart, on two nonstick baking sheets.

4 Bake the cookies in batches, for 12–15 minutes each, or until golden brown at the edges. Cool them on the baking sheets until firm enough to handle, then transfer to a wire rack to cool completely. You can store the cookies in an airtight container for up to 5 days, or freeze them for up to 8 weeks.

PLAN AHEAD
You can wrap the dough in plastic wrap and chill it for up to 3 days ahead, or freeze it for up to 3 months. Defrost overnight in the fridge before baking.

Ginger

Maple pecan

🕐 **30 mins** plus chilling and cooling   🍴 **MAKES 25**

SABLÉS maple pecan

Pecans are full of flavor and bring crunch to these sablés. Be sure to chop the nuts finely, so that it is easy to slice the log of dough.

1 Place **8 tbsp softened unsalted butter** in a large bowl. Add ¼ **cup granulated sugar** and ½ **cup light brown sugar**, and beat with a handheld mixer until light and fluffy.

2 Add ¼ **cup maple syrup**, **1 egg yolk**, and ½ **tsp vanilla extract** and beat well to combine. Sift in 1½ **cups all-purpose flour** and ¼ **tsp fine sea salt**. Add ¾ **cup finely chopped pecans** and bring the mixture together to form a dough. Shape it into a 10 x 2in (25 x 5cm) log, wrap tightly in parchment paper, and chill for 1 hour.

3 Preheat the oven to 350°F (180°C). Remove the paper and place the dough on a cutting board. Use a sharp knife to cut it into ½in (1cm) thick rounds. Place the rounds, spaced apart, on two nonstick baking sheets and transfer to the oven.

4 Bake the cookies in batches, for 15 minutes each, until they are golden brown at the edges. Cool them on the baking sheets for about 15 minutes before placing on a wire rack to cool completely. You can store the cookies in an airtight container for up to 5 days, or freeze them for up to 8 weeks.

PLAN AHEAD
You can wrap the dough in plastic wrap and chill it for up to 3 days ahead, or freeze it for up to 3 months. Defrost overnight in the fridge before baking.

🕐 **30 mins**
plus chilling and cooling   🍴 **MAKES 25**

SABLÉS chocolate

Green pistachios add flecks of color to these dark chocolate sablés. For the fullest pistachio flavor, use raw, unsalted nuts.

1 Place **8 tbsp softened unsalted butter** and **¾ cup granulated sugar** in a large bowl and beat with a handheld mixer until light and fluffy. Add **2 egg yolks** and **2 tsp vanilla extract** and beat well to combine.

2 Sift **1¾ cups all-purpose flour**, **½ cup cocoa powder**, and **½ tsp fine sea salt** into the bowl. Add **½ cup finely chopped pistachios** and bring the mixture together to form a dough. Shape the dough into a 12 x 2in (30 x 5cm) log, wrap it tightly in parchment paper, and chill for 1 hour.

3 Preheat the oven to 350°F (180°C). Remove the paper and place the dough on a chopping board. Use a sharp knife to cut it into ½in (1cm) thick rounds. Place the rounds, spaced apart, on two nonstick baking sheets and transfer to the oven.

4 Bake the cookies, in batches, for 12–15 minutes. Cool them on the baking sheets for 15 minutes before placing on a wire rack to cool completely. You can store the cookies in an airtight container for up to 5 days, or freeze them for up to 8 weeks.

PLAN AHEAD
You can wrap the dough in plastic wrap and chill it for up to 3 days ahead, or freeze it for up to 3 months. Defrost overnight in the fridge before baking.

Chocolate

Dips and double dips
Plunge sablés into rich chocolate, melted over a bainmarie. As always, make sure the bottom of your bowl does not touch the water in the pan.

Half dips Melt 6oz (175g) dark chocolate in a heatproof bowl over a pan of simmering water. Remove from the heat. Dip a Classic sablé (see pp260–61) halfway into the chocolate. Allow excess to drip off into the bowl, then place on a lined baking sheet to set. Repeat with the remaining sablés.

Double dips Half-dip Classic sablés (see p260–61) in dark chocolate, as above, and let dry on a lined baking sheet. Melt 6oz (175g) white chocolate in a separate bowl, then remove from the heat. Dip in the other half of each sablé and let set.

Dipped edges Prepare the Chocolate sablés (see left), reserving the crushed pistachios from the dough. Bake them and let cool. Roll the edges in a shallow plate of melted dark chocolate (see above) and then in the reserved bowl of crushed pistachios. Let set.

Total immersion Melt 6oz (175g) dark chocolate (see above). Remove the bowl from the heat and immerse each of the Ginger sablés (see opposite) into the chocolate. Place on a lined baking sheet, sprinkle with ⅓ cup chopped crystallized ginger, and let set.

🕐 **20 mins**
plus cooling

🍴 **MAKES 16**

TUILES simple

Classic tuiles are easy to make, but the art lies in timing and shaping them properly. Serve them with cream and fruit, or use them to decorate desserts such as possets, mousses, and sorbets.

INGREDIENTS

4 tbsp unsalted butter, softened

⅓ cup confectioners' sugar, sifted

1 egg, beaten

¼ cup all-purpose flour, sifted

vegetable oil, for greasing

whipped cream, to serve (optional)

raspberries, to serve (optional)

1

Preheat the oven to 400°F (200°C). Place the butter and sugar in a large bowl and beat together until light and fluffy. Add the egg and mix well to combine, then fold in the flour.

Gently fold in the flour with a metal spoon, making sure not to overmix.

2

Draw four 3¼in (8cm) wide circles on four sheets of parchment paper, turn them over, and place on baking sheets. Spoon the batter into the traced circles, using the back of a wet spoon to smooth it out to a thin layer. Bake on the top rack of the oven for 5-7 minutes, until the edges are golden brown.

3

Remove from the oven and use a palette knife to lift and drape the tuiles over a greased rolling pin. You have only seconds to shape them before they harden. Bake for another minute to soften them, if needed.

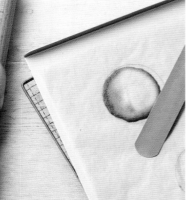

Leave the tuiles to cool on the rolling pin for 2-3 minutes.

Once cooled, gently transfer the tuiles to a wire rack to cool and dry completely. Serve them with whipped cream and raspberries, if desired. You can store the tuiles in an airtight container for up to 5 days.

4

TUILES lime and coconut

These cookies are so thin that any additions to the mixture must be very finely chopped or sliced. Simple fruit zest and coconut flakes add flavor and texture.

INGREDIENTS
4 tbsp unsalted
  butter, softened
½ cup confectioners' sugar
1 egg
grated zest of 1 lime
½ cup all-purpose flour
3–4 tbsp unsweetened,
  dried coconut flakes
vegetable oil, for greasing

1 Preheat the oven to 400°F (200°C). Place the butter and sugar in a bowl and beat until light and fluffy. Add the egg and beat to combine. Then beat in the lime zest, gently fold in the flour, and mix well.

2 Draw four 3¼in (8cm) wide circles on each of four sheets of parchment paper, turn them over, and place on baking sheets. Spoon the batter onto the traced circles and use the back of a wet spoon to smooth it out to a thin layer.

3 Sprinkle the coconut over the circles. Bake for 6–8 minutes, until golden brown at the edges. Remove, cool, and shape the tuiles over a greased rolling pin for 2–3 minutes. Place on a wire rack to cool completely before serving. You can store the tuiles in an airtight container for up to 2 days.

BRANDY SNAPS

A classic British treat, these crisp cookies are best served filled with whipped cream and dusted with confectioners' sugar.

INGREDIENTS
7 tbsp unsalted butter,
  diced
½ cup granulated sugar
¼ cup corn syrup
¾ cup all-purpose flour,
  sifted
1 tsp ground ginger
finely grated zest of
  ½ lemon
1 tbsp brandy
vegetable oil, for greasing

For the filling
1 cup heavy cream,
  whipped
1 tbsp confectioners' sugar
1 tsp brandy

SPECIAL EQUIPMENT
piping bag fitted with a
  large nozzle

PLAN AHEAD
You can store the
unfilled brandy snaps
in an airtight container
for up to 2 days ahead.

1 Preheat the oven to 350°F (180°C). Melt the butter and granulated sugar in a saucepan over medium heat. Add the syrup and mix well. Remove from the heat and beat in the flour, ginger, and lemon zest until well combined. Add the brandy and mix well to combine.

2 Draw four or five 3¼in (8cm) wide circles each on each of four sheets of parchment paper, turn them over, and place on baking sheets. Spoon the batter onto the traced circles (see Lime and coconut tuiles, step 2).

3 Bake on the top rack of the oven for 6–8 minutes, until they are golden brown and the edges have darkened slightly. Let them cool on the baking sheets for 3 minutes, until soft enough to shape and move with a spatula. Return to the oven for 1–2 minutes to soften, if needed.

4 Shape the cookies over the greased handle of a wooden spoon. Let cool and harden on the spoon before transferring to a wire rack to cool completely. Place the filling ingredients in a bowl and mix well to combine. Pipe the filling into the cooled, rolled brandy snaps. Once filled, the cookies will soften, so serve them immediately.

⏲ **30 mins** plus cooling   🍴 **MAKES 12**

CANNOLI TUILES Amaretto

Traditional Italian cannoli are deep fried. For a lighter variety that is easy to make, try these baked tuiles that are stuffed with an Amaretto and ricotta filling.

INGREDIENTS

½ cup granulated sugar

2 tbsp honey

4 tbsp unsalted butter, softened

2 tbsp heavy cream

1 tbsp Amaretto

½ cup all-purpose flour

vegetable oil, for greasing

For the filling

5½oz (150g) ricotta cheese

10oz (300g) mascarpone

½ cup confectioners' sugar

zest of 1 large lemon

1–2 tbsp Amaretto

1 tsp vanilla extract

½ tsp cinnamon

1oz (30g) grated dark chocolate, to decorate

SPECIAL EQUIPMENT

piping bag fitted with a large star nozzle

PLAN AHEAD

You can store the unfilled cannoli in an airtight container for up to 2 days ahead.

1 Preheat the oven to 400°F (200°C). Melt the granulated sugar, honey, butter, cream, and Amaretto in a saucepan over low heat for 5 minutes, stirring, until the mixture is smooth and the sugar has melted.

2 Remove from the heat, add the flour, and beat well to combine. Use a greased tablespoon to place spoonfuls of the mixture on lined baking sheets in neat circles, spaced well apart. Place only 2–3 tablespoons on each sheet to avoid overcrowding.

3 Bake on the top rack of the oven for 5–7 minutes, until golden brown all over. Let the tuiles cool on the baking sheets for 2–3 minutes until set, but still soft enough to shape.

4 Wrap the tuiles loosely around the greased handle of a large wooden spoon. Bake them for another 1–2 minutes to soften, if they cool too quickly. Let set and harden on the spoon, then transfer to a wire rack to cool completely.

5 For the filling, beat the ricotta in a bowl until smooth. Beat in the remaining ingredients until thick and smooth, and pipe the mixture into the cannoli. Sprinkle each end of the cannoli with chocolate. Once filled, the tuiles will soften, so serve them immediately.

Cups and cones

Warm tuile cookies (see pp264–65) are flexible and perfect for shaping. Cool them for a few seconds, then shape while they are still pliable.

Cones Mold tightly crumpled tin foil into a cone shape and wrap a still-warm tuile cookie around it to form the cone. It cools and sets in a few seconds. Serve with a small ice cream scoop, if desired.

Spirals Shape your tuile dough into 1¼ x 4in (3 x 10cm) strips on a lined baking sheet. Bake in the oven, and when warm, wrap around the handle of a greased wooden spoon. Slide them off once hardened.

Cigars Wrap the warm rounds of baked tuiles tightly around the handle of a greased wooden spoon. Once cool, dip them in 6oz (175g) dark chocolate, melted in a heatproof bowl over a pan of simmering water.

Brandy snap baskets Use an upturned, lightly buttered ramekin to mold still-warm and flexible Brandy snap rounds (see opposite) into a basket shape. Let cool and set, fill with fresh fruit or sorbet, and serve immediately.

FROZEN

Ice creams and sorbets ▪ Iced desserts

INGREDIENTS

2 cups heavy cream

1¼ cups whole milk

1–2 tsp pure vanilla extract

pinch of salt

½ cup granulated sugar

¼ cup light brown sugar

4 large egg yolks

SPECIAL EQUIPMENT

ice cream maker

2-quart shallow freezer-
proof airtight container

PLAN AHEAD

You can prepare, cover,
and store the custard in
the fridge up to 1 day
before freezing.

 **25 mins**
plus chilling and freezing   **SERVES 4**

ICE CREAM vanilla

Nothing beats the smooth, creamy flavor of good vanilla ice
cream. Homemade ice cream is surprisingly simple. Store the
bowl of the ice cream maker in the freezer, if possible, so
that you can whip up a treat whenever you feel like it.

1

Prepare the ice cream maker
as per the instructions. Heat
the cream, milk, vanilla extract,
salt, and both types of sugar
in a saucepan over low heat,
stirring until the sugar dissolves.
Whisk the egg yolks in a large
heatproof bowl.

2

When it is steaming, whisk
a little of the milk mixture
into the egg yolks. Then
whisk in the remaining milk
until combined. Transfer
back to the pan and cook
over medium–low heat
until thick enough to coat
the back of a spoon.

3

Remove from the heat and pour the custard back into a large bowl set over an ice bath. Let cool for about 20 minutes, then remove the bowl from the ice bath, cover with plastic wrap, and chill for 6–7 hours, or overnight, until completely chilled.

Remove the mixture from the fridge and pour into the ice cream maker. Churn for 10–15 minutes, until thick. Pour the ice cream into the airtight container and freeze for 4–5 hours, until firm. Remove from the freezer 20 minutes before serving. You can store the ice cream in a freezer-proof container in the freezer for up to 2 months.

4

🕐 **50 mins**
plus chilling and freezing 🍴 **SERVES 4**

ICE CREAM pecan and salted caramel

The addictive marriage of salt and caramel works perfectly for ice cream. Use good-quality sea salt flakes that dissolve easily.

INGREDIENTS
2 cups heavy cream
1¼ cups whole milk
⅛ tsp sea salt flakes
½ cup granulated sugar
¼ cup light brown sugar
7 large egg yolks, beaten
1 tsp pure vanilla extract
¾ cup chopped pecans

For the caramel
½ cup granulated sugar
½ cup heavy cream
1 tbsp unsalted butter
½ tsp salt
¾ tsp vanilla extract

SPECIAL EQUIPMENT
ice cream maker
3-quart shallow, freezer-
proof container with a lid

PLAN AHEAD
You can prepare, cover, and store the custard in the fridge up to 1 day ahead of freezing.

1 Prepare the ice cream maker as per the instructions. For the caramel, boil the granulated sugar and 2 tablespoons of water in a saucepan over medium–high heat, brushing down the sides of the pan with a damp pastry brush. Cook the sugar for 5 minutes, swirling the pan to ensure it cooks evenly. Remove from the heat.

2 Gradually add the remaining caramel ingredients, stirring with a wooden spoon. Melt again over medium–low heat. Transfer to a bowl and let cool. Heat the cream, milk, salt, and both types of sugar in a saucepan over low heat, stirring until the sugar dissolves.

3 In a bowl, whisk a little cream mixture into the beaten yolks until combined. Whisk in the rest of the cream mixture. Transfer the custard to a clean pan. Cook over medium–low heat until it is thick enough to coat the back of a spoon. Remove and stir in the vanilla extract.

4 Strain the custard into a bowl set over an ice bath. Let cool completely. Cover with plastic wrap and chill for 1–2 hours. Pour into the ice cream maker and churn, adding the pecans halfway through, until thick.

5 Pour half of the ice cream into the airtight container followed by half the caramel. Then repeat with the remaining ice cream and caramel, creating a swirl effect with a knife. Cover and freeze for 4–5 hours, until firm. Remove from the freezer 20 minutes before serving. You can store the ice cream for 1–2 months in the freezer.

🕐 **55 mins–1 hr**
plus chilling and freezing 🍴 **SERVES 4**

ICE CREAM peach

This simple fruity ice cream gives you delicious good-quality ice cream without an ice cream maker.

INGREDIENTS
4 peaches, halved
and pitted
2½ tbsp light brown sugar
2¼ cups heavy cream
1 cup whole milk
¾ cup granulated sugar
¾ tsp pure vanilla extract
pinch of salt
2½ tsp lemon juice

SPECIAL EQUIPMENT
3-quart shallow, freezer-
proof container with a lid

PLAN AHEAD
You can prepare and store the peach puree in an airtight container up to 1 day ahead.

1 Place the airtight container in the freezer. Preheat the oven to 400°F (200°C). Place the peaches in a shallow ovenproof dish and sprinkle the brown sugar over the top.

2 Bake the peaches for 25–30 minutes, until they are tender and lightly caramelized on top. Then transfer them to a food processor and pulse until smooth. Strain the peach puree into a bowl, cover, and place in the freezer until cold, but not frozen.

3 Combine the cream, milk, granulated sugar, vanilla extract, salt, and lemon juice in a bowl, stirring until the sugar dissolves. Then add the peach puree, mix until smooth, and pour the mixture into the airtight container. Cover and freeze for 50–60 minutes.

4 Mix the ice cream to break up any crystals that may have formed, repeating every 45–55 minutes until fully frozen. Remove from the freezer 20 minutes before serving. You can store the ice cream for 1–2 months in the freezer.

Simple alternatives

An ice cream base is so easy to adapt. Some ideas require an ice cream maker (see pp270–71), whereas some take on the handmade varieties (see opposite).

Cookies and cream Prepare the Vanilla ice cream (see pp270–71, steps 1–4) and stir in 2oz (60g) coarsely crumbled Oreos before freezing.

Coffee Combine 1 tbsp medium-strength coffee powder and 1 tbsp hot water in a small bowl and let cool. Prepare the Vanilla ice cream (see pp270–71, steps 1–4) and stir in the coffee mixture before freezing.

Rum and raisin Place ½ cup raisins and 3 tbsp dark rum in a small bowl. Let steep overnight. Prepare the Vanilla ice cream (see pp270–71, steps 1–4) and stir in the steeped raisin mixture before freezing.

Chocolate bar Coarsely chop about 2¼oz (65g) of your favorite chocolate bars into small pieces. Prepare the Vanilla ice cream (see pp270–71, steps 1–4) and stir in the chocolate before freezing.

Apple and cinnamon Replace the peaches (see Peach ice cream, steps 1–4), with 4 apples, cored and quartered, add 1 tsp ground cinnamon, and continue with the recipe.

Mint chocolate chip Replace the lavender (see Lavender ice cream, steps 1–4) with 1 tsp finely chopped mint and 1 tsp green food coloring paste. Add 2oz (60g) finely chopped good-quality dark chocolate just before freezing in step 2.

Cherry and walnut Replace the peaches (see Peach ice cream, steps 1–4) with 14oz (400g) ripe pitted cherries. Add ⅓ cup chopped walnuts to the ice cream mixture before freezing.

🕐 **20 mins** plus chilling and freezing   🍴 **SERVES 4**

ICE CREAM lavender

Culinary lavender gives a gentle floral fragrance to this ice cream, which does not require an ice cream maker.

INGREDIENTS

2 cups heavy cream

1¼ cups whole milk

¼ cup clover honey

¼ cup granulated sugar

3½ tbsp dried culinary lavender, plus extra to serve

pinch of salt

¼ tsp pure vanilla extract

SPECIAL EQUIPMENT

3-quart shallow, freezer-proof container with a lid

1 Place the airtight container in the freezer. Heat all the ingredients in a large saucepan over medium heat, stirring constantly until the sugar dissolves. Remove from the heat once the mixture begins to simmer and let infuse for 30 minutes.

2 Strain the mixture through a fine mesh strainer into a large bowl, discarding the lavender. Chill for 1–2 hours, then pour the mixture into the airtight container. Cover and freeze for 1 hour.

3 Remove the ice cream from the freezer and mix gently with a wooden spoon to break up any crystals that form. Return to the freezer and repeat every 45–55 minutes, until the ice cream is fully frozen.

4 Remove the ice cream from the freezer 20 minutes before serving, spoon into bowls, and sprinkle with the reserved lavender. You can store the ice cream for 1–2 months in the freezer.

🕐 **35 mins**
plus cooling and freezing

🍴 **SERVES 8**

SEMI FREDDO coffee

An Italian dessert, *semi freddo* translates as "half frozen." To make a classic semi freddo, freeze a combination of mousse, custard, cream, and flavorings—the texture of the finished dessert will be somewhere between a mousse and an ice cream.

INGREDIENTS

4 eggs, separated

¾ cup granulated sugar

2 tbsp instant coffee powder, plus extra for dusting

1¼ cups heavy cream, whipped to soft peaks

scant 1oz (25g) good-quality dark chocolate

SPECIAL EQUIPMENT

9 x 5in (22 x 12cm) loaf pan

1 Line the pan with plastic wrap and set aside. Place the egg yolks and ¼ cup of the sugar in a heatproof bowl over a saucepan of simmering water, making sure it does not touch the water.

2 Beat the mixture with a handheld mixer for 5 minutes, until it is pale, light, and has tripled in volume.

3 Combine the coffee powder with 2 tablespoons of boiling water in a cup. Gradually beat the coffee mixture into the egg yolk mixture, then remove from the heat and beat for 3–5 minutes, until cool.

4 Beat the egg whites and remaining granulated sugar in a separate heatproof bowl over the pan of simmering water (see step 1) to form stiff peaks. Remove from the heat and beat for another 3–5 minutes, until it cools. Fold a little of the meringue into the coffee mixture.

5 Carefully fold the remaining meringue into the coffee mixture, so that you lose as little air as possible, until combined. Gently fold in the whipped cream and pour the mixture into the pan. Cover with plastic wrap and freeze for 4–6 hours.

6 Melt the chocolate in a heatproof bowl over a pan of simmering water (see step 1). Invert the semi freddo onto a plate, discarding both sheets of plastic wrap. Dust with coffee powder, decorate with the melted chocolate, and serve. You can store it, covered in the freezer, for up to 1 month.

SEMI FREDDO dark chocolate and brandied prune

You can serve this rich semi freddo as an alternative to a festive yule log—it is the perfect make-ahead dessert.

INGREDIENTS

1 cup soft prunes, diced

3 tbsp brandy

7oz (200g) good-quality dark chocolate, broken into pieces

4 eggs

½ cup granulated sugar

1¼ cups heavy cream

dark chocolate curls, to decorate

SPECIAL EQUIPMENT

1lb (450g) loaf pan

1 Line the pan with plastic wrap. Place the prunes and brandy in a small saucepan. Add just enough water to cover the prunes and bring to a boil. Reduce the heat to a low simmer and cook for 5 minutes. Remove from the heat and let steep until needed.

2 Melt the chocolate in a heatproof bowl over a pan of simmering water, making sure it does not touch the water. Remove from the heat. In a separate bowl, beat the eggs and sugar over a pan of simmering water until the mixture is pale, fluffy, and has tripled in volume.

3 Remove from the heat and beat for another 3–5 minutes, until cool. Whisk a spoonful of the egg mixture into the chocolate and combine, then add it all back into the egg mixture and fold it in gently. Beat the cream in a bowl to form soft peaks.

4 Gradually fold the cream into the egg mixture, so that you lose as little air as possible. Then gently fold in the prunes until evenly combined. Pour the mixture into the prepared pan, cover with plastic wrap, and freeze for at least 4–6 hours.

5 Remove the pan from the freezer and turn out the semi freddo, discarding both sheets of plastic wrap (see Yogurt, honey, and pistachio semi freddo, steps 2–3). Serve decorated with dark chocolate curls. You can store the semi freddo, covered in the freezer, for up to 1 month.

SEMI FREDDO yogurt, honey, and pistachio

Because eggs are omitted from this recipe, this modern take on semi freddo has a firm texture—this also means that it keeps for much longer in the freezer.

INGREDIENTS

1¾ cups full-fat Greek yogurt

6 tbsp honey, plus extra to serve (optional)

grated zest of 1 large orange

¾ cup heavy cream

¼ cup unsalted and skinned pistachios, finely chopped

SPECIAL EQUIPMENT

1lb (450g) loaf pan

1 Line the pan with plastic wrap. Beat the yogurt, honey, and orange zest in a large bowl until smooth and well combined. In a separate bowl, beat the cream to form soft peaks and carefully fold into the yogurt mixture. Fold in three-quarters of the pistachios.

2 Pour the mixture into the prepared pan, cover with plastic wrap, and freeze for at least 6 hours. Then remove from the freezer, take off the plastic wrap, and invert the pan over a large serving plate. Shake the pan lightly, if needed, to release the semi freddo.

3 Peel off the plastic wrap. Sprinkle with the reserved pistachios and a drizzle of honey, if desired, and serve immediately. You can store the semi freddo, covered in the freezer, for up to 3 months.

🕐 **35 mins**
plus cooling and freezing   🍴 **SERVES 8**

SEMI FREDDO
raspberry meringue

This dessert takes inspiration from a classic raspberry pavlova. Freezing meringue, cream, and fruit creates a light and creamy semi freddo that is ideal for the summer months.

INGREDIENTS
4 eggs

½ cup granulated sugar

¾ cup heavy cream, whipped to soft peaks

1½oz (45g) store-bought meringues, broken into small pieces, plus extra to decorate

4½oz (125g) raspberries, lightly crushed, plus extra to serve

SPECIAL EQUIPMENT
1lb (450g) loaf pan

1 Line the pan with plastic wrap. Place the eggs and sugar in a heatproof bowl over a saucepan of simmering water, making sure it does not touch the water. Beat with a handheld mixer, until the mixture is pale, fluffy, and has tripled in volume. Remove from the heat and beat for another 3–5 minutes, until cool.

2 Fold the whipped cream carefully into the egg mixture, so that you lose as little air as possible. Then fold in the meringues and raspberries. Pour the mixture into the prepared pan, cover with plastic wrap, and freeze for at least 4–6 hours, until frozen.

3 Remove the pan from the freezer and turn out the semi freddo, discarding both sheets of plastic wrap (see Yogurt, honey, and pistachio semi freddo, steps 2–3). Serve with crushed meringue pieces and raspberries. You can store the semi freddo, covered in the freezer, for up to 1 month.

🕐 **35 mins**
plus cooling, chilling, and freezing   🍴 **SERVES 8**

SEMI FREDDO
coconut, lime, and mango

This tropical iced indulgence has the perfect balance of flavors, thanks to sweet mango and sharp lime.

INGREDIENTS
3 egg yolks

¼ cup granulated sugar

1 tbsp cornstarch

1 x 14oz (400ml) can coconut milk

¾ cup heavy cream

¼ cup confectioners' sugar

6oz (175g) ripe mango, diced and chilled

grated zest of 2 limes

toasted coconut shavings, to decorate

SPECIAL EQUIPMENT
1lb (450g) loaf pan

1 Line the pan with plastic wrap. Beat the egg yolks, granulated sugar, and cornstarch in a large heatproof bowl. Gently heat the milk in a small, heavy-bottomed saucepan until hot, but not boiling. Carefully pour the milk over the egg yolk mixture, beating constantly until combined.

2 Return the custard mixture to the pan and heat gently for 4–5 minutes, stirring constantly, until thick enough to coat the back of a spoon. Pour it into a shallow bowl and let cool completely. Cover the surface with plastic wrap and chill until needed.

3 Beat the cream and confectioners' sugar in a bowl to form soft peaks. Chill until cold, then fold the cream into the custard, followed by the mangoes and lime zest. Pour the mixture into the prepared pan, cover with plastic wrap, and freeze for 6 hours, until frozen.

4 Remove the pan from the freezer and turn out the semi freddo, discarding both sheets of plastic wrap (see Yogurt, honey, and pistachio semi freddo, steps 2–3). Decorate with the coconut shavings to serve. You can store the semi freddo, covered in the freezer, for up to 1 month.

🕐 **45–50 mins**
plus cooling, chilling, and freezing

🍴 **SERVES 4–6**

SORBET lemon

To make a refreshing sorbet, churn and freeze a mixture of sugar syrup and flavorings. There are thousands of flavor combinations to try, but lemon sorbet is the classic, and, some would argue, the best.

INGREDIENTS
1¼ cups granulated sugar
zest of 2 lemons, plus extra to serve
1¼ cups lemon juice

SPECIAL EQUIPMENT
ice cream maker
1½ pint (800ml) airtight freezer-proof container

PLAN AHEAD
You can prepare and store the syrup in the fridge up to 3 days ahead.

Prepare the ice cream maker as per the instructions. Heat the sugar and 1¼ cups cold water in a saucepan for 5 minutes, stirring occasionally, until the sugar dissolves.

1

Pour the syrup into a large heatproof bowl. Let cool completely, then chill until cold. Add the lemon zest to the syrup.

2

Strain the lemon juice and discard the seeds. Add it to the syrup and whisk the mixture well to combine.

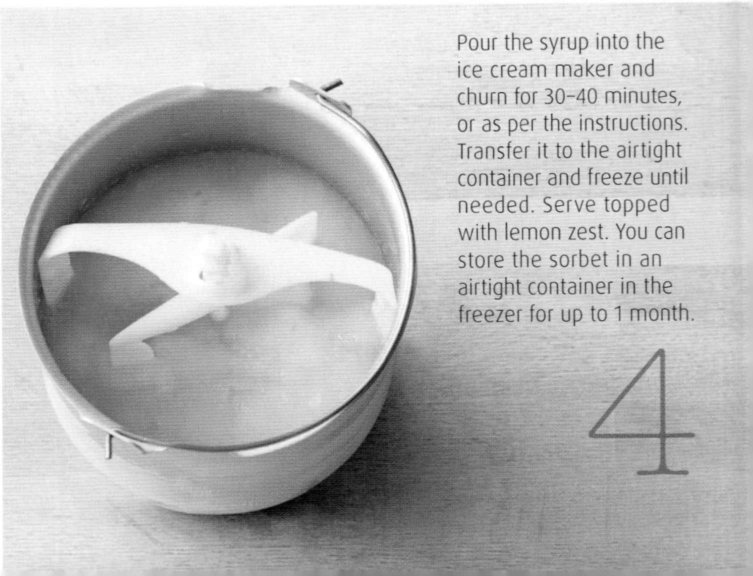

3

Pour the syrup into the ice cream maker and churn for 30–40 minutes, or as per the instructions. Transfer it to the airtight container and freeze until needed. Serve topped with lemon zest. You can store the sorbet in an airtight container in the freezer for up to 1 month.

4

🕐 **30 mins**
plus cooling, chilling, and freezing   🍴 **SERVES 4–6**

SORBET raspberry and hibiscus

Dried hibiscus flowers impart a gorgeous dark red color. You can find them in health food stores.

1 Prepare the **ice cream maker** as per the instructions. Place **1¼ cups granulated sugar**, **½ cup dried hibiscus flowers**, and **2 cups cold water** in a large saucepan and bring to a boil. Then reduce to a simmer and cook for 5 minutes, stirring occasionally, until the sugar dissolves. Pour into a heatproof bowl.

2 Let the juice cool, then chill overnight. The next day, strain the juice into a blender, pressing the flowers with the back of a spoon. Discard the flowers. Add **1lb 2oz (500g) raspberries** and **juice of 1 lime** to the blender and pulse until smooth.

3 Strain the liquid into a large pitcher, pressing down with the back of a spoon. Pour it into the ice cream maker and freeze as per the instructions. Then transfer it to a **2¾ pint (1.5 liter) shallow freezer-proof container** and freeze until needed. You can store the sorbet in the container in the freezer for up to 1 month.

🕐 **15 mins**
plus chilling and freezing   🍴 **SERVES 4–6**

SHERBET pink grapefruit and rose water

A sherbet is a cross between an ice cream and a sorbet. It is simple to prepare, and does not require an ice cream maker.

1 Place **1¼ cups granulated sugar**, **grated zest of 1 large pink grapefruit**, **2 cups pink grapefruit juice**, and **1 tbsp rose water** in a blender. Pulse for 2 minutes, until it is well combined and the sugar has dissolved.

2 Transfer the mixture to a bowl and chill for 1 hour. Then transfer to a blender, add **1½ cups whole milk**, and pulse until well combined. Pour the liquid into a **2¾ pint (1.5 liter) shallow freezer-proof container**.

3 Transfer to the freezer, scraping the frozen edges into the center of the container with a fork every 45 minutes, breaking up any larger ice crystals with the back of the fork. Repeat this process for 3 hours, or until the mixture is well frozen, but not solid, then freeze until needed.

4 Whisk **1 large egg white** in a bowl and use to brush **12–16 washed and dried large edible rose petals**. Sprinkle the petals evenly with **granulated sugar**, shake off any excess, and let dry. Serve the sherbet decorated with the rose petals. You can store the sherbet in the container in the freezer for up to 1 month.

Raspberry and hibiscus sorbet

Pink grapefruit and rose water sherbet

Coffee granita

🕐 **15 mins**
plus cooling, chilling, and freezing

🍴 **SERVES 4**

GRANITA coffee

With its signature crystallized texture, this is a refreshing alternative to after-dinner coffee. It is easy to make—there is no need for an ice cream maker.

1. Place **2 tbsp espresso powder**, **2 tbsp granulated sugar**, **2 tbsp coffee liqueur**, and **1 tsp vanilla extract** in a large heatproof pitcher. Pour in **2 cups boiling water**, whisking until the sugar dissolves.

2. Pour the liquid into the **2 pint (1.2 liter) shallow freezer-proof container**. Cool to room temperature, chill until cold, then transfer to the freezer.

3. Scrape the frozen edges of the granita into the center of the container with a fork every 45 minutes, breaking up any larger ice crystals with the back of the fork.

4. Repeat this process for 3–4 hours, until the mixture is well frozen, but not solid. Serve. You can store the granita in the container in the freezer for up to 1 month.

 **25 mins** plus cooling **MAKES 4**

SUNDAE vanilla and chocolate with pecan brittle

Whether you make your own vanilla ice cream (see p270–71) or buy it at the store, there is no better way to serve it than as the basis of this sundae—drenched with warm chocolate sauce and sprinkled with crunchy brittle.

INGREDIENTS
⅓ cup pecans, halved
⅔ cup granulated sugar
1 pint good-quality vanilla ice cream

For the sauce
4 tbsp unsalted butter
2½oz (75g) good-quality dark chocolate, chopped into small pieces
¾ cup condensed milk
½ tsp vanilla extract
¼ tsp sea salt flakes

SPECIAL EQUIPMENT
4 x 5½fl oz (160ml) sundae glasses

PLAN AHEAD
You can prepare and store the brittle in an airtight container up to 2 weeks ahead. You can prepare and store the sauce in an airtight container in the fridge up to 1 week ahead.

1

Preheat the oven to 350°F (180°C). Spread the pecans on a baking sheet and bake on the top rack of the oven for 5 minutes, until lightly toasted. Remove from the heat and let cool.

2

Coarsely chop the pecans and place them in a tight, single layer on a baking sheet lined with parchment paper. Heat the sugar in a heavy-bottomed saucepan over medium heat for 5 minutes, without stirring, until it begins to melt at the edges.

3

Cook the sugar, stirring gently, to form a light-colored caramel. Pour it over the pecans and tip the pan gently to help spread it out evenly. Let cool completely, then break the brittle into small pieces and set aside.

4

For the sauce, melt the butter and chocolate in a small heatproof bowl over a pan of simmering water, making sure it does not touch the water. Stir well until smooth and remove from the heat.

5

Remove the water from the heat. Whisk the remaining ingredients into the chocolate mixture until combined. Keep the sauce warm over the pan of water.

6

Divide the ice cream between the glasses and pour the sauce over the top. Sprinkle with the brittle and serve immediately.

🕐 **35 mins**
plus cooling and drying

🍴 **MAKES 4**

SUNDAE salted caramel and chocolate crunch

Salt has become a dessert staple, and it's easy to see why—good-quality salt contrasts with sweet flavors, while accenting them at the same time.

1 For the salted caramel, heat ¾ **cup granulated sugar** in a heavy-bottomed saucepan over medium heat until it has melted. Then whisk for 7–10 minutes, until the sugar is amber brown in color. Add **8 tbsp diced unsalted butter** and whisk well to combine.

2 Remove from the heat and add ½ **cup heavy cream**, whisking constantly until smooth. Then whisk in **1 tsp vanilla extract** and **1 tsp sea salt flakes** until well combined. Set aside to cool.

3 Melt 2½oz (75g) **good-quality dark chocolate chips** in a heatproof bowl over a pan of simmering water, making sure it does not touch the water. Dip **10 pretzels** two-thirds of the way into the chocolate, dripping off any excess. Place them to dry on a lined baking sheet.

4 Divide **1 pint good-quality vanilla ice cream** between **4 x 5½fl oz (160ml) sundae glasses**. Reserving four of the pretzels, coarsely crush the rest and scatter over and around the ice cream. Drizzle with the salted caramel and top each sundae with one of the reserved pretzels. Serve immediately.

Salted caramel and chocolate crunch

🕐 **20 mins**   🍴 **MAKES 4**

SUNDAE summer fruit

This stunning and sophisticated sundae benefits from the hint of vanilla, which adds incredible depth to the sauce and the crunch of meringue.

1. Combine **5½oz (150g) blackberries**, **3½oz (100g) halved and pitted cherries**, and **3½oz (100g) blueberries** in a small heavy-bottomed saucepan with a lid. Add **¼ cup granulated sugar**, **½ tsp vanilla extract**, and **2 tbsp of water** to the pan.

2. Cover and bring the mixture to a boil, then reduce the heat to low, uncover, and cook for another 5–7 minutes, until the berries start to break down and release their juices. Remove the compote from the heat and let cool slightly.

3. Beat **½ cup heavy cream** in a bowl to form soft peaks. Break **2oz (60g) store-bought meringues** into small pieces. Place **1 scoop vanilla ice cream** into **4 x 5½fl oz (160ml) sundae glasses**.

4. Reserving a little for decoration, sprinkle over the meringue pieces. Top with **1 scoop of ice cream** and spoon over the warm berry compote. Top the sundae with a spoonful of the whipped cream and a sprinkling of the reserved meringue. Serve immediately.

PLAN AHEAD
You can prepare and store the compote in the fridge up to 3 days ahead. Reheat gently to serve.

Summer fruit

🕐 **15 mins**   🍴 **MAKES 4**

SPLIT banana

Give an old-fashioned sundae an update with a homemade warm chocolate sauce, pistachios, and good-quality vanilla ice cream.

1. For the sauce, heat **2oz (60g) chopped good-quality dark chocolate** and **⅓ cup heavy cream** in a small, heavy-bottomed saucepan. Stir constantly until the chocolate has melted, then remove from the heat and keep warm.

2. Beat **½ cup heavy cream** in a bowl to form soft peaks. Peel **4 ripe bananas** and split them down the middle, lengthwise, to create two long slices. Place two slices each, cut-side up, in **4 x 10in (25cm) glass sundae dishes**.

3. Top the banana slices with **2 small scoops good-quality vanilla ice cream** and **1 small scoop good-quality milk chocolate ice cream**. Make sure that the chocolate ice cream is in the center.

4. Top the ice cream with small spoonfuls of the cream and drizzle over the chocolate sauce. Sprinkle the sundaes with **¼ cup chopped unsalted and skinned pistachios** and **¼ cup halved and pitted cherries**. Serve immediately.

Banana split

20 mins plus freezing   **SERVES 8**

BOMBE chocolate and cherry

This showstopping bombe is surprisingly easy to prepare. If cherry ice cream is difficult to find, a good-quality soft-serve raspberry ice cream works just as well. Make sure not to over-whisk the ice cream, or it will no longer hold its shape.

INGREDIENTS
3 pints chocolate ice cream, or chocolate chip ice cream
2½ pints cherry ice cream
1 pint dark chocolate ice cream

For the glaze
6oz (175g) good-quality dark chocolate
3 tbsp coconut oil

SPECIAL EQUIPMENT
10 cup freezer-proof bowl, about 8in (20cm) wide

PLAN AHEAD
You can prepare and store the glaze in the fridge up to 2 days ahead. Reheat it gently before use.

1

Line the freezer-proof bowl with plastic wrap, leaving some overhang. Place it in the freezer until needed. Place the milk chocolate ice cream in a large bowl and beat with a handheld mixer until slightly softened.

2

Cover the inside of the bowl with ice cream.

Spread the ice cream in an even layer in the prepared bowl, pressing it into shape. Place the bowl back in the freezer for 30–45 minutes, until the ice cream is solid.

3

Smooth out the chocolate layer before adding the second layer.

In a separate bowl, soften the cherry ice cream (see step 1). Remove the frozen bowl from the freezer and spread the cherry ice cream over the chocolate layer (see step 2). Freeze for another 30 minutes, or until firm.

4

Soften the dark chocolate ice cream (see step 1) and pack it into the center of the bombe. Freeze for 40 minutes.

5

Heat a large pan of water. Dip the bottom of the bombe bowl into the water for 15–20 seconds. Invert the bombe over a large serving dish and remove the bowl. Take off the plastic wrap and place the bombe in the freezer.

6

For the glaze, melt both the ingredients in a heatproof bowl over a pan of simmering water, making sure it does not touch the water. Leave for 1–2 minutes, then drizzle it over the bombe and serve immediately. You can store the bombe, covered in the freezer, for up to 3 days.

20 mins plus freezing **SERVES 8**

BOMBE mango and coconut

With a little patience and a simple technique, you can craft an ice cream bombe that is sure to wow your guests. Coconut ice cream is usually available in specialty supermarkets.

INGREDIENTS
2 quarts coconut ice cream
1 quart mango sorbet

For the glaze
6oz (175g) white chocolate
3 tbsp coconut oil

SPECIAL EQUIPMENT
10 cup freezer-proof bowl, about 8in (20cm) wide

PLAN AHEAD
You can prepare and store the glaze in the fridge up to 2 days ahead. Reheat gently before using.

1 Line the freezer-proof bowl with plastic wrap, leaving some overhang, and place it in the freezer. Beat half the ice cream in a bowl with a handheld mixer until slightly softened. Spread it evenly in the prepared bowl, covering the inside of the bowl completely. Press it into shape and freeze for 40–45 minutes, until solid.

2 Soften the mango sorbet (see step 1). Spread it evenly over the ice cream layer and freeze for another 30 minutes, or until firm. Beat the remaining ice cream in a bowl until softened and use to fill the center of the bombe. Freeze for 40 minutes.

3 Heat a large saucepan of water and dip the bottom of the bombe bowl in it for 15–20 seconds. Then invert the bombe over a large serving dish, remove the bowl, and discard the plastic wrap. Freeze until needed.

4 For the glaze, melt both ingredients in a heatproof bowl over a pan of simmering water, making sure it does not touch the water. Let it warm up briefly. Pour the glaze over the bombe and serve immediately. You can store it, covered in the freezer, for up to 3 days.

20 mins plus freezing **SERVES 8**

BOMBE banana, toffee, and salted peanut

Mixing ice cream through the banana layer gives this bombe a light, soft texture. You can also top with peanuts.

INGREDIENTS
3 bananas, sliced
2 quarts toffee ice cream
¼ cup salted peanuts, chopped
1 quart vanilla ice cream

SPECIAL EQUIPMENT
10 cup freezer-proof bowl, about 8in (20cm) wide

1 Line a large baking sheet with parchment paper. Spread the banana slices on the parchment, spaced well apart. Freeze for 1 hour, or until they are solid.

2 Line the freezer-proof bowl with plastic wrap, leaving some overhang, and place it in the freezer. Beat the toffee ice cream in a large bowl with a handheld mixer until slightly softened.

3 Spread the ice cream evenly in the prepared bowl, covering the inside of the bowl completely. Press it into shape and freeze for 40–45 minutes, until solid. Place the frozen banana slices in a bowl. Blend with a hand-held blender until smooth and fold in the peanuts.

4 Soften 2½ cups of the vanilla ice cream (see step 2) and fold into the banana and peanut mixture. Spread this mixture over the toffee ice cream evenly and freeze for 30 minutes, or until firm. Then soften the remaining vanilla ice cream and use to fill the center of the bombe. Freeze for another 40 minutes.

5 Using a large saucepan of hot water, turn out the bombe over a large serving dish (see Mango and coconut bombe, step 3). Remove the bowl, take off the plastic wrap, and serve immediately. You can store the bombe, covered in the freezer, for up to 3 days.

ICE CREAM BOMBES
Alternative sauces

A sauce can add fresh flavor to an ice cream bombe. Some of these sauces are designed with bombe recipes in mind, but they also work well drizzled over a serving of ice cream.

◄ Dulce de leche sauce

Whisk 1 x 14oz (400g) can dulce de leche with ½ cup half-and-half. Add a pinch of sea salt. This sauce makes a delicious accompaniment to the Banana, toffee, and salted peanut bombe (see opposite). Pour it over the bombe while still warm, since it thickens as it cools.

Pineapple and rum sauce ▲

Place 1 x 14½oz (425g) canned pineapple chunks in a blender, along with ¼ cup of the juices. Add 2 tbsp dark rum, blend to a smooth sauce, and chill until needed. You can serve it alongside the Mango and coconut bombe (see opposite).

◄ Strawberry sauce

Place 14oz (400g) coarsely chopped strawberries, 1 heaping tbsp granulated sugar, and juice of 1 lemon in a saucepan with a lid. Cover and simmer for 10 minutes, then puree and strain the sauce before chilling. Serve with any ice cream bombe.

◄ Warm chocolate fudge sauce

Serve this with the Banana, toffee, and salted peanut bombe (see opposite). Melt 4 tbsp unsalted butter and 1¾oz (50g) diced dark chocolate in a heatproof bowl over a pan of simmering water, making sure it does not touch the water. Remove from the heat and whisk in ¾ cup condensed milk and ½ tsp vanilla extract. Serve warm, or at room temperature.

Chocolate mocha sauce ►

Heat ½ cup heavy cream and ¼ cup corn syrup until hot, but not boiling. Pour it over 4oz (115g) finely chopped dark chocolate and 1 tsp espresso powder, and whisk until melted. Serve warm since it thickens when it cools. Perfect with the Chocolate and cherry bombe (see pp286–87).

Dark cherry sauce ▲

Place 7oz (200g) pitted cherries, 2 tbsp granulated sugar, and 1 tbsp water in a small saucepan with a lid. Cover and heat gently for about 10 minutes, until the cherries start to release their juices and soften. Puree until completely smooth, chill, and serve drizzled over your choice of ice cream bombe.

⏱ **40 mins**
plus chilling and freezing

🍴 **MAKES 6**

PARFAIT white chocolate and rose water

A parfait is a soft and light frozen dessert that combines eggs and cream and sweetens them with sugar syrup. It doesn't require an ice cream maker, but you do need a cooking thermometer to get the syrup to the correct temperature.

INGREDIENTS
1 cup heavy cream
4½oz (125g) white chocolate, finely chopped
½ cup granulated sugar
⅛ tsp salt
4 large egg yolks
1 tsp rose water

¼ cup unsalted and skinned pistachios, coarsely chopped

SPECIAL EQUIPMENT
sugar thermometer
6 x 5fl oz (150ml) freezer-proof glasses

1 Beat the cream in a bowl to form soft peaks and chill until needed. Melt the chocolate in a heatproof bowl over a saucepan of simmering water, making sure it does not touch the water. Remove from the heat and set aside, stirring frequently to ensure it does not burn.

Stir the chocolate gently to ensure it is smooth.

2 Heat the sugar, salt, and ¼ cup water in a pan over low heat, stirring occasionally, until the sugar dissolves. Bring to a boil, then reduce the heat to a simmer and cook until the temperature reaches 230°F (110°C). Remove from the heat.

Check the temperature at regular intervals.

3 Meanwhile, in the bowl of a standing mixer, beat the egg yolks for 4–5 minutes, until pale and smooth. Then beat in the hot sugar syrup in a steady stream, until combined. Add the rose water, beat well, then fold in the chocolate. Beat for another 1 minute, or until well combined.

4 Gently fold in the whipped cream, until no streaks remain. Pour it into the glasses and freeze for 1 hour. Sprinkle the parfait with pistachios to serve. You can store the parfait, covered in the freezer, for 2–3 days.

🕐 **45 mins**
plus chilling and freezing

🍴 **MAKES 6**

PARFAIT vanilla and honey with strawberries

This is a summery twist on a classic parfait. Ripe strawberries and crisp sliced almonds provide a fantastic contrast in texture. Layer your dessert quickly, as parfaits tend to melt at room temperature.

INGREDIENTS
1 cup heavy cream
4 large egg yolks
¼ cup granulated sugar
3 tbsp honey
⅛ tsp salt
1 tsp vanilla bean paste
1lb (450g) strawberries, hulled and diced
⅓ cup sliced almonds

SPECIAL EQUIPMENT
sugar thermometer
6 x 5½fl oz (160ml) glass jars

PLAN AHEAD
You can prepare and store the parfait mixture in an airtight container in the freezer 2–3 days ahead.

1 Beat the cream in a bowl to form soft peaks and chill until needed. In a separate bowl, beat the egg yolks vigorously for 4–5 minutes, until they are pale yellow in color. Set aside.

2 Heat the sugar, honey, salt, and ¼ cup water in a small saucepan over low heat, stirring frequently, until the sugar dissolves. Bring to a boil, then reduce the heat and simmer until the temperature reaches 230°F (110°C).

3 Remove the sugar syrup from the heat. Pour it into the egg yolk mixture, in a steady stream, beating constantly until the mixture thickens and cools slightly.

Gently fold in the vanilla bean paste, then the cream, until no streaks remain. Transfer to an airtight container and freeze for at least 3 hours.

4 Remove from the freezer 10 minutes before serving. Place one scoop of the parfait mixture in each glass and top with a layer of the strawberries and almonds. Repeat the process to make another layer of each and serve immediately.

🕐 **25 mins**
plus chilling and freezing

🍴 **MAKES 4**

PARFAIT tropical fruit

Flavor a simple parfait with coconut, and then, just before serving, layer it with small diced tropical fruit to create a sundae-style dessert.

INGREDIENTS
1 cup heavy cream
4 large egg yolks
½ cup granulated sugar
⅛ tsp salt
1¼ tsp coconut extract
2–3 kiwis, diced
6oz (175g) pineapple, diced
½ cup coconut shavings,
  plus extra to serve
1 mango, diced

SPECIAL EQUIPMENT
sugar thermometer
4 x 5½fl oz (160ml) glass jars

PLAN AHEAD
You can prepare and store the parfait mixture in an airtight container in the freezer 2–3 days ahead.

1 Beat the cream in a bowl to form soft peaks and chill until needed. In a separate bowl, beat the egg yolks and set aside (see Vanilla and honey parfait, step 1).

2 Heat the sugar, salt, and ¼ cup water in a small saucepan over low heat, stirring, until the sugar dissolves. Bring to a boil, then reduce the heat and simmer until the temperature reaches 230°F (110°C).

3 Pour the sugar syrup into the egg yolks and beat well (see Vanilla and honey parfait, step 3). Then add the coconut extract and beat until combined. Fold in whipped cream. Transfer the mixture to an airtight container and freeze for 3 hours.

4 Remove from the freezer 10 minutes before serving. Make two layers each of the parfait mixture, fruit, and coconut in each glass jar (see Vanilla and honey parfait, step 4). Serve immediately.

Drips and drizzles

Parfait is often neutral in color, so go wild with contrasting drizzled sauces—either on top or over serving plates.

Zigzag Heat ¼ cup store-bought dulce de leche in a small bowl over gently simmering water until it is just warm. Transfer it to a disposable piping bag, snip off a corner, and zigzag the sauce over scoops of Vanilla and honey parfait (see opposite).

Feather coulis Serve a mango coulis with the Tropical fruit parfait (see left). Puree the flesh of 2 mangoes with the juice of 1 lemon and 1 tbsp confectioners' sugar until smooth. Pour into a piping bag and pipe lines over your plate, then drag a skewer through the lines at an angle for a feathered effect.

Chocolate crème anglaise Prepare crème anglaise (see Blueberry upside-down cakes with crème anglaise, p69), adding 1¾oz (50g) finely grated dark chocolate at step 5. Pool it on a serving plate and place a scoop of Vanilla parfait (see opposite) on top. Serve.

Chocolate toppers For simple chocolate shapes, pipe 2oz (60g) melted and cooled chocolate onto parchment paper in decorative patterns. Let harden before peeling them off and using to decorate servings of parfait.

 **30 mins**
plus cooling, chilling, and freezing

SERVES 8

ICE CREAM PIE
rocky road

This ice cream pie is the perfect dessert for the whole family—it especially appeals to children and is really easy to prepare. It keeps for a while in the freezer, so you can prepare it days in advance. Use good-quality ice cream for best results.

INGREDIENTS
9oz (250g) graham crackers, finely crushed

¼ cup granulated sugar

9 tbsp unsalted butter, melted and cooled

For the filling
1 quart good-quality chocolate ice cream, softened

½ cup mini marshmallows, plus extra to serve

⅓ cup pecans, coarsely chopped, plus extra to serve

⅓ cup blanched almonds, coarsely chopped, plus extra to serve

SPECIAL EQUIPMENT
9in (23cm) deep loose-bottomed, fluted tart pan

PLAN AHEAD
You can store the blind-baked cracker base, wrapped in plastic wrap, in the fridge up to 2 days ahead.

1
Preheat the oven to 350°F (180°C). Combine the cracker crumbs, sugar, and butter in a large bowl until the mixture resembles fine bread crumbs.

2
Spread the mixture evenly in the pan, packing it down well to make a firm base with a 1in (2.5cm) side. Bake the base for 10 minutes. Remove from the heat, let cool, then chill until needed.

3
For the filling, pulse the ice cream in a food processor, a little at a time, until thick, creamy, and smooth. Transfer it to a large bowl.

4
Fold in the marshmallows and nuts. Spread the filling in the crust evenly and freeze for at least 1 hour, until firm. To serve, thaw the pie in the fridge for 20–30 minutes, remove from the pan, and top with marshmallows and nuts. You can store the pie, covered in the freezer, for up to 2 months.

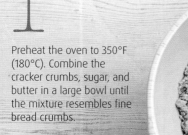

50 mins plus cooling and freezing

SERVES 8

ICE CREAM PIE triple chocolate

The sponge cake in this ice cream pie does not harden in the freezer, giving the dessert a yielding texture that you can eat straight from frozen. Other flavors of ice cream, such as cherry, could also work very well with the chocolate cake.

INGREDIENTS

3 eggs
½ cup granulated sugar
¼ cup all-purpose flour
¼ cup cocoa powder

For the filling

2 cups chocolate ice cream
2 cups vanilla ice cream
2oz (60g) Oreos, filling removed, finely crushed

SPECIAL EQUIPMENT

8in (20cm) deep springform cake pan

PLAN AHEAD

You can store the unfilled sponge cake in an airtight container up to 2 days ahead.

1 Preheat the oven to 375°F (190°C). Line the pan with parchment paper. Whisk the eggs and sugar in a bowl for 5 minutes, until the mixture is pale, thick, and has tripled in size. Sift in the flour and cocoa and fold gently until combined.

2 Pour the batter into the prepared pan evenly. Bake for 20–25 minutes, until the sponge cake is well risen and an inserted toothpick comes out clean. Let cool in the pan for 10 minutes before releasing the sides and transferring to a wire rack to cool completely.

3 For the filling, place the chocolate ice cream in a bowl for 10–15 minutes, to soften. Then beat it briefly with a handheld mixer until smooth. Slice the cake in half, lengthwise.

4 Place the bottom slice, cut-side up, in the pan and spread over the chocolate ice cream evenly. Top with the second cake half, cut-side down, and freeze for at least 30 minutes.

5 Soften the vanilla ice cream in a separate bowl (see step 3). Remove the cake from the freezer and spread over the vanilla ice cream evenly. Sprinkle with the Oreo crumbs evenly. Cover the pie with plastic wrap and freeze for at least 4 hours, until frozen solid.

6 Remove the pie from the freezer at least 10 minutes before serving and transfer it to a large serving platter. Serve immediately. You can store the pie, covered in the freezer, for up to 1 month.

25–30 mins
plus freezing

SERVES 6

ICE CREAM PIE
pear and ginger

Three forms of ginger combine to give a complex warmth to the refreshing pear and cream filling of this ice cream pie.

INGREDIENTS

5 tbsp unsalted butter plus extra for greasing

9oz (250g) gingersnaps, crushed

For the topping

1 quart good-quality vanilla ice cream

5 pieces stem ginger, preserved in syrup, drained, plus extra to decorate

2 tbsp stem ginger syrup, plus extra for drizzling

1 x 14oz (400g) can pear halves in natural juice, drained and finely chopped

SPECIAL EQUIPMENT

9in (23cm) springform cake pan

PLAN AHEAD

You can store the blind-baked gingersnap base, wrapped in plastic wrap, in the fridge up to 2 days ahead.

1 Grease and line the pan with parchment paper. Place the ice cream in a bowl and let soften. Place the gingersnaps in a separate heatproof bowl. Melt the butter in a saucepan and mix with the gingersnaps.

2 Spread the gingersnap mixture evenly in the pan, pressing down with the back of a spoon to form a firm base. For the topping, pulse the ice cream, ginger, and ginger syrup in a food processor until smooth, thick, and creamy. Stir in the chopped pears.

3 Pour the topping over the gingersnap base and freeze for at least 2 hours, until completely frozen. Before serving, let soften in the fridge for 30 minutes. Transfer the pie to a serving plate. Drizzle with a little ginger syrup, scatter with the ginger pieces, and serve. You can store the pie, covered in the freezer, for up to 2 months.

Index

Entries in **bold** indicate ingredients.

About the authors

CAROLINE BRETHERTON is the author of five cookbooks including DK's best-selling *Illustrated Step-by-Step Baking* and *Pies: Sweet and Savory*. She has a passion for fresh ingredients and contemporary recipes, particularly of the sweet variety. With a career in the food industry spanning 20 years, she founded Manna Café in London's Notting Hill, has run a successful catering company, and has written for various newspapers and magazines. She works from her home in North Carolina.

KRISTAN RAINES is a recipe writer and photographer. She is author of the blog *The Broken Bread*, which was shortlisted for *Saveur*'s 2014 Best Baking and Desserts Blog. She is passionate about sourcing local and seasonal produce, whenever possible, and incorporates this approach into everything she cooks and bakes. She lives with her husband John in Seattle.

Acknowledgments

Caroline Bretherton would like to thank Peggy Vance and all the DK team; all at Deborah McKenna; and most of all Luke, Gabriel, and Isaac.
Kristan Raines would like to thank her husband John for supporting her beyond all measure, her family for their hospitality, and Martha Burley for constant aid.

DK would like to thank the following: **Photography**: Charlotte Tolhurst for recipe photography and Kristan Raines for the recipe photography on pages 10–13, 18–21, 26–30, 44–49, 70–73, 90–92, 140–43, 145–53, 198–201, 228–31, 244–47, 270–73. **Photography art direction**: Sara Robin, Geoff Fennell, Penny Stock. **Food styling**: Jane Lawrie, Kate Wesson, Fern Green. **Prop styling**: Linda Berlin. **Design assistance**: Vikas Sachdeva, Era Chawla, and Sourabh Challariya. **Recipe testing**: Jane Bamforth, Chris Gates, Anne Harnan, and Jan Stevens. **Proofreading**: Claire Cross, Arani Sinha, and Janashree Singha. **Indexing**: Vanessa Bird. All photography © Dorling Kindersley

Conversions

Oven temperature equivalents

For a convection oven, reduce the temperature by at least 25°F/10°C.

Fahrenheit	Celsius	Description
225°F	110°C	Cool
250°F	130°C	Cool
275°F	140°C	Very low
300°F	150°C	Very low
325°F	160°C	Low
350°F	180°C	Moderate
375°F	190°C	Moderately hot
400°F	200°C	Hot
425°F	220°C	Hot
450°F	230°C	Very hot
475°F	240°C	Very hot

Volume equivalents

Imperial	Metric
1fl oz	30ml
2fl oz	60ml
2½fl oz	75ml
3½fl oz	100ml
4fl oz (½ cup)	120ml
5fl oz	150ml
6fl oz	175ml
7fl oz	200ml
8fl oz (1 cup)	240ml
10fl oz	300ml
12fl oz	350ml
14fl oz	400ml
15fl oz	450ml
16fl oz (1 pint)	500ml
1¼ pints	600ml
1½ pints	750ml
1¾ pints	800ml
2 pints	950ml
2¼ pints	1 liter
2½ pints	1.2 liters
2¾ pints	1.3 liters
3 pints	1.5 liters
4 pints	1.9 liters
5 pints	2.3 liters

Weight equivalents

Imperial	Metric
½oz	15g
¾oz	20g
1oz	30g
1½oz	45g
1¾oz	50g
2oz	60g
2½oz	75g
3oz	85g
3½oz	100g
4oz	115g
4½oz	125g
5oz	140g
5½oz	150g
6oz	175g
7oz	200g
8oz	225g
9oz	250g
10oz	300g
1lb	450g
1lb 2oz	500g
1lb 8oz	675g
2lb	900g
2lb 4oz	1kg
3lb 3oz	1.5kg